Typical and Atypi
Adolescent Development 6

Emotions, Temperament, Personality, Moral, Prosocial and Antisocial Development

This concise guide offers an accessible introduction to the development of communication and language in infancy and childhood. It integrates insights from both typical and atypical development to reveal the fundamental aspects of human growth and development, and common developmental disorders.

The topic books in this series draw on international research in the field and are informed by biological, social and cultural perspectives, offering explanations of developmental phenomena with a focus on how children and adolescents at different ages actually think, feel and act. In this volume, Stephen von Tetzchner explains key topics including: emotions and emotion regulation, temperament and personality, moral development, and prosocial and antisocial development.

Together with a companion website that offers topic-based quizzes, lecturer PowerPoint slides and sample essay questions, *Typical and Atypical Child and Adolescent Development 6 Emotions, Temperament, Personality, Moral, Prosocial and Antisocial Development* is an essential text for all students of developmental psychology, as well as those working in the fields of child development, developmental disabilities and special education.

Stephen von Tetzchner is Professor of Developmental Psychology at the Department of Psychology, University of Oslo, Norway.

The content of this topic book is taken from Stephen von Tetzchner's core textbook *Child and Adolescent Psychology: Typical and Atypical Development*. The comprehensive volume offers a complete overview of child and adolescent development. For more information, visit www.routledge.com/9781138823396

Topics from Child and Adolescent Psychology Series
Stephen von Tetzchner

The **Topics from Child and Adolescent Psychology Series** offers concise guides on key aspects of child and adolescent development. They are formed from selected chapters from Stephen von Tetzchner's comprehensive textbook *Child and Adolescent Psychology: Typical and Atypical Development* and are intended to be accessible introductions for students of relevant modules on developmental psychology courses, as well as for professionals working in the fields of child development, developmental disabilities and special education. The topic books explain the key aspects of human development by integrating insights from typical and atypical development to cement understanding of the processes involved and the work with children who have developmental disorders. They examine sensory, physical and cognitive disabilities and the main emotional and behavioral disorders of childhood and adolescence, as well as the developmental consequences of these disabilities and disorders.

Topics books in the series

Typical and Atypical Child and Adolescent Development 1
Theory and Methodology

Typical and Atypical Child and Adolescent Development 2
Genes, Fetal Development and Early Neurological Development

Typical and Atypical Child and Adolescent Development 3
Perceptual and Motor Development

Typical and Atypical Child and Adolescent Development 4
Cognition, Intelligence and Learning

Typical and Atypical Child and Adolescent Development 5
Communication and Language Development

Typical and Atypical Child and Adolescent Development 6
Emotions, Temperament, Personality, Moral, Prosocial and Antisocial Development

Typical and Atypical Child and Adolescent Development 7
Social Relations, Self-awareness and Identity

For more information on individual topic books visit www.routledge. com/Topics-from-Child-and-Adolescent-Psychology/book-series/ TFCAAP

Typical and Atypical Child and Adolescent Development 6

Emotions, Temperament, Personality, Moral, Prosocial and Antisocial Development

Stephen von Tetzchner

Routledge
Taylor & Francis Group

LONDON AND NEW YORK

Cover image: © Mike Harrington/Getty Images

First published 2023
by Routledge
4 Park Square, Milton Park, Abingdon, Oxon OX14 4RN

and by Routledge
605 Third Avenue, New York, NY 10158

Routledge is an imprint of the Taylor & Francis Group, an informa business

British Library Cataloguing-in-Publication Data
A catalogue record for this book is available from the British Library

Library of Congress Cataloging-in-Publication Data
A catalog record has been requested for this book

ISBN: 978-1-032-27402-7 (hbk)
ISBN: 978-1-032-26779-1 (pbk)
ISBN: 978-1-003-29253-1 (ebk)

DOI: 10.4324/9781003292531

Typeset in Bembo
by Apex CoVantage, LLC

Access the companion website: www.routledge.com/cw/vonTetzchner

Contents

PART IV
Prosocial and Antisocial Development 147

Introduction

Emotions are essential in human life – as well as in the lives of other species. Emotions reflect an appraisal of the environment and may give direction for action. The understanding and expression of emotions are also a foundation of human interaction. From a developmental perspective, the question is how emotional reactions and reactions to emotions change in early and later childhood, and how children and adolescents evaluate and react to people and events. Children's emotion regulation abilities affect how they perceive the world and their behaviors and social relationships. Personality is an individual characteristic, and individual patterns of emotional reactions and reactions to emotions constitute a first basis of personality. Moral appraisal is a necessary element of everyday life, which may represent many moral dilemmas. With age, children learn what is right and wrong but also to evaluate the circumstances of particular actions. Moral reasoning may be reflected in the behavior of children and adolescents, but emotion understanding and emotion regulation abilities may also influence their development of prosocial and antisocial actions.

Development can be defined as an age-related process involving changes in the structure and functions of humans and other species. The four parts of this book present core issues related to the development of emotions and emotion regulation, temperament and personality, moral reasoning, and prosocial and antisocial behavior, building on the models of development and the developmental way of thinking presented in Part I of Book 1, *Theory and Methodology*. Most individual differences in mental and physical features and abilities emerge not directly from a particular biological or environmental factor, but rather as a result of *interaction effects*, where biological or environmental factors are moderated by one or several other factors. Moreover, development is never a one-way process: it is a *transactional process*, characterized by reciprocal influences between the child and the environment over time. Readers may find it useful to consult the part on developmental models in Chapter 6 of Book 1 or the corresponding chapter in the complete book before reading the present topic book.

The topics in the present book include both typical development, which is the most common course, with unimpaired functions and ordinary individual differences between children, and atypical development, which represents various degrees of unusual or irregular development, including the development of children and adolescents who have emotional and behavioral disorders. The issues presented in this topic book are particularly relevant for teachers and special educators, as well as mental health professionals. They concern the processes underlying the variation in typical as well as atypical development and help the reader get a deeper understanding of the individual variation in development of emotional understanding and regulation, personality, moral reasoning, and prosocial and antisocial behavior.

Part I Emotions and Emotion Regulation is about the development of emotional understanding and expression and the gradual transition from other-regulation to self-regulation of emotions. Emotions constitute an organizing system that helps children understand the world and is a basis for social and societal participation and adaptation. The core developmental issues concern what emotional expressions children produce and understand and what emotional traits, skills and strategies characterize them at different age levels.

Human development to maturity stretches over about 20 years. Emotions are part of the human endowment from the very start; in the first months of life, children already express interest, pleasure and discomfort. The primary emotions are shared by nearly all humans, but children need emotional experiences to learn the functional aspects of the emotions, what they may express in particular situations, and how other people react to different emotional expressions. Children's emotional expressions are limited at first, but they gradually become more complex and encultured. The emergence of self-referential emotions such as pride and shame, based on the child's own standards or norms, represents an important developmental milestone.

The emotional expressions of parents and other people inform infants about the qualities of their surroundings, the infants' current experiences and the presence of possible dangers or joys. Children start early to search for and use this information actively as a means to know how they should feel in a situation and to regulate their emotional reactions and expressions. Conversations with parents and other adults are an important source of emotional knowledge. Parents may provide information about the emotional content of past events and prepare their children emotionally for what is likely to happen – both positive excitements and negative events. During development, children show an increasing variety of emotions, and there are also changes in how and when children express feelings. They learn to regulate their emotional expressions in stressful situations and to avoid expressing emotions when social conditions or cultural norms require it. A 2-year-old may just put an unpopular Christmas gift aside, whereas a 3-year-old may smile and say *Thank you* – and then quickly pass the gift on to the mother. With age, children develop empathy and sympathy and learn to cope with negative emotions from others. Emotional knowledge and regulation continue to develop throughout childhood and adolescence.

The emotional system influences children's perceptual, cognitive and social development, and development in these areas influences children's emotional development. The understanding of emotional development is, therefore, woven into the understanding of child development in general. As in other developmental areas, there are considerable individual differences in how children react to and cope with emotions in stressful situations. Emotional disorders such as anxiety and depression are among the most common disorders in childhood and adolescence. Some children show difficulties with emotional understanding and regulation and develop regulation disorders or behavioral disorders (see Part IV and Book 1, *Theory and Methodology*, Chapter 33).

Part II Temperament and Personality is about individual differences in how children and adolescents meet the world and cope in social and societal life. Infants differ in irritability, activity level and how they react to newness and changes. Some respond more than others to sounds and other forms of sensory stimulation. Some need time to "warm up"; others seem to enjoy rapid changes in activities and stimulation. Some frequently show strong emotional reactions; others rarely do. All of these traits may belong under the heading "temperament." They constitute a fundamental part of children's individuality and influence how people in the environment react to the children.

Emotional development and personality formation are related. The child's emotionality, emotional regulation and other temperament traits are considered important starting points for the development of personality traits. Children evaluate people and events and develop individual patterns of emotional reactions and actions. Some are generally cautious, whereas others seem to seek excitement. Such characteristics constitute the individual's reaction tendencies and typical mode of action in relation to the positive possibilities and challenges he or she faces. Assessment of personality traits is based on the assumption that each individual has a set of relatively permanent personal characteristics that are stable across situations, places, tasks and the people with whom they interact, but some theoreticians point to how the reactions and actions of children and adolescents may vary across situations.

The classic theories of personality structure and development differ in their assumptions about developmental phases and experiences that may lead to the development of particular personality traits. These theories have been, to a large extent, replaced by more general assumptions about the genetic bases and environmental influences on the way children and adolescents interact with other people and cope with challenges. In the modern approaches, the roots of personality are assumed to be in children's genes and biological constitution, the qualities of their environments and their unique adaptations to the surroundings. Early neglect, maltreatment and abuse may negatively impact personality formation and, in some individuals, lead to the development of personality disorders. Personality formation is a transactional process from childhood to adulthood (see Book 1, *Theory and Methodology*, Chapter 6, or the corresponding chapter in the original book).

Morality is an understanding of what is right and wrong. *Part III Moral Development* is about the emergence of moral reasoning and conscience, and the social and cultural bases of ethical values and moral reasoning about the dilemmas of everyday life. Theories of moral development describe and explain children's understanding of right and wrong, how this changes with age, and how children at different age levels evaluate their own and others' actions based on their consequences and the intentions behind them. Conscience implies an assessment of one's own actions and is closely related to the emotions shame and guilt. Conversations with parents and other adults guide children and adolescents to gradually acquire their culture's view of what is morally acceptable and unacceptable. There is a relation between the child's pattern of emotional reactions and development of moral reasoning. Some children show atypical moral transgressions and seem to lack the typical emotional reactions to moral transgressions and understanding of how others react emotionally to immoral actions. They fail to develop ordinary moral values and insights and may show psychopathic traits.

Part IV Prosocial and Antisocial Development concerns how children develop behaviors that may benefit others and behaviors that may inflict harm on others. Prosocial behavior and attention to the needs of others represent a positive developmental course for the individual and constitute a necessary basis for collaboration and life in a society. Antisocial attitudes and behaviors may negatively influence both the life of the individual and society at large. The presence of these behaviors may reflect how children perceive the social world. Most children show both prosocial and antisocial behaviors, but some children show relatively more prosocial or antisocial behavior compared with their peers. Insights into how children perceive the social world and develop prosocial and antisocial behaviors are important for understanding children's emotional and behavioral development in a broader social context and for being able to support the development of prosocial behaviors and prevent antisocial behaviors.

Some of the terminology used in developmental psychology may be unfamiliar to some readers. Many of these terms can be found in the Glossary.

Part I

Emotions and Emotion Regulation

1

Children's Emotional Life

Emotions are part of the basic equipment that allows human beings to understand and act in a social world. Children become aware of other people's emotions early in life, showing signs of happiness when they can play and be silly, or getting angry or upset when they cannot have a toy they want or when they see someone get hurt. They can be proud or ashamed of something they have done. Children who are upset look for someone to comfort them; happy children look for playmates or others who can share their happiness. Children who feel ashamed often react by withdrawing, while proud children seek interaction and recognition. Emotional **development** deals with the types of emotions children understand and express at different ages, and their ability to gradually adapt their emotional expressions and actions to different activities and social contexts.

DOI: 10.4324/9781003292531-2

2

Emotions

There is no generally accepted definition of "**emotion**," but it is commonly agreed that emotions include feeling states as a reaction to an event or the result of evaluating a past or present situation or event, including social cues from others (Camras & Shuster, 2013). Emotions comprise seven key elements: *expression* includes facial and other **gestures**, posture, movements, vocalization and linguistic content. *Understanding* is the **recognition** of emotional expression in other people. *Experience* is the conscious recognition of one's own emotions, while *bodily responses* include changes in heart rate, skin temperature and the like. Fear, for example, results in increased heart rate, shortness of breath and sweating, while shame can lead to a lower heart rate and blushing. *Direction* reflects the fact that emotions always are directed *at* something, such as being in love or angry with someone, being afraid of something or someone and so on. *Action* means that emotions activate and govern human actions toward or away from something. Happiness serves to maintain an individual's **activity**, while anger can lead to attempts at overcoming obstacles. *Regulation* involves **adaptation** to a given situation by modification of one's emotional experience or expression and related actions.

Primary emotions are associated with evaluating an entire situation, or specific aspects of it, and include joy, sadness, fear and anger. **Secondary** or **self-referential emotions** are rooted in self-perception and an individual's evaluation according to a personal standard; they include pride, shame, embarrassment, guilt and envy. *Relational emotions*, such as love, hate and jealousy, are directed at others. They will be discussed in Book 7, *Social Relations, Self-awareness and Identity*.

DOI: 10.4324/9781003292531-3

Reason and emotion are often seen as opposites, but there is no absolute dividing line between emotional and cognitive development. Any emotional response implies an appraisal of the situation – whether it is safe or dangerous, gives reason for concern or joy, and so on (Moors et al., 2013). In order for children to make such evaluations, they must have knowledge of their physical and social environment.

3

Emotion Regulation

Emotion regulation refers to the monitoring and control of one's own emotional experiences and expressions and the ability to adapt them to one's personal goals and sociocultural conditions (Campos et al., 1989). Although, traditionally, it has been common to distinguish between *generating* and *regulating* emotions as two processes with a different neurological basis (Gross & Barrett, 2011), both perceived emotion and emotional expression will depend on the context, one's own preparedness for what will or will not happen, and how well one knows and masters the situation. An emotional expression in itself will thus always be the result of regulation (Campos et al., 2004; Kappas, 2011; Thompson, 2011).

Hence, **self-regulation** can occur before, during or after an emotion has been expressed and can include the emotion itself, its particular expression and its intensity. Behavior is regulated by adapting emotional expressions and actions to a situation. A child may show less anger, suppress a smile or tears or refrain from taking an attractive toy. Children can avoid or seek out emotional situations, or someone can prepare them for what is about to happen, such as a blood test, in order to avoid an excessively strong emotional reaction. New and unexpected events will generally elicit stronger emotions than events that are expected, but, in some cases, expectations about an emotionally positive or negative event can amplify a child's reactions. Children's expectations about their own birthday, for example, often lead to increasing emotional arousal as the day approaches. As children grow older, their development goes from seeking **protection** and help from adults to regulating their own emotional state and seeking help from peers (see Figure 3.1), but most people faced with a difficult situation will seek help from others throughout life.

DOI: 10.4324/9781003292531-4

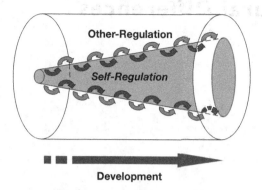

Figure 3.1 From other-regulation to self-regulation.

Early in development, children need a great deal of external help to regulate their emotions. With age, they steadily improve at self-regulation, but even adults may need external help when their stress levels are high (based on Sameroff & Fiese, 2000, p. 6).

Many studies focus on children's ability to control anxiety, anger and similar emotions, but regulation is more than control. Emotions and regulation strategies are neither good nor bad in themselves but depend on the context. Even strong negative emotions can be adaptive if the child is facing a threatening or dangerous situation. Both over control and under control lead to a more limited emotional repertoire and poorer emotion regulation in children (see Chapter 17, this volume). The goal of regulation is adaptation, but the process can lead to **maladaptation** when children make the wrong connections between emotions, **cognition** and actions. In such cases, the developmental outcome can be emotional or **behavioral disorders**.

4

Cultural Differences

The issue of universal emotions and cultural differences is central to an understanding of emotional development. Some emotions, such as fear of dangerous animals, are probably universal in the sense that they share the same type of expression and are triggered by similar situations in all **cultures**. Other, more complex emotions are likely to be culturally determined. There are significant cultural differences in regard to the types of expressions that are used, the extent to which emotions are valued and the ways in which children are expected to show emotions and regulate them at different ages (Halberstadt & Lozada, 2011; Keller & Otto, 2009), for example between Cameroon and Germany (Figure 4.1).

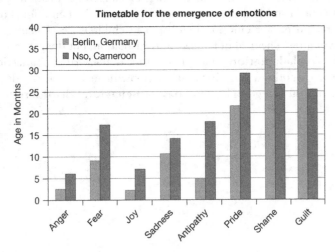

Figure 4.1 Mothers in Germany and Cameroon expect their children to show particular emotions at different ages (after Keller & Otto, 2009, p. 1002).

DOI: 10.4324/9781003292531-5

For example, the function of anger is to overcome obstacles in order to achieve goals, and how and when anger is accepted varies between cultures. Inappropriate anger may repel others, and it is, therefore, an important developmental task to learn to express anger in culturally acceptable ways (Lemerise & Harper, 2010), as illustrated in Box 4.1.

Box 4.1   Child Anger in Different Cultures

The Yanomami tribe in northern Brazil raises children to develop anger and **aggression**. Among the Inuit in Arctic regions of America, children show little anger after the age of 6. In Kenya, Kipsigi children are raised not to show pain or grief. Children of the Tamang people in Eastern Nepal explained that it is useless to get angry at someone who has done something wrong to them, and that they should instead feel shame. Children of the Brahman tribe in Western Nepal believed anger is acceptable, but should not be shown. Likewise, children in Gujarat in India said they felt anger, grief and pain, but did not express these feelings because others might find it unacceptable. Children in the northeastern part of the United States said they could both feel and show anger as long as they did so in a socially acceptable way (Cole et al., 2002; Oatley et al., 2006; Raval et al., 2007; Wilson et al., 2012).

Children express a variety of emotions; some are shy, others are direct.

The cultural differences are noticeable early on. In an experimental study, 11-month-old Japanese children waited on average for 48 seconds before approaching an attractive toy after their mother had said something with an angry voice. American children waited for

18 seconds. When the mother's voice expressed joy or fear, there were no differences between the children (Miyaki et al., 1986). The results reflect that Japanese mothers protect their children against expressions of anger, especially in public places. The Japanese children were not accustomed to these types of expressions and reacted more strongly to them than US children, who were more accustomed to anger. Another **experiment** showed stronger negative emotions among German 5-year-olds than among Japanese 5-year-olds when an adult hindered them from reaching a goal by taking away a puzzle before the children were done with it (Holodynski & Friedlmeier, 2006). Differences go beyond Eastern and Western cultures, however: Japanese 1-year-olds are more expressive than their Chinese peers (Camras et al., 2003).

The fact that studies have found early differences in emotion regulation among Japanese and American children does not mean that Japanese children merely suppress their *expressions* of anger because showing anger is culturally unacceptable, but that they actually *feel* less anger as a result of cultural influences. Thus, emotional development is part of the **enculturation** process (Lutz, 1988).

Main Theories of Emotional Development

Most theories of emotional development are based on Darwin's (1872) hypothesis that the emotional expressions of human beings are the result of evolutionary adaptation. According to *differential emotions theory*, children begin with two innate forms of *general arousal*: one that may be called "discomfort" or "restlessness," and another that may be called "comfort" or "contentment." These arousals are divided into progressively more demarcated and structurally consistent emotions. Crying and smiling can be seen as part of a warning system that, from the moment of birth, signals important changes in the child or the environment and may involve discomfort, contentment or danger for the child and caregiver (Mayer & Salovey, 1997). Early emotional expressions are primarily the result of *physiological* reactions. Over time, they are increasingly driven by *psychological* factors, meaning that emotions are governed by the child's evaluation of people and events in the environment. Children's evaluations change in line with their general cognitive and social development and are determined by their experiences and the cultural meaning they have learned to attribute to different events (Camras, 2011; Sroufe, 1996; Thompson, 2011).

Theories of *discrete emotions* are based on the assumption that human beings have a set of basic innate emotions that are activated early on and appear quickly and automatically (see Table 5.1). According to Izard (2007), children are unable to regulate their emotional expressions in the first 6 months of life, as they are triggered almost **reflexively**. However, children and adults rarely have a need for spontaneous, automatic reactions. Gradually, children learn to distinguish feelings and facial expressions and become better able to modify their own emotions and expressions, while the importance of the **basic emotions** decreases as a result of **maturation**, emotional

DOI: 10.4324/9781003292531-6

Table 5.1 Basic emotions according to Izard (based on Tomkins & McCarter, 1964; Izard, 2007)

Emotion	Description
Interest	Eyebrows down, eyes track, look, listen
Enjoyment, joy	Smile, lips widened up and out, smiling eyes (circular wrinkles)
Grief	Arched eyebrows, mouth down, tears, rhythmic sobbing
Anger	Frown, clenched jaw, eyes narrowed, red face
Disgust	Sneer, upper lip up
Fear	Eyes frozen open, pale, cold, sweaty, facial trembling, with hair erect

enculturation, cognitive development and social **learning**. This process gains momentum as children begin to talk and develop more advanced cognitive skills (Izard et al., 2002).

According to Izard's theory, children are born with a system of emotions that lays the foundation for experiencing and expressing a number of basic emotions. This system gradually undergoes change and transformation as children consciously and non-consciously learn to adapt their emotional states and expressions to a situation. In contrast to theories of differential emotions, discrete emotions are indivisible but can be *combined* into more complex emotions (Camras, 2011; Camras & Shutter, 2010).

From a *behaviorist* point of view, crying and smiling are innate physiological reactions to certain events, such as loss of a supporting surface, hunger, loud sounds or pain. In **classical conditioning**, neutral stimuli are associated with stimuli that trigger emotional responses, causing the neutral stimuli to elicit more differentiated emotional responses (see Book 4, *Cognition, Intelligence and Learning*, Chapter 35). Consequently, emotional development is the result of a differential response (Schlinger, 1995). In one of developmental psychology's most widely discussed experiments, 9-month-old Albert was exposed to an extremely loud sound while playing with a white rat. The sound was intended as an **unconditioned stimulus** that would elicit fear, leading Albert to associate the rat with the sound and in turn become afraid of the rat (Watson & Rayner, 1920). The results, however, are unclear, and it is uncertain whether Albert actually developed a fear of rats and similar animals (Griggs, 2015; Harris, 1979).

Functionalist theories focus on the relationship between emotions and the "object" at which they are directed. Often, this can be another person, and development reflects the changes in children's goals and ability to regulate their emotions and the social environment. The purpose of emotions is to maintain or change critical aspects of the child's inner state or the environment, and preparing for action is part of the emotion itself (Barrett & Campos, 1987; Campos et al., 2010, 2011).

Early Emotional Development

Human beings show emotions in different ways, such as by vocalizing or sweating, but above all by movements of the mouth and eyebrows (Figure 6.1). As they develop, children's comprehension and production of emotions change, as well as the situations in which emotions are used and the way in which they are perceived by others.

Emotional Expressions

Positive Emotions

Smiling is the first expression of contentment and joy, and a **reflexive** *smile* is present from birth. The *social smile*, characterized by open eyes and a focused gaze, usually occurs for the first time when children are 6–10 weeks old. Reflexive smiles and social smiles have different social consequences: parents tend to interpret the reflexive smile as an expression of the child's physiological state, whereas the social smile is seen as an expression of the feelings experienced by the child. Many parents report that the social smile, together with eye contact, represented the first clue that their child looked at them with interest, so that they themselves began to look at their child as a person (Freedman, 1974; Wolff, 1963).

Early smiles are most easily elicited when the infant is awake and inactive. At the end of the **neonatal period**, infants also begin to smile in response to external stimulation. They smile when they *recognize* something, such as a colorful toy or a familiar voice. In the first 6 weeks, infants smile more at voices than at faces, and more at hearing the voice of their mother than that of a stranger. At 3 months, the maternal voice is no longer enough. The sound of her voice leads

DOI: 10.4324/9781003292531-7

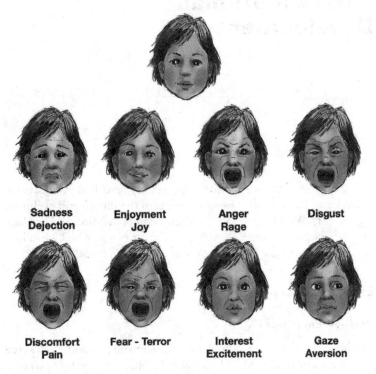

Sadness   **Enjoyment**   **Anger**   **Disgust**
Dejection   **Joy**   **Rage**

Discomfort   **Fear - Terror**   **Interest**   **Gaze**
Pain   **Excitement**   **Aversion**

Figure 6.1 Some emotional expressions in children.

infants to search for her face, and their smile first appears once they have found it (Sroufe, 1996; Wolff, 1963, 1966).

Both people and interesting objects can elicit early infant smiles. Three-month-olds smile most during interaction with others, and there is little difference between familiar and unfamiliar faces. At 5–6 months, regardless of the situation, a stranger will no longer elicit a smile, and, if the stranger's face shows no expression, children begin to look worried. Eight-month-olds smile when they see their mother looking at them from a distance, but not when she is reading and not looking at them. In other words, the sight of the mother's face is not enough for children at this age to smile – they must perceive that they have her attention as well (Jones & Hong, 2005).

Infants also smile when they *master* something. Infants 2–8 months old smiled more often in response to a music box playing a tune when they moved their foot (a ribbon attached to their foot activated the music box) than same-age children who heard the music box just as often, but independent of their own actions (Lewis et al., 1990).

Although the development of smiling does not depend on visual stimulation, a lack of visual stimulation leads to delayed development. Blind children smile before the age of 3 months, but their smile has a reflexive quality and differs from the smiles of sighted infants of the same age. Their smiles are more difficult to elicit and seem vague and unclear. A prolonged and distinct smile that corresponds to the social smile of sighted children first appears at the age of 6 months (Fraiberg, 1971; Freedman, 1964). Also, deafblind children show a variation in emotional expression, but to a lesser degree than sighted children (Eibl-Eibesfeldt, 1973). The fact that children who are unable to see the emotional expressions of others still develop the same types of expressions indicates the presence of a relatively specific genetic basis for expression.

Laughter appears in the first months of life and already then closely resembles that of adults (Kawakami et al., 2006; Sroufe & Waters, 1976). Children often laugh in connection with an abrupt change in activity, such as when someone lifts them up into the air or engages them in other romp and play. In the first year of life, a change takes place in what makes children laugh. Initially, tactile stimulation is most effective, but gradually, social and humorous visual stimulation is most likely to elicit laughter (Sroufe, 1996).

Smiles express joy.

Negative Emotions

Crying is the first expression interpreted as distress and discomfort. In newborns, crying is associated with high levels of physiological activation and can be triggered by internal and external stimulation. Sound, visual stimulation and room temperature, among other things, can affect how much or how little a child cries. To begin with, crying is acoustically quite uniform, and parents often do not know what it means. During the first weeks of life, crying becomes more varied in its sound patterns and subject to more varied interpretations. There is a certain relationship between the sound of the crying and how it is interpreted, but parents tend to focus on its possible cause, with major differences in whether they believe children cry because they long for company or because they are being difficult or unreasonable (Newson & Newson, 1965). Changes in crying patterns are not only the result of maturation but also of changes in the activities children participate in. The enculturation of crying starts early.

The earliest signs of *fear* in infants are interpreted based on facial expressions and crying. Although newborns blink reflexively when an object approaches, this is hardly an expression of fear. It is not until the age of 8–9 months that children begin to show defensive reactions, an increase in heart rate and other signs of fear in situations that could reasonably be thought to cause the child to be afraid. This development is generally attributed to maturation, as children at this age have no experience with being struck by objects. At about 5 months of age, many infants begin to show fear of strangers. They are now better able to distinguish between familiar and unfamiliar, and it is the unfamiliar itself to which infants react, as they usually have no previous experience that could give rise to fear of strangers. They also begin to show fear of loud noises, heights, masks and unfamiliar toys (Scarr & Salapatek, 1970).

It is during early **childhood** that children show most fear of things. Their fear response is strongest at the end of the second year, after which it decreases, but fear of loud noises and unfamiliar toys, for example, begins to decline in the beginning or middle of the second year. At the same time, there is considerable variation between individuals: some children easily respond with fear, others seem fearless. There is also individual variation across situations. "Strong" fear-eliciting situations trigger fear in nearly all children, whereas fear responses in "weak" situations differ depending on the children's experiences. For example, children show little reaction to strangers when engaged in free play, whereas many will respond with fear to

Crying is a clear emotional expression, but it is not always easy to find the cause.

a remote-controlled robot or spider. Children who respond to non-threatening situations with fear are often socially reticent (Buss & McDoniel, 2016; Mischel et al., 2002).

Ethologists (see Book 1, *Theory and Methodology*, Chapter 16) point out that fear is determined by nature as well as culture (Hinde, 1992). This is illustrated in a study where 7–18-month-olds were shown two films at the same time, one with a snake and one with another exotic animal. They looked longer at the film of a snake when they heard a fearful voice than when the voice had a happy character. Without voiceover, they looked equally long at the snake film as at the other animal film (DeLoache & LoBue, 2009). This demonstrated a special attention to snakes with fearful voices, but not that fear of snakes was innate. In a similar study, infants did not demonstrate accelerated heart rate or a large startle magnitude when they saw the snake film, which are usual physiological reactions indicating fear. However, the special attention to snakes may make children prepared for learning fast to be afraid of snakes (Thrasher & LoBue, 2016). In ethological theory, fear of snakes has evolutionary survival value and is, therefore, easily established, but also depends on specific experiences (Hinde, 1992).

Early in children's lives, parents also interpret crying as an expression of *anger*, for example when the child cries after losing a pacifier, although clear expressions of anger do not usually show up until the age of 4–6 months. Infants typically show anger when they are impeded in their movements or when parents and other adults do not fulfill their expectations, such as taking an object they are sucking on from their mouth (Stenberg et al., 1983). Pain can lead to expressions of anger as well (Izard et al., 1987). In the course of **toddlerhood**, parents show increasingly less tolerance for expressions of anger and try to get children to regulate their emotions according to the cultural standards by "labeling" their expressions, diverting their attention and similar strategies (Lemerise & Dodge, 2008).

There is less research on *sadness* and *grief* than on discomfort, anger and fear. A possible reason for this may be that sadness is not always linked to a specific aspect of a situation but appears to be more of a basic mood. Children are perceived as sad when they show little facial expression, activity and positive response. This can, for example, be observed in 3-month-olds who are separated from their caregiver and in infants who live in orphanages with little social stimulation. From an ethological perspective, sadness is associated with loss or expected loss of a loved one (Bowlby, 1980). Sadness reduces children's activity level and preserves their energy in situations in which the caregiver is not available to protect them (LaFreniere, 2000). Children can also show sadness when the people in their environment fail to be emotionally responsive to them. Children of depressed mothers, for example, appear sadder or more despondent than other children.

Distinguishing between Early Emotional Expressions

Infants' earliest facial expressions can be difficult to differentiate. Although they often resemble the emotional expressions of adults, they do not always occur in relevant situations, and observers may be uncertain as to their interpretation (Camras & Shutter, 2010). One study observed 10–12-month-olds in situations designed to elicit joy (playing with an interesting toy), fear (being placed near a visual cliff) and surprise (seeing an object "disappear"). The happy situation almost exclusively elicited expressions of joy. The fear situation elicited a greater amount of fearful expressions than the other situations, in addition to many other emotional expressions. Although the infants showed more surprise than any other emotion in the surprising situation, surprise was just as frequent in the other situations (Hiatt et al., 1979). Other studies have found that infants show approximately the same facial expression in situations designed to elicit fear or anger (Camras & Witherington, 2005).

There is little doubt that children have a number of innate emotional expressions, as demonstrated by observations of blind children (see p. 17, this volume). However, the expressions of newborns do not reflect any expectations. It takes several months for emotions to gain more direction and content and for infants to begin to expect certain reactions from the environment (Emde, 1992; Sroufe, 1996). This means that infants' repertoire of facial expressions gradually finds application and meaning, counter to Izard's assumption that children are born with a limited number of discrete emotional expressions. Instead, the results indicate that children start with relatively undifferentiated states of arousal, and that the various emotional expressions initially reflect differences in intensity only (Camras, 2011; Oster et al., 1992). Perhaps they represent a form of "emotional **babbling**" on the way to a broader emotional repertoire.

Children must be able to adapt to the possibilities as well as the dangers in their environment. They need both the motivation to explore and a set of reactions to possible dangers ranging from caution to escape. Fear of steep cliffs or unknown predators (enemies in the environment) cannot be learned by trial and error. Children would have fallen down the cliff or been devoured before they had the chance to learn how to avoid these dangers. At the same time, it would be unfeasible to maintain a repertoire of hundreds of specific reactions that nonetheless would be insufficient to cover all the environmental dangers a child may face. This means that an open, **dynamic system**, along with a handful of action tendencies capable of providing new responses quickly, affords the best adaptation to the environment. A key element of such a system is the ability to learn from the emotional expressions of others. This requires children to quickly develop an understanding of a number of relatively unambiguous emotional expressions.

Understanding Emotional Expressions in Others

The **perception** of emotions involves the ability to *detect, differentiate* and *recognize* expressions, that is, to ascribe value or meaning to them in a given context and decide a course of action (Walker-Andrews, 1997; Walle & Campos, 2012). Initially, the perception of emotional expressions is *global*, as children have not yet learned to distinguish between different contextual elements. Over time, they perceive emotions as more *referential* (directed at a particular aspect of the situation) and linked to specific types of situations.

Voices

At birth, hearing is more developed than vision, and vocal emotional expressions attract more attention than facial expressions during early development. Hearing does not need to be focused in the same way as vision, and acoustic stimulation is suitable for waking children up as well as to capture their attention. Three-month-olds dishabituate to a happy voice after **habituation** to a sad voice, but they first dishabituate to a happy face after having habituated to a sad face at the age of 5 months (Caron et al., 1988). This indicates that the voice represents an earlier cue to emotional information than the face.

Around the age of 3 months, infants look for their mother's face when they hear her voice, but they do not associate facial expressions with the voice until later. Seven-month-old children, unlike children 4 months younger, spent more time looking at a video with a **correspondence** between vocal emotional content and facial expression than at a video in which voice and face expressed different emotions (Walker-Andrews, 1986). Infants, thus, are more attentive to emotional expressions that are presented synchronously in different modalities (see also Book 3, *Perceptual and Motor Development*, Chapter 6).

Facial Expressions

The recognition of facial expressions undergoes gradual development in the first 2 years of life. Field and colleagues (1982) found that 2-day-old children responded differently to faces showing joy, surprise and grief, while Farroni and colleagues (2007) found that 1-day-old children **discriminated** between a happy and a fearful facial expression, but not between a fearful and a neutral face. This suggests a certain ability to discriminate facial expressions, but also shows that they must be quite dissimilar for newborn infants to notice the difference. Three-month-olds are able to differentiate faces with different intensities of the same emotion, such as a smiling face (Bornstein & Arterberry, 2003; Kuchuk et al., 1986).

Around the age of 5 months, children begin to distinguish between sad, fearful and angry facial expressions (Schwartz et al., 1985).

Seven-month-olds generally look longer at a fearful face than a happy one, but reactions are *asymmetrical*: after habituation to a happy face, 7-month-olds dishabituated to a face showing fear, but did not dishabituate to a face showing joy or astonishment after habituation to a fearful face (Nelson & de Haan, 1997). These results suggest that fearful facial expressions have greater attention value than faces showing joy. One possible explanation may be that children have an innate tendency to perceive a fearful face as a danger signal. A more likely explanation is that infants generally have far more experience with happy than with fearful faces, and that they spend more time looking at what is least familiar. Infants at this age rarely see their mothers showing negative facial expressions (Malatesta & Haviland, 1982).

Children's perception of emotional expressions remains limited throughout the first year, and expressions need to be distinct. Ten-month-olds dishabituated to more mixed positive expressions following habituation to prototypically happy expressions, but not vice versa (Ludemann, 1991). This probably reflects the categories the children formed during habituation to facial expressions. When they were shown only typical expressions of joy, they formed a narrow category and dishabituated to mixed facial expressions because they perceived them as novel. After habituation to more mixed expressions, however, they formed a broader category that also could include typical happy expressions. They failed to dishabituate because they did not perceive the typical happy expressions as a change in stimulation (see Book 1, *Theory and Methodology*, Chapter 25). The results of these studies show that early emotional perception is not exclusively governed by a biologically predetermined course of development, but a process based on experience.

Imitation of Emotional Expressions

It is generally agreed that children are able to perceive and produce emotional facial expressions early on; there is considerable disagreement about *when* children begin to imitate the expressions they observe in others (see Book 4, *Cognition, Intelligence and Learning*, Chapter 35). According to Field and colleagues (1982), 2-day-old infants showed evidence of imitating some aspects of happy, sad and surprised facial expressions. The infants reacted with eye and mouth widening more often when the face showed surprise than when it showed one of the other two emotions, lip tightening when they saw a sad face, and lip widening when they saw a smile. As 2 days are unlikely to be enough to learn to recognize facial expressions, Field interprets the results to suggest a connection between newborn infants' systems for perception and action, for example in the form of a **mirror neuron** system (see Book 2, *Genes, Fetal Development and Early Neurological Development*, Chapter 15).

However, other researchers have pointed out that Field's study does not necessarily demonstrate **imitation** but only the fact that the adult expressions elicited an emotional response in the infants (Anisfeld, 2005; Kaitz et al., 1988; Ray & Heyes, 2011). The children's reactions may rather reflect the same type of emotional "contagion" that leads newborns to cry when they hear other infants cry (Geangu et al., 2010). In line with this, Provine (1997) describes this type of response as a preparation for later imitation of emotional expressions. Contrary to this view, Meltzoff (1993) maintains that not only do infants imitate the expressions, imitation leads the infants to experience the emotion that corresponds to the expression they are imitating. Meltzoff thus views imitation as the underlying mechanism for emotional contagion, rather than emotional contagion as the basis for imitation, as Provine argues.

Meltzoff and Moore (1999) suggest that the imitation of emotional expressions and other facial movements leads children to discover they are human beings: infants' sense of human **identity** is strengthened when they experience belonging to the ones "who do like that with their faces." Furthermore, imitation leads to recognition and affection between parent and child and, from an evolutionary point of view, increases the likelihood of children being cared for and surviving. Parents often imitate the facial expressions of their child, usually with some form of variation. In the first 12 months, parents actually imitate their child more often than the child imitates them. Positive emotional expressions in particular are subject to imitation, while the child's negative emotions are often overlooked or met with a different emotion, such as concern and interest in response to the child's anger (Ray & Heyes, 2011; Lemerise & Dodge, 2008).

Emotion Regulation

In early **infancy**, children lack the cognitive and neurological prerequisites to regulate their innate emotional expressions (Izard, 1991). They need help calming down but also need to learn how to calm down without the help of others, a process that begins at birth when parents respond to the infant's **signals** and offer comfort (Kopp, 1989). In early infancy, parents establish routines to avoid sudden shifts in the child's state and help regulate the child's level of arousal by interpreting the child's signals and adjusting stimulation to a suitable level. Stern (1998) uses the term **affect attunement** to describe adults' adjustment of emotional actions and expressions to those of the child, as in this example (p. 207):

A nine-month-old boy bangs his hand on a soft toy, at first in some anger but gradually with pleasure, exuberance, and humor. He sets up a steady rhythm. Mother falls into his rhythm and says, "kaaaaa-bam, kaaaaa-bam," the "bam" falling on the stroke and the "kaaaaa" riding with the preparatory upswing and the suspenseful holding of his arm aloft before it falls.

The mother "reformulates" the child's emotional actions. According to Stern, affect attunement helps children understand the emotions that underlie actions (see also Book 7, *Social Relations, Self-awareness and Identity*, Chapter 20).

With age, children learn to delay as well as to moderate their expressions. Delaying an emotional response is the first step on the way to emotion regulation, a window of time that allows perceptual and cognitive processes to affect the perceived emotion and expression and reduce excessive stimulation. Six-month-olds, for example, show less distress when, after a little while, they stop looking at a toy fire truck with flashing lights and blaring sirens that they see for the first time (Crockenberg & Leerkes, 2006). An infant who smiles and interacts with the mother may turn away from the mother for a short moment to moderate his emotional arousal and subsequently turn back to continue the interaction with the mother. Sucking on the thumb is an early form of emotional self-regulation that helps children calm down (Saarni et al., 2006). Adults contribute to expanding children's repertoire by allowing them to perceive the state of their own body and form simple patterns of behavior. Without the help of adults to regulate their emotions, children experience discomfort and emotional disorganization (Field, 1994).

Parents are often worried that they might "spoil" their children by picking them up when they cry and cause them to cry more often, that picking up will function as a reinforcer and increase crying, as might be expected based on behaviorist theories (see Book 1, *Theory and Methodology*, Chapter 12). However, a classic study found that infants whose mothers responded quickly to their child's crying during the first half year cried less during the second half (Bell & Ainsworth, 1972). This means that a quick response to children's expression of discomfort did not cause them to be "spoiled" and more demanding. Instead, the results indicate that the maternal responsiveness helped the children learn to cope with the causes of their crying. They appeared less overwhelmed by emotions, managed to regulate their own emotions and cried less. Moreover, the decrease in crying allowed the children more time to become familiar with other activities, sounds and movements. When the mothers waited longer, the intensity of the crying tended to increase, and it was more difficult to calm the infants down (Thompson, 1991).

Social Referencing

Children react to the emotional expressions of others early on, and, toward the end of their first year of life, children begin to use other people's expressions as a cue to how they themselves should feel, think and act in unfamiliar and insecure situations. *Emotional* **social referencing** means that children use the emotional content of other people's expressions as cues for their own feelings in a given situation. *Instrumental referencing* involves using others as a cue to how they themselves should act in a situation. Social referencing provides children with information they cannot extract from the situation itself based on their own experience alone (Feinman et al., 1992). Thus, in these situations, children try to identify other people's emotions not to find out how others feel, but to find out more about their own current situation.

In a classic study of social referencing in 12-month-olds, the infants used the mother's emotional expression to guide them in an uncertain situation (Box 6.1). A similar study found that children crawled across faster when the mother smiled *and* spoke positively than when she spoke with her back turned so the child could not see her face. The children waited the longest time when their mother smiled but did not say anything (Mumme et al., 1996).

Emotional expressions are an important part of children's social world, and many situations involve children's use of emotional information. In one study, 14-month-olds were given either a sad or a fearful message by their mother about a doll that had lost its leg. The children who received a sad message tried to comfort the doll, while the children who received a message accompanied by a fearful expression avoided playing with the doll (Campos et al., 1985). This type of emotional information can affect young children far longer than the situation itself. Eleven- and 14-month-old infants watched an

Box 6.1   Visual Cliff and Social Referencing (Sorce et al., 1985)

The study utilized a customized version of a visual cliff covered by a glass plate (see Book 3, *Perceptual and Motor Development*, Chapter 3). The cliff was shallow but appeared so deep that several of the 12-month-old children were unsure whether it was dangerous as they were led toward the edge. Many of them looked at their mothers, who had been instructed to show expressions of joy, fear, anger, sadness or interest. There was a clear relation between the mothers' emotional expressions and the children's actions. When the mothers showed fear, none of the 17 children crawled across the drop-off. When they looked angry, 2 of 18 children moved across, while 6 of 18 children crossed the cliff when their mothers looked sad. When the mothers showed interest, 11 of 15 children traversed the cliff, while 14 of 19 children crawled across when their mothers looked happy. The children thus used the mothers' emotional expression as a cue to their safety in an uncertain situation.

Photograph courtesy of Joe Campos.

unfamiliar toy that was out of reach being lowered from the ceiling while the experimenter repeated the nonsense phrase "tat fobble" several times, with a voice and a facial expression that expressed either joy or disgust, and then raised the toy to the ceiling again (Hertenstein &

Campos, 2004). When the children were allowed to explore the toy an hour later, the 14-month-olds who had heard the voice expressing disgust waited longer before touching the toy than those who had heard the cheerful voice. The 11-month-olds who had been exposed to the disgust condition waited a little longer as well, but the difference from those who had heard the cheerful voice was minor. In other studies, the object **exploration** of 15- and 18-month-olds was influenced by the observation of a conversation with angry or neutral information not directed at them (Repacholi & Meltzoff, 2007; Repacholi et al., 2014).

The studies show that adults' reactions and attitudes are important for how young children meet new and unfamiliar people and things. Infants who are 12–18 months old are more kindly disposed to strangers when their parents smile and talk about them in a positive emotional voice. Concerned parents usually have a serious demeanor when their toddler is examined by a doctor. This can lead the child to be reluctant and cry, as the parents' facial expressions are perceived to mean something is wrong with the doctor. Physical exams at the doctor's office may go more smoothly if parents smile and laugh, even though they are concerned for their child.

Research on emotional expression has commonly used the child's mother as an emotional reference, but children just as readily follow the father's cues as those of the mother. Siblings, too, can function as a reference when young children feel uncertain (Blackford & Walden, 1998; Hirshberg & Svejda, 1990a, b). In a laboratory environment, 12-month-old infants may spend more time looking at a friendly experimenter than at their own mother (Stenberg, 2009). Thus, children seek emotional information from people they trust, whether they are very familiar to the child or they seem to have control and are part of the situation in which the children find themselves (Walden & Kim, 2005).

The information children gain through social referencing does not alone determine how they relate to new and unfamiliar situations. Some situations are so obviously positive or negative from the child's point of view that no help is needed to define them. Other situations are so unclear that adults represent children's only source of appraisal, but most situations lie somewhere in the middle. Children seek information or use the information adults voluntarily offer to varying degrees. Some may feel uncertain about what to do in a given situation, and some will always act contrary to the information they have been given. In the study involving a visual cliff, 5 of 19 children did not crawl to their mother when she smiled, and 2 moved toward her when she looked angry. Some of these differences are due to children's subjective perception of the situation. In addition to individual **temperament**, children react differently to novelty and unknown things (see p. 68, this volume). Earlier experiences can lead to a different perception of the situation as well. Some toddlers, for example, are afraid of Santa Claus in stores at Christmas time, while others readily sit on his lap (Blackford & Walden, 1998).

Although information from adults is important, it is only one of several cues used by children to assess a situation. Sometimes, the temptation to touch and explore something is simply too strong for children, even if their mother has conveyed that it is "dangerous." When this happens, children will occasionally turn to their mother and smile. This is often perceived as defiant or teasing behavior, but the child may just as well intend to reassure the mother and let her know that it was not dangerous after all. Children do not always understand why they are not supposed to touch something, such as an object that can easily break.

Many 1-year-olds act first and look at their caregiver afterwards. With increasing age, children improve at evaluating new situations and using the emotional information provided by adults. Young toddlers often look at their caregiver before they approach an unfamiliar object. Once they are slightly older, children increasingly ask direct questions to obtain emotional information. Three-year-olds often ask questions about dangerous things. As children grow older and more independent in their evaluations, "negotiations" about the emotional content of different situations become more common (Walden & Ogan, 1988).

One of the characteristics of emotional referencing is its focus on external circumstances, such as a particular person, object or event. A mere mood change in the child does not qualify as social referencing. The child's feelings must be directed at something the adult has reacted to as well. When an adult shows a particular emotion, the child always seeks to identify the aspect of the situation associated with the emotion. A child who takes the initiative must be able to direct the adult's attention at the element of concern to find out how the adult reacts to this particular element, for example a nearby dog. The principle is the same as for establishing **joint attention**, which appears around the same age (see Book 5, *Communication and Language*

Development, Chapter 2). Occasionally, children can misinterpret the source of the expression of an adult, but, in order to be useful at all, social referencing must essentially be secure – information that appears uncertain would undermine its very function. As children also have to trust the other person, they usually use parents, siblings and other familiar or clearly competent persons for social referencing.

7

Emotional Development in Childhood and Adolescence

With age, children recognize a greater range of emotions and become more familiar with the relationship between emotions and external events, desires and beliefs. At about 3–4 years of age, children are able to name the types of emotions that commonly accompany different situations and, around the age of 5, they begin to gain a broader understanding of the expressions and causes of emotions (Gross & Bailif, 1991; Pons et al., 2004).

Self-referential Emotions

Children's emerging recognition of themselves as a *self-as-known*, or *me*, at the end of the second year (see Book 7, *Social Relations, Self-awareness and Identity*, Chapter 20) represents the beginning of **self-referential** (or **self-conscious**) **emotions** (Figure 7.1). These emotions are founded on **self-evaluation**, personal standards and assumptions about how one is evaluated by others and are primarily related to social relations (Lagattuta & Thompson, 2007; Zinck, 2008). Emotions based on a personal moral standard are often called *moral emotions* (Dahl et al., 2011; Eisenberg, 2000). Guilt and pride are examples of self-directed emotions that may have their basis in a personal standard, whereas contempt and disgust are examples of moral emotions that can be directed at others (Tangney et al., 2007; Tracy & Robins, 2004).

Additionally, self-referential emotions have a regulating function. Shame and guilt reduce the likelihood of repeating the action that triggered the emotion, whether it is something unreasonable a child has said or the inability to master a skill that is expected at a certain age. Younger children can feel proud to be able to eat by themselves and feel ashamed when they make a mess. At the same time, expressions

DOI: 10.4324/9781003292531-8

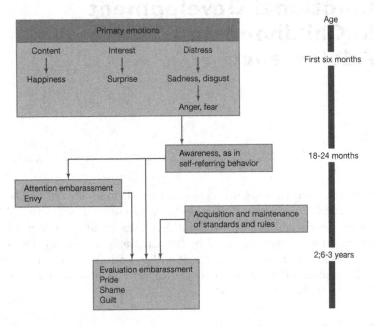

Figure 7.1 Self-referential emotions.

Early development of self-referential emotions (elaborated from Lewis, 1993, p. 232, 2007, p. 135).

of guilt and shame show that children have insight into their own actions and, thus, reduce the likelihood of negative reactions from others. Pride over good grades will usually increase the time and effort a child spends on homework in the future (Beer & Keltner, 2004).

Pride

Pride is a combination of feeling joy and mastery. In early childhood, pride is a general feeling of doing "well," often as a result of adults' praise or recognition, such as a positive comment about a child's drawing. With age, children begin to develop a personal standard (Sroufe, 1996). Winning a race, for example, increasingly leads to expressions of joy in 2–5-year-olds (Stipek et al., 1992). Pride is associated with achievement. Three-year-olds only show pride when they are able to master a task they find difficult; mastery of simple tasks does not lead to expressions of pride (Tracy & Robins, 2007). Children will not feel proud when they are praised for something they have been able to do for a while, but may instead believe that the person praising them has little confidence in their abilities (Dweck, 1999).

The understanding of pride develops somewhat later than the expression of pride. Around the age of 4 years, children begin to recognize pride in the facial expressions and posture of others (without supporting situational cues), but, until the age of 7, expressions of pride are often perceived as joy. All the way up to the age of 11,

Pride of mastery.

Shame of failure.

children have trouble differentiating between the happiness of getting something they like without having done anything in particular, such as Grandpa buying an ice cream, and the pride of getting something after making an effort, such as an award for throwing a ball a long distance after practicing for a long time (Kornilaki & Chlouverakis, 2004; Tracy et al., 2005). The ability to differentiate self-referential emotions thus requires both cognitive skills and social insight.

Shame and Guilt

Shame is related to the violation of personal standards. Toddlers only show shame when their wrongdoing is discovered by others. Around 3 years of age, children begin to feel ashamed when they are unable to accomplish a given task. Girls show more shame than boys, but also display significant **individual differences** early in development. Children who often show shame during **preschool age** have a tendency to continue to do so at **school age** as well (Mills, 2003; Mills et al., 2010).

Shame reflects children's perception of how they are evaluated by others. Children who have experienced social trauma or being rejected typically describe feelings of shame. Girls who have been subjected to neglect show less pride when they master something and generally show more shame than girls who have not been victims of neglect. Boys who have been subjected to neglect show less pride as well as shame. Children who have been sexually abused often blame themselves and feel ashamed about the abuse (Mills, 2005).

Guilt is defined as an intense feeling of having transgressed one's own standards. It differs from shame in that it focuses on a failed task rather than a failed **self** (Lewis, 2007). In one study, the leg of a doll had been attached so it would fall off while 2-year-olds played with it and the experimenter was in another room. Some of the children – the avoiders – reacted in a way similar to shame – they avoided the experimenter when she returned and waited to tell her what had happened. Other children – the amenders – showed more guilt-related behavior: they repaired the doll and promptly told the experimenter about the incident (Barrett et al., 1993). However, most likely, the children's expression of guilt merely reflected their expectations that the adult would scold them or react negatively in other ways. Children usually do not show guilt based on a personal standard until the age of 3–5 years, when they also begin to show signs of a moral standard. Girls' expressions of guilt are more pronounced than those of boys, but only after the age of 3 years (Kochanska et al., 2002). Shame and guilt are complex emotions, and children are well into school age before they are able to distinguish between them based on the underlying events (Ferguson et al., 1991).

Shame and guilt are important for children's social adjustment but can also contribute to maladjustment and a poor **self-image**. Children who have suffered neglect and abuse often react with shame (see previous page), but children who have been subjected to excessive control by their parents can also develop strong feelings of shame and guilt. Some children take responsibility for situations in which they have no part. They may believe, for example, that it is their fault that their depressed mother or father is distressed (Zahn-Waxler et al., 1984). There is a relationship between excessive guilt and shame and the development of depression and other mental health disorders (Dost & Yagmurlu, 2008; Mills, 2005), while lack of shame and guilt is related to the development of psychopathic traits (Frick et al., 2014) (see Chapter 24, this volume).

Embarrassment

Embarrassment is social. *Exposure embarrassment* is an unpleasant emotion associated with feeling observed and exposed, while *evaluative embarrassment* stems from an assumption or fear of being evaluated by others against one's own will (see Figure 7.1). Feelings of insecurity and an inability to take the perspective of others can cause children to think that others pay particular attention to them and focus on their negative sides and, thus, lead to embarrassment and social anxiety (Miller, 2007). Children with social-cognitive disorders, such as high-functioning children with **autism spectrum disorder**, are often anxious and easily embarrassed when they think someone is watching them (Kuusikko et al., 2008).

Cultural Differences

The basis for self-referential emotions varies with each culture. Shame, for example, is related to violating the norms of modesty in Japan and China, whereas, in the United States, it is usually associated with a shortcoming in personal qualities. Similarly, pride is related to individual traits in the United States, whereas it is associated with contributing to the benefit of others in China. Chinese parents talk about shame when their children do not behave as expected by society (Fung et al., 2003; Mesquita & Karasawa, 2004).

Further Emotional Development

The ability to recognize more differentiated and subtle emotional expressions continues to evolve throughout childhood and **adolescence** (Montirosso et al., 2009). Children gradually gain a better understanding of the types of emotions they might expect and express in different situations. They realize that there are differences in what people feel and how they express themselves, and that they can hide their feelings from others. They can talk about emotions they have experienced in the past and discuss what leads up to emotions and the consequences they can have (Bretherton et al., 1986). In adolescence, self-referential emotions are increasingly related to comparisons with peers.

Toward school age, children become better at putting a name to their own emotional states, as well as those of others. They can explain that they look forward to something or that someone is angry with them because they have done something wrong. Ten-year-olds know, on average, eight words for happy feelings, six words for sad feelings and six words for scary feelings. Fourteen-year-olds know about the same number of words for happy and scary feelings, but they know more words for sad feelings, at least when it comes to girls (Doost et al., 1999). Both children and adolescents are better at labeling the emotions in stories than in facial expressions alone (Widen et al., 2015).

Children also begin to understand mixed emotions, for example that people can feel both pride and sadness at the same time (Denham, 2007). In one study, 5–10-year-olds were told a story about a girl who had been rejected by her best friend and then asked what the girl felt when she met her friend again. The youngest children simply based their responses on the current situation and the idea that children are happy to meet their best friends and answered that the girl would feel happy. The older children also took into account what had happened earlier and said the girl would be upset when she met her friend (Gnepp & Gould, 1985). In late childhood, children begin to understand that the emotional content of a situation can be seen from several angles, and that people can have conflicting feelings (Pons et al., 2004).

Emotion Regulation

Throughout childhood, children continue to regulate their emotions in cooperation with adults and older children. Parents communicate how and when it is appropriate to express emotions, such as not to laugh at someone who has been hurt, how to react to others' emotional expressions and how children can regulate their emotional expressions in culturally appropriate ways (Eisenberg et al., 1998; Halberstadt & Lozada, 2011; Morris et al., 2007). Once children are about 6 years old, parents in many cultures begin to expect them to express their emotions according to the culture's norms and rules. Japanese mothers expect more emotional control of their children than American mothers, such as refraining from crying and coping with their anger on their own (Hess et al., 1980).

Preschool children regulate their emotions mostly through action or by seeking help from others. They might crawl underneath the bed to avoid something they do not like, hug a teddy bear when they are upset or ask an adult for comfort. Children evolve from "being their emotion" to representing their emotional state through **symbols** and language and by processing it through play, imagination and conversations with adults (Greenspan & Greenspan, 1985). Once they reach school age, children make increasing use of *cognitive strategies*, such as saying to themselves "I can do it," redefining the situation or trying to think of something else. Five-year-olds need help with this, whereas 10-year-olds make spontaneous use of these types of strategies (Brenner & Salovey, 1997).

Children also become better at both hiding their emotions and knowing what situations require it. At preschool age, they are to some extent aware of when to modify, amplify or suppress their emotional expressions. Children of 3–4 years who have hurt themselves cry more often when they know that a familiar adult is watching them (Blurton-Jones, 1967). They clearly express disappointment when they open an uninteresting present by themselves, but moderate their expression when the person who gave the present watches them open the package. Six-year-old girls hide their disappointment more than boys of the same age when receiving a gift that is too childish for their age (Cole, 1986; Saarni, 1984). Children express anger more often when provoked by their peers than when provoked by adults (Gross & Harris, 1988; Saarni, 1988).

The ability to regulate emotions and deal with distress and stress independently and together with one's peers is important for the development of independence in childhood and adolescence. When children of early school age are asked who gives them emotional support, most of them mention their parents. Older children more often respond that they would seek help from friends (Asher & Parker, 1989). Adolescents often ask their peers for advice on how to deal with unfamiliar social and emotional situations (Steinberg & Silk, 2002). Sharing feelings and giving emotional support are key elements in adolescents' descriptions of friendship (see Book 7, *Social Relations, Self-awareness and Identity*, Chapter 13), and adolescents particularly turn to their friends when they need support in dealing with emotionally difficult situations, also via online contact (Dolev-Cohen & Barak, 2013; Rossman, 1992).

Emotionality in Adolescence

Adolescence is often described as a turbulent and emotional period. In one study, 12–15-year-olds reported more events involving negative emotions related to family, school and friends than 9–11-year-olds (Larson & Ham, 1993). Higher levels of **emotionality** among adolescents are related to puberty and the body's physical changes, but also to a **role** that varies between being child and adult. The transfer of responsibility and control from the parents to the adolescent implies greater demands on self-regulation, and social embarrassment and anxiety are common (Cui et al., 2014). Adolescents are sensitive to being evaluated by others, and feelings of both shame and pride increase in frequency and intensity. Many adolescents experience stress in connection with change of school and growing academic and social demands. Taken together, these factors can lead to greater emotional lability, anxiety and depression among adolescents (Laugesen et al., 2003; Zeman et al., 2006).

8

The Influence of the Environment on Children's Emotions

Children's earliest emotional experiences usually occur within the family, and the family's emotional climate has an impact on how children express and regulate emotions. Toddlers tend to spend much time together with their mothers, and, when the latter show many positive emotions, the children show more positive emotions than negative ones as well. Toddlers with mothers who are often angry show negative emotions more frequently than positive ones, while toddlers with emotionally intense mothers tend to be more emotional than toddlers whose mothers are less intense (Denham, 1989; Denham & Grout, 1993).

Sensitivity

Parental **sensitivity** and reactions help shape children's feelings about themselves and others and are important for whether a child learns that it is acceptable to show emotions and seek help and support from others. A study of maternal reactions to anger in 2-year-old children found that children of mothers who responded quickly to anger were angry less often and reacted more positively to other people when their mother was absent than children whose mothers reacted more slowly to their child's anger. When the mothers responded quickly to their child's expressions of fear, the children showed less fear in other situations and more joy and interest in their surroundings. The children who were encouraged to show emotions when they felt anxious were also more popular in kindergarten and rarely showed anger in socially unacceptable ways. The children whose parents tried to get them to show little emotion, for example by asking them not to make such a fuss about what bothered them, were perceived to be socially less competent by their kindergarten teachers (Denham, 1993).

DOI: 10.4324/9781003292531-9

When parents show little reaction to their child's expressions of distress, children can learn to inhibit these expressions. They may be less likely to seek contact or may adopt other strategies to reduce their own distress (Bridges & Grolnick, 1995). Likewise, children who are punished for crying and showing negative emotions learn to inhibit these expressions (Morris et al., 2007), with possible consequences for their ability to self-regulate. One study found that boys of mothers with a restrictive attitude to negative emotional expressions showed physiological arousal when they saw negative emotions in others, while at the same time denying that they felt distress (Eisenberg, 1991). For children to learn to manage negative emotions, they need experience with emotionally demanding situations. If children are not given the opportunity to show these types of emotions, they will not be able to learn to regulate them and will feel insecure in situations in which they are likely to occur. It is notable that children who are told by their parents to restrain their display of emotions in order not to hurt someone do not react in this way. It is parents' repeated request for emotional restraint when they themselves are upset or anxious that can lead children to become more aroused in situations involving negative emotions.

The previously mentioned studies suggest that sensitive parents who react quickly are advantageous to children's emotional development, but the relationship between parental reaction and children's emotional regulation is not so simple. Roberts and Strayer (1987) found that children with moderately responsive parents showed the highest level of social competence. Their explanation for this is that adults who are highly responsive to children's negative emotions can hinder children from engaging in difficult social interactions with others and prevent them from getting sufficient opportunities to learn to cope with negative emotions. Other studies have found that children whose parents try to regulate their child's negative emotions with "time out," telling them to go into another room when they are crying, show little anger when together with other children. The same applies to children whose parents react with **sympathy** and comfort (Eisenberg & Fabes, 1994). Consequently, it seems that children who receive help in regulating their own negative emotions show fewer such emotions in interaction with other children. The way in which help is offered is not a deciding factor. At the same time, it is important to remember that parental reactions are affected by children's temperament (see Part II, this volume). The ability to regulate emotions is the result of interaction between the child's characteristics and the way in which the environment supports the child's self-regulation.

Talking about Emotions

Talking with others about emotions and emotional situations is important for the development of emotion regulation. Children first talk about emotions within the family. In early childhood, mothers largely talk about emotions when children have pain or feel happy, but also when they are angry, upset or agitated about something. These conversations give children insight into emotional states, what they are called, how they are expressed, how they affect others and how they can regulate them. Most 2-year-olds use language to express concern, comfort and sympathy when others seem upset. One study found that half of the emotional explanations relating to everyday situations among 3-year-olds involved internal or mental causes, such as: *She is upset because she misses her mom*, or *She was angry because she thought it was her turn*. Most explanations had to do with children not getting their way or their wishes fulfilled (Fabes et al., 1991). Another study found that 3-year-olds who often talked with their parents about the cause of emotions showed better emotional skills 3 years later than children who had not had these types of conversations as often (Dunn et al., 1991).

Girls seem to talk more about emotions than boys. In an American kindergarten, 77 percent of the children's emotional statements came from girls, and, at school age, the girls used more emotional words than boys (Doost et al., 1999). One reason for this may be that parents and older siblings of kindergarten-age children ask more questions and comment more on the emotional life of girls than of boys of the same age, although boys and girls initiate these types of conversations equally often (Dunn et al., 1987). There are also differences in the types of emotion talk boys and girls are engaged in. Mothers of 3-year-olds discuss sad emotions in greater detail with their daughters and anger in more detail with their sons. In addition, they focus more on restoring relationships when their daughters are angry with a girlfriend, whereas they show more acceptance of retaliation when their sons are angry with a friend (Fivush, 1991). **Gender differences** continue into later childhood and adolescence. More often than boys, girls say they want to talk to siblings or others when they are sad. They also focus more on the emotion itself than boys do and use more cognitive strategies to try to suppress feelings. Boys are more likely to use strenuous physical activity to regulate their emotions, for example in situations in which they feel bad, nervous or worried (Brenner & Salovey, 1997).

9

Reacting to Emotions in Others

Children's social world contains a myriad of emotional situations and expressions. Their reactions to the emotional expressions of others reflect their interpretation of these expressions and situations, as well as their own emotional regulation abilities.

Empathy and Sympathy

Empathy and sympathy are not emotions in their own right but *emotional reactions* to the condition or situation of another person. *Empathy* means to feel *with* someone else and to experience an emotion similar to that of the other person. This can be pain or sadness, but also joy or anger, depending on the other person's situation. *Sympathy* or *cognitive empathy* means to feel *for* someone else and implies an understanding that the other person has the feelings he or she has. Both reactions require an awareness of the fact that another person feels something specific; it is not enough for the child to be affected by someone else's mood (de Waal, 2008; Eisenberg et al., 1992).

Hoffman (1987) describes four **stages** in the development of empathy (Table 9.1). In the first stage, infants can show expressions similar to those they perceive in others, but probably reflecting the child's perception of the situation more than the other person's emotional state (see also social referencing, p. 26, this volume). In the second stage, children are aware that someone else is unhappy, rather than they themselves. They try to give comfort, for example by fetching an adult or offering a favorite toy to a crying child. In the third stage, beginning at the age of 2–3 years, children's attempts at comforting are more adapted to the person being comforted. They might fetch the crying child's mother, rather than just any adult (Eisenberg, 1992; Zahn-Waxler et al., 1992). The fourth stage starts during school age.

DOI: 10.4324/9781003292531-10

Table 9.1 Four stages in the development of empathy (Hoffman, 1987)

1 Global empathy	In the first year of life, children are able to express an emotion they have witnessed, for example by crying when another child is crying, but their emotions are involuntary and undifferentiated.
2 "Egocentric" empathy	Beginning in the second year, children actively offer to help others. They make appropriate efforts to empathize, but in a way they themselves would find comforting and is thus egocentric.
3 Empathy for another's feelings	In the third year of life, when they also begin to engage in **role-play**, children become aware that other people's feelings can differ from their own. Their response thus becomes more adapted to the needs of others.
4 Empathy for another's general plight	Late childhood or early adolescence brings a growing awareness of the fact that other people have feelings beyond the immediate situation that extend to other general life conditions. Older children and adolescents can feel empathy for entire groups, such as poor or oppressed people, and thereby go beyond the immediate situational experience.

Now, empathy includes an understanding not only of someone else's immediate feelings but also of the person's experiences and situation. Children aged 10–12 years, for example, are better than younger schoolchildren at regulating the impact of someone else's grief in order to be able to offer comfort (Saarni, 1992).

The social environment is important for children's development of empathic and sympathetic reactions. Parents who react with empathy and sympathy when children are upset or anxious also seem to foster children who respond with empathy and sympathy when others are sad or upset (Spinrad & Stifter, 2006). Personal negative experiences do not lead to insight and empathy but rather to the contrary. In a study of 1–3-year-olds who had been victims of neglect, the children showed little concern for other children who were crying. Some of them threatened or physically attacked the crying child; others became agitated and anxious. Both reactions can be the result of the children's rejection and the lack of help they received in coping with their own and others' emotions. Children of the same age who had not been subjected to neglect also reacted differently, but were generally more caring. They looked at the crying child, touched and caressed her or tried to comfort her in other ways (Main & George, 1985).

A low degree of empathic arousal can lead to poor motivation to help and comfort others, but a strong empathic response does not necessarily lead to more concern for others. Children who experience strong empathy with another child can become extremely aroused, feel distress and focus more on their own discomfort than on the other child's problems. When they see a child get hurt and start to cry, they can withdraw to avoid having to hear the sound of crying instead of offering help. Children with more moderate emotional reactions to such situations, or with good emotion regulation, are not as overpowered by their own emotional reactions and are able to help and support the crying child (Eisenberg et al., 1997). Therefore, empathy is not always an advantage. A high degree of empathy can increase children's worry and guilt and, thus, represent **vulnerability** for developing **internalizing disorders** (Tone & Tully, 2014). For example, children who become too involved with their depressed mother tend to blame themselves for the mother's problems and develop excessive guilt (Zahn-Waxler & Kochanska, 1990).

Reactions to Negative Emotions in Others

Children seem to be especially aware of anger and other negative emotions in other people (LoBue, 2009; Vaish et al., 2008). They often become distressed and have problems regulating themselves when they experience such emotions in others. Parental conflicts with lots of quarreling and aggression in children's first months of life increase the likelihood that they will react with withdrawal, negativity and distress to novelty at the age of 6 months (Crockenberg et al., 2007).

In one experiment, 2-year-old children, accompanied by their mother and a friend of the same age, witnessed two women pretending to argue for 5 minutes, followed by a 2-minute conversation during which they resolved their differences. Half of the 2-year-olds became quite distressed during the quarrel, moved toward their mother and expressed verbal and non-verbal concern. One-third of the children did not move during the exchange. Furthermore, children who had witnessed the pretend quarrel were later more aggressive toward their friend or took away the friend's toy slightly more often than they had done previously. One month later, some of the children witnessed a similar type of quarrel. On this occasion, an even larger number of children became anxious, and their subsequent aggressive behavior was more frequent and intense (Cummings et al., 1985). Hence, the effect increased with the number of experiences.

A similar study found that 4–5-year-olds became more distressed than the 2-year-olds had been, but had a larger repertoire of regulatory strategies and showed more varied responses. Some of them tried to get away, while others smiled. Some watched the arguing adults and looked back and forth between their mother and their friend, maybe to see how they reacted. The most ambivalent children – those who were both distressed and smiled – also showed the most aggressive behavior afterwards (Cummings, 1987).

Harris (1994) points out that there is no clear explanation for why witnessing a quarrel would lead to greater aggression in young children. Their reaction was not simply imitative: the adults only had a verbal argument, whereas the children displayed non-verbal aggressive behavior. One explanation may be that seeing adults quarrel counteracted the **inhibitions** children were brought up to have in connection with both verbal quarrels and physical acts of aggression (Bandura, 1986). Another possibility is that the quarrel elicited greater emotional arousal and, in turn, led the children to interpret their peers' behavior as provocative rather than positive. The latter explanation is supported by the observation that the most aggressive boys were more aroused after witnessing a pretend quarrel than the boys who showed less aggression. It is also important to stress that not all children in Cummings's study responded the same way. Although some showed aggressive behavior, others seemed concerned and tried to offer comfort. Several children attempted to get away, perhaps because they were overwhelmed by their own feelings of empathy. In a study of 6–9-year-old children, boys had a tendency to react to anger and aggression by showing anger and aggression themselves, whereas girls expressed distress and anxiousness instead (Cummings et al., 1989). In another study involving a pretend quarrel, 9–11-year-olds showed the strongest aversion to anger in adults, while 17–19-year-olds showed the least (Cummings et al., 1991). This suggests that children are more vulnerable to such experiences than adolescents, who have developed a higher level of self-regulation.

The results of these studies emphasize the importance of children's emotional environment. Studies have furthermore shown that children who grow up in families with many conflicts involving anger and aggression have less **emotional competence**, perform more aggressive actions and more often develop internalizing and **externalizing disorders** than other children. It is possible that parents who frequently have conflicts expose their children to more stress than parents who quarrel less, and offer their children less help with emotional regulation (Katz et al., 2007; Morris et al., 2007; Raver,

2004). Additionally, parents serve as role models for solving interpersonal problems, and children and adolescents with frequent exposure to parental conflicts have a tendency to try to resolve conflicts with physical aggression and similar strategies (Cummings & Davies, 1994, 2002; Duman & Margolin, 2007; Maxwell & Maxwell, 2003). Some children and adolescents live in conflict areas with high levels of negative emotions. They react with distress and anxiety but may also experience desensitization, with reduced reactions to anger and conflict (Cummings et al., 2009, 2017; Tarabah et al., 2016).

Parents with Depressive Traits

Depressive symptoms are relatively common in mothers of infants and toddlers and somewhat less common in fathers (Dix & Meunier, 2009; Wilson & Durbin, 2010). Depressive mothers are typically passive and despondent, and their children show fewer positive emotions and look less often at their mother's face than other children (Silk et al., 2006). Many of the mothers' emotional expressions are related to their general condition and do not give the child information about the emotional content of the situation, for example the presence of something funny or dangerous. This reduces the children's basis for emotional learning through social referencing (see p. 26, this volume) and leaves them with a more limited repertoire of strategies for emotional regulation (Field, 1984; Field et al., 1988, 2009).

Peers

Children share many experiences, norms, challenges and perspectives with their peers. Peer interaction is therefore important for children to learn when and how to express emotions (Burleson & Kunkel, 2002; Denham, 2007). Children typically meet joy with joy, whereas they meet other children's expressions of sadness with attempts to include them in play or other activities (Strayer, 1980). The reactions change with age. Toddlers react more often to other children's expressions of anger than to expressions of sadness (Denham, 1986). Preschoolers rarely react to someone who seems hurt or angry and show the strongest reactions to expressions of joy. As they tend to stay away from children who often seem angry, the latter have poorer chances of social learning and participation (Barth & Archibald, 2003). Children who frequently show anger and little ability to self-regulate are at **risk** of being teased and bullied by their peers (Hanish et al., 2004).

10

Emotional Disorders

Symptoms of anxiety, depression and regulation disorders are relatively common in childhood and adolescence, and some children meet the criteria for a diagnosis (see Book 1, *Theory and Methodology*, Chapter 33). This also applies to children who show **atypical development** in other areas, such as children with autism spectrum disorders (Gillberg et al., 2016; Joshi et al., 2010). Anxiety and depression illustrate the complexity in the development of **mental disorders** in children and adolescents. Children with anxiety often show symptoms of depression, but the two disorders develop along somewhat different paths. An unstable home environment and negative life events seem to have a greater impact on the development of depression than of anxiety (Karevold et al., 2009; McLaughlin & King, 2015).

Depression and anxiety disorders tend to have a major impact on peer relations and school performance, but many children and adolescents are not referred for treatment. Programs at school may increase the likelihood of detecting and preventing disorders (Werner-Seidler et al., 2017).

Anxiety Disorders

Among all mental disorders, those involving anxiety appear earliest in life, perhaps because they are so closely associated with children's fundamental need for security (see Book 7, *Social Relations, Self-awareness and Identity*, Chapter 3). Attention to potential danger is important for children's well-being and survival, and fear fulfills an important function in children's ability to adapt and cope with the environment. The border between natural apprehension and fear on the one hand, and anxiety disorders requiring treatment on the other, is not always

DOI: 10.4324/9781003292531-11

clear, and milder forms can be particularly difficult to identify. Unlike fear, anxiety is characterized by excessive and pervasive emotions that occur in situations that are not immediately dangerous or threatening but are perceived as such by the child (Pine & Klein, 2015).

When and how anxiety disorders present themselves coincide to some degree with other developmental traits (Vasey et al., 2014). Phobias emerge at the same time as children begin to show a normal fear response. Separation anxiety is most common in the years following the child's first reactions to being separated from **attachment** figures (see Book 7, *Social Relations, Self-awareness and Identity*, Chapter 4). In adolescence, social anxiety is the most common disorder, but adolescents generally show more symptoms of worry and anxiety than children and adults (Pine & Klein, 2015). Thus, the basis for anxiety disorders can differ throughout life. Most children with early anxiety disorders do not develop anxiety disorders in adulthood, but many adults with anxiety disorders have experienced problems with anxiety in childhood (Gregory et al., 2007). Most adolescents with symptoms of anxiety do not develop anxiety disorders as adults (Pine & Fox, 2015).

Developmental psychopathology (see Book 1, *Theory and Methodology*, Chapter 9) emphasizes the importance of temperament and attention regulation in the development of anxiety (Ollendick & Hirshfeld-Becker, 2002; Pérez-Edgar et al., 2014). Genetic vulnerability seems to play a role (Feigon et al., 2001). Although heritability is higher in childhood than in adulthood, it also stabilizes over time. This suggests an age-related increase in the impact of cultural and social factors on children's ability to cope with anxiety and stressful situations (Nivard et al., 2015; Zheng et al., 2016). It is possible that the genetic basis is the same as for inhibited temperament (see Part II, this volume). Toddlers with this type of temperament are vulnerable to developing anxiety, but only a small percentage of all children with inhibited temperament develop anxiety disorders (Buss & McDoniel, 2016; Pérez-Edgar et al., 2014). One explanation for the relation between inhibited temperament and anxiety disorders may be that children with this temperament type tend to be careful, do not get to know their emotional environment and therefore are unable to distinguish between what is and what is not safe. Their constant alertness to potential threats shows up in the form of anxiety symptoms (Kalin, 1993).

Children with symptoms of anxiety are more attentive to novel events and facial expressions reflecting a possible threat than other children (Dudeney et al., 2015; Mathews & MacLeod, 2005). Although attention to potentially threatening events is important, it becomes non-functional when it persists over time, and can promote and maintain anxiety. A number of factors can contribute to developing this type of sustained attention. One possibility is that toddlers with an inhibited temperament are particularly sensitive to novelty and threatening expressions and events and therefore overestimate the importance of such events. Another explanation is that the children fail to unlearn the early innate attention with quick reactions to new and uncertain events (Pérez-Edgar et al., 2011, 2014). They develop an attention bias to threats that involve many, or nearly all, novel and slightly more complex situations, including neutral **communication** from other children and adults (Briggs-Gowan et al., 2015). Britton and colleagues (2011) suggest that these blurred lines between threat and safety may contribute to the development of chronic anxiety disorders in adulthood.

There is no evidence that the family's overall level of functioning and **parenting styles** contribute to the development of anxiety, but there is a link between anxiety disorders and overprotective, "hostile" upbringing with little **autonomy** encouragement (Jongerden & Bögels, 2015; Lebowitz et al., 2014). In addition, studies have shown transactional effects: children of anxious parents can become especially attentive to potential dangers, and anxiety in children can lead to overprotective parents (Rapee et al., 2009; Vasey et al., 2014). Mothers of anxious children can become over-involved and controlling and thereby contribute to increasing their child's anxiety (Eley et al., 2010, Hudson et al., 2009, 2011).

Anxiety thus seems to be related to social stress and insecurity (Rapee et al., 2009). Research has found that negative life events only have a limited impact, but that an unsafe or threatening childhood environment can increase children's vigilance about non-specific threats. Children's sensitivity to potential threats can furthermore amplify the effect of exposure to domestic violence. Studies have described symptoms of anxiety and depression in underage refugees and others who have experienced war (for example in Vietnam, Bosnia, Kuwait and Lebanon). These symptoms can be exacerbated by factors that maintain children's psychological distress after they have come to more peaceful areas, such as uncertain asylum status, long waiting times, frequent relocations, social isolation and poor housing conditions (Ehntholt & Yule, 2006). Correspondingly, early intervention and social support for children exposed to war trauma can help reduce anxiety many years later (Llabre et al., 2015). Studies of children who experienced Hurricane Katrina in Louisiana in 2005 found that the deployment of social support, especially from parents, had a protective effect (Lai et al., 2015).

Anxiety disorders can lead to negative cascading effects. For example, separation anxiety may manifest itself in sleep disorders during early school age, somatic complaints in late childhood and school refusal in adolescence (Vasey et al., 2014). Avoidance is a common strategy to reduce anxiety, and many children with anxiety try to avoid their peers. A possible consequence of this is that children miss out on play and interaction with their peers, while stress and worries lay hold of their cognitive resources and draw attention away from social interaction and schoolwork. Children with anxiety disorders have fewer friends than other children, are perceived as less competent and are at greater risk of being bullied (Buss & McDoniel, 2016; Rubin et al., 2009).

The extent of the disorder varies: in some adolescents, social anxiety is limited to specific situations; others struggle in many situations. Anxiety may interfere with both learning and social life at school, as well as romantic relationships (Kagan & Snidman, 2004). Social anxiety can lead to poor school performance and difficulties coping with the work environment (Ollendick & Hirshfeld-Becker, 2002). Some children with anxiety disorder also fulfill the criteria for behavioral disorders; this group generally does not cope as well as children who have anxiety disorder without behavioral disorders (Halldorsdottir & Ollendick, 2014).

It can be easier to affect the course of the disorder earlier rather than later in development (Pérez-Edgar et al., 2014), and the many potentially negative consequences make a strong argument for preventive measures and early intervention (Paulus et al., 2015). Prevention is especially targeted at children who appear anxious and socially inhibited and aims to teach them to master new situations and deal with their own anxiety, thereby supporting their **self-esteem**, social participation and well-being (Macklem, 2014). A number of studies have shown that it is possible to influence the developmental course of anxious children as early as preschool age (Chronis-Tuscano et al., 2015; Rapee et al., 2010). For example, the intervention program *Strengthening Early Emotional Development* (SEED) consists of gatherings and group training in socio-emotional skills for preschool children with mild and moderate anxiety symptoms, as well as concurrent discussion groups for parents (Fox et al., 2012).

Late childhood and adolescence are vulnerable periods for developing anxiety, and most preventive programs target this age group. Studies, however, indicate that prevention at age 9–10 is more effective than at 14–16 years of age (Lau & Rapee, 2011). *Coping Cat* includes individual intervention and prevention in groups. Based on **cognitive behavioral therapy**, it aims to help children and adolescents recognize and cope with difficult situations and anxiety (Gosch et al., 2012; Kendall, 1994). *Friends* (Barrett & Turner, 2001; Barrett et al., 2014) is based on *Coping Cat* and consists of several age-specific programs with positive group activities for preventing anxiety: *Fun Friends* (4–7 years), *Friends for Life* (8–11 years) and *My Friends Youth* (12–16 years) (Higgins & O'Sullivan, 2015). *Emotion*, designed for children aged 8–13 years, aims to raise awareness about the relationship between experienced emotions and emotions and situations, and to promote a positive sense of self and active social participation (Martinsen et al., 2016). In line with a transactional point of view, several studies involving parents and children have shown reduced levels of anxiety in children and of distress and anxiety in parents (Anticich et al., 2013; Fox et al., 2012).

Treatment includes relaxation exercises, emotional training, strategies for coping with situations involving anxiety, controlled mental or physical exposure to anxiety-inducing things or situations (desensitization), and educating children and parents about anxiety and its treatment (Neil & Christensen, 2009; Weems & Varela, 2011). Medication of children with anxiety disorders is common in the United States but less accepted in other countries (Pine & Klein, 2015). *Cognitive behavioral therapy* aims to change negative thinking patterns and teach children with social anxiety disorder to cope with difficult situations. Treatment includes gradual exposure to situations that trigger anxiety, such as separation from parents or phobia of things or places, and use of relaxation techniques and cognitive strategies. Parents often have a central role in following up these initiatives on a daily basis (Rapee et al., 2010). *Attention modification* is a relatively new cognitive method. Treatment uses computer programs that lead the child's attention from threatening to neutral stimuli on the screen (such as faces with an angry expression to faces with a neutral expression) or from neutral to positive expressions (Bar-Haim, 2010; MacLeod & Clarke, 2015). Only a limited number of studies have been conducted with children, but the preliminary results indicate that the method may help reduce symptoms of anxiety, including in children who have had little benefit from traditional cognitive behavior therapy (Bar-Haim et al., 2011;

Bechor et al., 2014; Lowther & Newman, 2014). However, not all children with anxiety disorders show increased attention to negative emotional expressions; it is therefore necessary to implement multiple strategies and adapt treatment to the individual child. **Assessment** of the child's abilities and other possible disorders will be important when choosing a treatment strategy. Moreover, it is important to look for positive resources as well as signs of other disorders in children who show symptoms of anxiety.

Depression

Depression is a **developmental disorder** with many possible causes and layers of symptoms and appears related to factors such as temperament, cognitive style and stress (Hankin, 2012). Whereas children with anxiety are wary of potential threats, children with depression ruminate on hopelessness and loss (Hankin, 2012; Hankin et al., 2010). There is some genetic vulnerability, but negative life events in childhood can have a major impact as well. Although adulthood depression is frequent in people subjected to physical, sexual or psychological abuse in childhood, not all individuals in this group develop depression. Children with the short **allele** of the 5-HTTLPR gene are susceptible to the influence of both good and bad environments (see Book 2, *Genes, Fetal Development and Early Neurological Development*, Chapter 6). Children with this allele who have been abused are more vulnerable to developing depression than abused children with other alleles of this gene (Saveanu & Nemeroff, 2012). Children of depressed parents have higher rates of depression. This may be owing to hereditary factors as well as the transmission of pessimistic attitudes and a negative cognitive style from parent to child (Restifo & Bögels, 2009).

Depression manifests itself somewhat differently depending on age, although it always implies a change of mood and behavior. Sleep problems are common during the preschool period; with increasing age, lack of energy and poor concentration become more prominent, along with an unwarranted sense of guilt and worthlessness (Reinfjell et al., 2016). Friends are central to young people's lives, and the breakup of a close friendship can be a difficult experience and lead to depression, guilt and anger (Rubin et al., 2013). Furthermore, depression is often accompanied by other impairments, including regulation disorders (see following page). Children and adolescents who have problems with online gaming have a higher **incidence** of depression, difficulties at school and behavioral disorders (Brunborg et al., 2014; Johansson et al., 2009). Adolescents with ADHD have more depressive symptoms than adolescents without ADHD (Seymour et al., 2012). Many children and adolescents with a mild **intellectual disability** have low self-esteem and symptoms of depression, feeling that others perceive them as "stupid" and look down on them (Dagnan & Sandhu, 1999; Masi, 1998).

Children and adolescents spend a lot of time at school. Here, their problems often become more apparent, and their depression is typically aggravated by social isolation and fewer friends. When adolescents are unable to solve the problems they face, they experience even more stress, low self-esteem and depression (Roberts, 2015). If left untreated, adolescent depression represents vulnerability to mental health problems in adulthood.

Different types of treatments are available for depression, including cognitive behavioral therapy and "interpersonal therapy," which builds on the notion that depressive symptoms affect social relations (Gladstone & Beardslee, 2009). Treatments aim to reduce negative thoughts and promote stress management, self-regulation and positive thinking (Corrieri et al., 2013; Horowitz & Garber, 2006; Roberts, 2015). Relaxation and participation in enjoyable activities are key elements, while attempts are made to change children's thinking and self-perception and improve their social and communication skills (Corcoran & Hanvey-Phillips, 2013). Conversations focusing on strengthening children's confidence and self-image can also help reduce depression (Roberts, 2015; Sowislo & Orth, 2013). At school, teachers can contribute by establishing good relationships with depressed children and helping them interact positively with other students (Patel et al., 2014). Studies have found that children and adolescents with symptoms of depression who attended the *Penn Resiliency Program* and the *Coping with Stress Course* showed fewer such symptoms after attending the program (Hetrick et al., 2015). Meta-studies, which combine results from many studies, however, have shown small or moderate effects of treatment on children (Bastounis et al., 2016; Forti-Buratti et al., 2016), possibly because a number of treatments place excessive demands on the cognitive, social and emotional skills of the individual child or adolescent (Garber et al., 2016).

The same treatment principles have also been applied to preventive measures for adolescents in general, as well as those who are vulnerable to developing depression. Some studies have found a lower incidence of depression in children and adolescents who followed this type of program, while other studies did not show a similarly positive effect. Many programs lack sufficient evidence, especially for long-term effects (Corcoran & Hanvey-Phillips, 2013; Gillham et al., 2007; Horowitz & Garber, 2006; Merry et al., 2012).

Regulation Disorders

Emotion dysregulation – both under- and **over-regulation** – can be found in descriptions of many psychiatric diagnoses (Kring & Werner, 2004; Mullin & Hinshaw, 2007), and developmental psychopathology places particular emphasis on emotion regulation (see Book 1, *Theory and Methodology*, Chapter 9). Many studies have found relations between younger children's ability to regulate emotions and later disorders. Children who are emotionally unstable, restless, readily distracted and negative at preschool age tend to be inattentive, distractible, hyperactive and antisocial at later school age. Children with attention disorders are restless and have problems regulating their emotions (Shaw et al., 2014). Actively aggressive and **antisocial behavior** in children and adolescents (see Chapter 27, this volume) is related to low activation and lack of emotionality (Mullin & Hinshaw, 2007). There are different strategies for regulating emotions, and adolescents with a limited repertoire have a greater incidence of internalizing problems than adolescents with a broader repertoire (Lougheed & Hollenstein, 2012). In children with autism spectrum disorders, cognitive **rigidity** and poor emotion understanding and sensitivity to changes in the environment contribute to problems with emotion regulation (Mazefsky & White, 2014). Thus, the relationship between emotion regulation, social competence and disorders in children is a complex one.

The main focus of developmental studies has been on children's under-regulation of anger and other negative emotions, probably because these can have a highly negative effect on the relationship between children and parents and children's social life in general (Valiente et al., 2004). Emotional dysregulation, however, can involve excessively strong or weak emotional expression, uninhibited or inhibited behavior, *internalizing* disorders characterized by shyness and withdrawal, and *externalizing* disorders marked by aggressive, disruptive and antisocial behavior (Mullin & Hinshaw, 2007; Nigg, 2000). Depression in girls is usually related to **over-controlled** behavior and anxiety, whereas depression in boys seems to be related to **under-controlled** behavior and aggression (Caspi et al., 1995).

The relationship between over- and under-regulation remains somewhat unclear. Depression in girls may be the result of over-regulated positive emotions together with under-regulated fear and other negative emotions (Mullin & Hinshaw, 2007). Children who both over-regulate positive emotions and under-regulate negative emotions are particularly vulnerable to disorders.

As emotion regulation has a social basis, regulation disorders can have a serious impact on children's social development. Some years into school age, children begin to compare their skills, attitudes, possessions and families with those of their peers. According to Harter (1987), the most serious consequence of low self-esteem based on these types of comparisons is that children can develop mood disturbances or, in more severe cases, depression. This in turn leads to cascading effects of decreased interest and motivation to participate in peer activities, lower activity levels and little support and attention from the environment. Similarly, friends who use adaptive strategies can contribute to better self-regulation in adolescents who struggle with emotionally challenging situations (Reindl et al., 2016). **Resilience** to negative emotions is another factor that helps children cope with comparisons that put them at a disadvantage.

The development and consequences of emotional over-regulation are not as well studied as those of under-regulation. Over-regulation can lead to poor emotional expressivity and inadequate emotional adaptation, whereby children suppress emotions instead of seeking help to deal with them. Consequently, children may have fewer emotional experiences and receive little help and support from others in emotionally difficult situations. This can make for poorer learning and affect children's **attachment behavior**, which is a means of seeking security in uncertain and complex situations (Nigg, 2006).

Summary of Part I

1   *Emotional development* involves changes in an individual's understanding and use of emotional expressions and emotional regulation. Emotions comprise seven key elements: *expression, understanding, experience, bodily responses, direction, action* and *regulation.* There is no clear distinction between generating and regulating emotions. Development progresses from reactive to largely voluntary regulation, and from seeking adult protection and help to self-regulation and seeking help from one's peers.

2   Some emotions seem to be *universal*: they share similar expressions and are elicited by the same types of situations in all cultures. Others show significant cultural differences in expression, perceived value and the different ages at which children are expected to show and regulate particular emotions.

3   Nearly all theories of emotional development are based on Darwin. According to *differential emotions theory*, children start with two innate forms of general positive or negative arousal, which are divided into progressively more demarcated and structurally consistent emotions. Theories of *discrete emotions* maintain that infants have an innate capacity to experience and express a number of basic emotions that are gradually combined into more complex emotions. From a *behavioral* point of view, development is determined by classical conditioning and differential responses. *Functionalist theories* focus on the relationship between emotions and the "object" at which they are directed, often another human being. Development reflects the changes in children's goals and their ability to regulate themselves and their social environment.

4   The *reflexive smile* is present at birth, while the *social smile* usually appears at the age of 6–10 weeks. Laughter comes at 3–4 months of age. Blind children begin to smile later than sighted children.

This shows that experience is of importance, but also that the development of smiling does not depend on seeing others smile. Newborns *cry* when they experience high levels of physiological activation. Crying patterns are altered owing to both maturation and changes in children's activities.

5   In the middle of the first year of life, children begin to show *fear*, and the elicitation of fear depends on the child's development of other skills, such as independent locomotion. At preschool age, children are often scared of fantasy characters, whereas fear at school age is mostly related to physical injury and danger. In adolescence, social fear becomes dominant. Clear expressions of *anger* commonly emerge at 4–6 months, such as when children are impeded in their movements or when parents do not fulfill their expectations. In the course of early childhood, anger is increasingly less accepted by parents. Children are perceived to be *sad* when they show little facial expression, activity and positive response. Infants show many expressions resembling the emotional expressions of adults, but not always in relevant situations; interpreting the infant's inner state based on these expressions is unreliable.

6   Children show an early ability to distinguish the emotional expressions of voices a little before faces. Initially, expressions have to be distinct, but, with age, children gradually improve at recognizing more subtle emotional expressions. They also develop a better understanding of the relationship between emotions and events, desires and beliefs, the differences between other people's expressions and feelings, and the fact that emotions can be mixed or contradictory.

7   Researchers disagree on when children begin to *imitate* emotional expressions. Some maintain neonate imitation is made possible by a connection between the sensory and action systems, for instance in the form of a mirror neuron system. Others suggest the emotional expressions of adults can trigger emotional reactions in newborns, which prepare them for later imitation of emotional expressions.

8   Infants have a limited repertoire of self-regulating strategies and depend on help from caregivers. Stern uses the term *affect attunement* to describe adults' adaptation of emotional actions and expressions to those of the child, which helps children understand the emotions that underlie actions. *Social referencing* means that children use other people as a cue to what they themselves should

feel, think and do in uncertain situations. With age, children learn to delay, modify or hide their emotional expressions in accordance with the social situation.

9   Self-referential emotions are founded on a personal standard. *Shame* is related to violating this standard, whereas *pride* is related to exceeding it. Children can be *embarrassed* at being observed and evaluated by others. *Moral emotions* are based on a personal moral standard. *Guilt* and *pride* are aimed at oneself, whereas (justified) anger, contempt and disgust are directed at others. Self-referential emotions help to identify and correct social errors and vary across cultures.

10   Children's emotional experiences within the family affect their emotions. Parental sensitivity helps shape children's feelings about themselves and others. When children are prevented from showing negative emotions, they are unable to learn to regulate them and feel unsafe in situations that can give rise to these types of emotions. Children who receive help in regulating their negative emotions show fewer such emotions in interaction with other children. The way in which help is offered is not a deciding factor. Children who are able to deal with their emotions are also better at helping others than children with poorer emotional regulation. By the age of 3, conversations with parents often concern the causes of emotions. This gives children the opportunity to learn about emotional states, share their own feelings with others and understand and express emotions in new ways, in turn affecting their reaction to emotional situations.

11   *Empathy* and *sympathy* are emotional reactions to the situation of others. Hoffman describes four stages in the development of empathy. The emotional style of parents and other adults is important to children's development of empathy and sympathy. Negative experiences do not lead to insight and empathy in children. Children with self-regulation problems are often unable to help others who experience difficulties.

12   When parents or other adults show anger and aggression, children usually become anxious and find it difficult to regulate their emotions. Children are more vulnerable than adolescents, who have better self-regulation. Children growing up in families with high levels of anger and aggression are vulnerable to developing internalizing and externalizing problems. Children whose parents are depressed may develop a smaller repertoire for emotion regulation.

13   As peers share many of the same experiences, norms, challenges and perspectives, *peer interaction* is essential for learning when and how emotions are expressed. Children's ability to self-regulate and deal with anxiety and stress is important for how they are met by their peers and for developing independence and social participation in childhood and adolescence.

14   *Anxiety disorders* appear early in life, and their development seems related to the child's temperament, attention to threats and need for security. When and how they emerge depends on many factors. Although anxiety is not related to the family's overall level of functioning, there is a relation between anxiety disorders and overprotective, "hostile" upbringing with little autonomy encouragement. Anxiety disorders can have negative *cascading effects* on learning and social development. There are many programs to prevent and treat anxiety disorders in children and adolescents, but studies show varying efficiency of such programs.

15   Children and adolescents with *depression* tend to focus on hopelessness and loss, and temperament, cognitive style and environmental factors can contribute to the development of depression. Adolescence is a particularly vulnerable period. Studies of programs for the prevention and treatment of depression have shown varying results.

16   There is a relationship between behavioral disorders and underregulation of anger, but problems with emotion regulation can involve both excessively strong or weak expressions, uninhibited and inhibited behavior, *internalizing* disorders with shyness and withdrawal, and *externalizing* disorders with aggressive, disruptive and antisocial behavior. Depression in girls is usually related to *over-controlled* behavior and anxiety, whereas depression in boys seems to be associated with *under-controlled* behavior and aggression. Regulation disorders can have a major impact on children's social development and academic achievement.

Core Issues

- The presence of inborn discrete emotions.
- Early imitation of emotions.
- Culture and emotions.

Suggestions for Further Reading

Cummings, E. M., Ballard, M., & El Sheikh, M. (1991). Responses of children and adolescents to interadult anger as a function of gender, age, and mode of expression. *Merrill-Palmer Quarterly, 37*, 543–560.

Darwin, C. (1872). *The expression of the emotions in man and animals.* London: Oxford University Press (Reprint, 1998).

Denham, S. A. (2007). Dealing with feelings: How children negotiate the worlds of emotions and social relationships. *Cognitions, Brain, Behaviour, 11*, 1–48.

Dunn, J., Bretherton, I., & Munn, P. (1987). Conversations about feeling states between mothers and their young children. *Developmental Psychology, 23*, 132–139.

Hertenstein, M. J., & Campos, J. J. (2004). The retention effects of an adult's emotional displays on infant behavior. *Child Development, 75*, 595–613.

Hiatt, S. W., Campos, J. J., & Emde, R. N. (1979). Facial patterning and infant emotional expression: Happiness, surprise, and fear. *Child Development, 50*, 1020–1035.

Llabre, M. M., Hadi, F., La Greca, A. M., & Lai, B. S. (2015). Psychological distress in young adults exposed to war-related trauma in childhood. *Journal of Clinical Child and Adolescent Psychology, 44*, 169–180.

Spinrad, T. L., & Stifter, C. A. (2006). Toddlers' empathy-related responding to distress: Predictions from negative emotionality and maternal behavior in infancy. *Infancy, 10*, 97–121.

Tomkins, S. S., & McCarter, R. (1964). What and where are the primary affects? Some evidence for a theory. *Perceptual and Motor Skills, 18*, 119–158.

Part II

Temperament and Personality

Individual Differences

Temperament is often viewed as the starting point for children's **personality**. From the moment children are born, they meet the world in different ways. Some children are more active, emotional or irritable than others, or more reactive when hindered from doing something. Some children like to explore, while others respond with caution to changes and meeting new people, places and events. Nearly all 1-year-olds briefly check their activity when an unfamiliar adult wearing a mask enters the room, but, while some continue with what they were doing almost immediately, others remain still for a long time. Some children are particularly responsive to rewards; others are vulnerable to **punishment**. All of these differences reflect children's *temperament*, an individual reaction tendency, a behavioral and emotional disposition. *Personality* can be defined as a tendency to feel, think and act in ways that develop into individual patterns of an increasingly complex repertoire of thoughts, actions and emotions. It is commonly assumed that temperament has a strong biological basis, whereas personality also reflects the individual's experiences. Children with similar temperaments can develop highly different personalities depending on how they cope with the world and other people's reactions to them.

DOI: 10.4324/9781003292531-13

Temperament

Temperament can be categorized in a number of ways (see Bornstein et al., 2015; Zentner & Shiner, 2012). In a classic **longitudinal study**, Thomas and Chess (1977) found three main types of temperament. One group of children was generally cheerful, had regular sleeping and eating patterns, adapted easily to new situations, were positive toward strangers, showed moderate emotional reactions and were easily calmed down when they became aroused. This group with an "easy" temperament accounted for about 40 percent of the children. Another group had a tendency to withdraw in unfamiliar situations and generally appeared negative, with strong emotional reactions and irregular sleeping and eating patterns. These children with a "difficult" temperament accounted for about 10 percent. A third group of 15 percent was "**slow to warm up**." Although they adapted to new situations, they needed time to do so and were uneven in their daily routines. They were restless and easily started to cry, but their reactions were moderate. Initially, they often seemed similar to the difficult group but, after warming up, they mostly resembled the easy group. The remainder of the children, about one-third, could not be classified in any one of the three main groups.

More recent descriptions of temperament use slightly different categories, but most are related to activity, reactivity, emotionality and **sociability** (Shiner, 2015). "Activity level" describes the frequency and intensity of children's motor activities, and resistance to having to remain passive. "Positive emotionality" refers to the amount and intensity of positive emotions. "Negative emotionality" includes both fear and shyness, as well as **irritability**, discomfort, anger and resistance to control. "Sociability" describes the degree of children's **extraversion** and their interest and enjoyment in being with other

DOI: 10.4324/9781003329253I-14

people. "Self-regulation" refers to the effortful control of attention and distractions, as well as persistence. Some descriptions also include "likeability" or "kindness" and "adaptability" as basic temperamental traits (Rothbart & Bates, 2006; Zentner & Bates, 2008).

Some children are cautious, others actively seek new experiences.

As children experience many new things, **"reaction to novelty"** is a temperament trait of special importance. "High-reactive" or "inhibited" children tend to be cautious and shy and withdraw when meeting new people or things. They can find it emotionally challenging, for example, to meet lots of new children and adults when starting in kindergarten and may need help adapting. "Low-reactive" or "uninhibited" children are more likely to approach others and be social in these types of situations. Most children in this group enjoy meeting other children and adults in kindergarten. Shyness is more problematic for boys than for girls, and the relationship between mothers and shy daughters is usually better than that between mothers and shy sons (Coplan & Arbeau, 2008; Kagan & Snidman, 2004).

Measuring Temperament

There are different approaches to measuring temperament, each with strengths and weaknesses, and considerable discussion about which measures describe temperament best. Questionnaires and parent interviews are the most common methods, especially in investigations involving a large number of children (Caspi et al., 2005). However, many studies have found low **correlations** between different evaluations, such as between mothers and preschool teachers when the mothers evaluate their own child's temperament. The correlation is considerably higher when the child is not the mother's own (Seifer, 2002; Seifer et al., 1994). This indicates that a mother's evaluation reflects not merely the child's characteristics but also the mother–child relationship and maternal characteristics, such as the mother's stress level (Räikkönen et al., 2006). The subjective basis of such evaluations is also reflected in moderate correlations (0.29–0.49) between mothers' and fathers' assessments of their child's temperament (Neppl et al., 2010). Cultural beliefs also influence parents' evaluations of their child's temperament (deVries & Sameroff, 1984).

Kagan and Fox (2006) maintain that parent evaluations should be used with caution, as they are highly colored by parental traits and aspirations for the child, and should always be accompanied by observations of physiological measures such as heart rate and respiration. Rothbart and Bates (2006) object to Kagan's views that observations in practice rarely take place in different situations and do not last long enough for the observer to gain insight into how the child generally meets the world, whereas assessments by parents and preschool teachers reflect their contact with the child over time. They argue that observations cannot replace the information gathered by questionnaires and interviews, which additionally provides a solid basis for observation. Nonetheless, they agree with Kagan that one should not rely on a single method, but assess children's temperament using different approaches, such as both questionnaires and observations of children in various situations.

Heritability

It is a general view that the development of temperament is determined by both genetic and environmental factors (Goldsmith et al., 1999; Saudino, 2009; Saudino & Micalizzi, 2015). Twin studies have generally shown more similar temperaments in **identical twins** than in **fraternal twins**, but genetic influence seems to vary across traits. **Heritability estimates** vary from 0.2 to 0.6 (see Book 2, *Genes, Fetal Development and Early Neurological Development*, Chapter 6). Torgersen (1989), for example, found a relatively high degree of heritability for the temperament trait "activity level," while "emotionality" showed the lowest heritability.

In recent years, the relationship between temperament and specific genes has been the subject of study in both humans and apes. Current knowledge remains limited, but important genes appear to be those with a general effect on brain metabolism, such as 5-HTTLPR, MAOA and DRD4 (see Book 2, *Genes, Fetal Development and Early Neurological Development*, Chapter 6). This agrees well with Kagan's description of temperament traits as "root notes" in the nervous system. However, human biology is not about genes alone – prenatal nutrition and the health of the mother and child also affect the child's irritability. Even twins can have slightly different fetal environments (Riese, 1990; Saudino, 2009).

Stability of Temperament

Developmental research on temperament has focused on infancy, but temperament exists at all age levels. Adult temperament is often described as "introverted" or "extraverted," "inhibited" or "impulsive" (Eysenck, 1967). An important question is the degree to which an individual maintains the same temperament. Mathiesen and Tambs (1999) found moderate correlations, ranging from 0.37 to 0.60, based on maternal ratings of four temperament traits at 1½ and 4 years:

"activity," "reaction to novelty," "sociability" and "emotionality." This shows that changes in temperament occur even during the first years. Another study assessed children several times from the age of 2 to 12 years and found that the largest changes in temperament occurred between the ages of 3 and 5. After this, the children showed less intense reactions and better regulation, adaptability and mood, but their activity level as well as degree of sensitivity and reactivity continued to change throughout school age (Guerin & Gottfried, 1994). Parental evaluations of child temperament over extended periods of time show relatively low correlations of around 0.2–0.4 from early to later age levels (Putnam et al., 2002).

Kagan and Snidman's (2004) results illustrate the complexity of temperament development. In a study of 68 children with signs of a "high-reactive" or "inhibited" temperament at an early age, ten were described as shy with strangers at the age of 11. Only 1 of the 92 children with an early "low-reactive" or "uninhibited" temperament fit this description. Of the children in the early uninhibited group, 30 percent were described as "exuberant," whereas only 5 percent of those with an early inhibited temperament had this characteristic at the age of 11. At the same time, 30 percent of the early inhibited group and 15 percent of the early uninhibited group were described as energetic and talkative. Nine of the early uninhibited children and one inhibited child were described as rebellious at 11 years of age.

The issue of **stability** is further complicated by the fact that the behaviors used to measure temperament change with age. "Activity" and "emotionality" are expressed in quite different ways at the ages of 1, 7 and 15 years. Six-month-olds show negative emotionality by crying, whereas 6-year-olds show worry and concern and can appear depressed and sad. Children can thus change considerably while maintaining the same temperament (Neppl et al., 2010). Additionally, **continuity** of temperament is dependent on the environment. Children with early inhibition, for example, more often remain inhibited when their mothers are invasive and critical, whereas they become less reticent with mothers who actively try to counteract the child's shyness (Rubin et al., 2002).

Temperament and Parental Behavior

Children's activity level, irritability and reactions to unfamiliar people and situations have an impact on how parents perceive children and relate to them. For example, active children tend to look for a toy themselves, whereas passive children wait until someone brings a toy to them, and they will probably be treated differently. This in turn affects the children's activities and reactions, which then influence the parents, and so on, in a transactional chain (Cheah & Park, 2006; Räikkönen et al., 2006).

Parental response to the child's temperament changes as the child grows older. Studies have found that children whose mothers reported that their child had a **difficult temperament** at 6 months received more emotional contact and stimulation with objects than children with an easier temperament. The contact may have consisted of attempts to comfort and stimulation with objects in an effort to divert the attention of the crying child. At 2 years, the children with a difficult temperament and resistance to external control were exposed to more negative control by their mothers (Lee & Bates, 1985; Pettit & Bates, 1984). Shy and reserved children are often overprotected and over-controlled by their parents (Rubin et al., 1999). In addition, parents bring their own temperament, their ways of meeting others and their cultural values into the interaction with their child and show a relatively stable parenting style throughout early childhood and pre-school age (Dallaire & Weinraub, 2005; Smith, C. L., 2010).

Children with a difficult temperament can be a challenge for parents; it is particularly stressful when typical parenting strategies fail. The experience of not being able to manage their child has a very negative impact on parents with low self-esteem in the first place. Mothers who were insecure and anxious to begin with became more insecure when they failed to calm their child, whereas secure mothers were not affected by such experiences. Similarly, an irritable temperament in the child can lead vulnerable mothers to become depressed and feel incompetent (Ganiban et al., 2011). Several studies have found a relationship between irritability and negative emotions in children and poor caregiving and lack of response from parents. Correspondingly, there is a relationship between children's positive emotions and ability to self-regulate and parents' **responsivity**, social interaction and use of rewards (Hinde, 1989; Kiel & Buss, 2010). However, these correlations say nothing about the way in which the patterns arise – both are parts of a transactional chain and affect one another. The temperament and emotional style of the parent as well as those of the child contribute to the course of development (Gallagher, 2002; Sameroff, 2009).

Different temperaments are neither good nor bad in themselves, but the temperaments of parent and child can be more or less suited to one another, "**goodness of fit**" (Chess & Thomas, 1999; McClowry et al., 2008). The development of temperament is not merely a matter of the child's initial temperament alone, but also of how parents respond to it, and how the child in turn responds to the parents' temperament (Bates et al., 2012). This is well illustrated in Box 12.1. The only generally positive parental traits that can be singled out are sensitivity and ability to adapt to the child's temperament and help the child to cope with difficult situations and with self-regulation. This is true regardless of whether the child tends to be active or passive, emotionally positive or negative, or shows strong or weak reactions. The temperament of a child has less explanatory value for the course of development than the context in which the temperaments of the child and the parents interact (Lerner & Lerner, 1983).

Box 12.1 A Temperamental Journey (Thomas & Chess, 1986, pp. 48–49)

Carl was one of our most extreme cases of difficult temperament from the first few months of life through 5-years-of-age. However, he did not develop behavior disorder, primarily due to optimal handling by his parents and stability of his environment. His father, who himself had an **easy temperament**, took delight in his son's "lusty" characteristics, recognized on his own Carl's tendency to have intense negative reactions to the new, and had patience to wait for eventual adaptability to occur. It was clear without any orientation by us, that these characteristics were in no way his or his wife's influence. His wife tended to be anxious and self-accusatory over Carl's tempestuous course. However, her husband was supportive and reassuring and this enabled her to take an appropriate objective and patient approach to her son's development. By the middle childhood and adolescent years few new situations arose which evoked the difficult temperament responses. The family, school and social environment was stable and Carl flourished and appeared to be temperamentally easy rather than difficult. An occasional new demand, however, such as the start of piano lessons, again evoked his previous typical response of initial intense negative response, followed by slow adaptability and eventual positive zestful involvement. When Carl went off to college, however, he was faced simultaneously with a host of new situations and demands – an unfamiliar locale, a different living arrangement, new academic subjects and expectations, and a totally new peer group. Within a few weeks his temperamentally difficult traits reappeared in full force. He felt negative about the school [and] his courses, the other students, couldn't motivate himself to study and was constantly irritable. Carl knew something was wrong, discussed the situations with his family and us and developed an appropriate strategy to cope with his problem. He limited new demands by dropping several extracurricular activities, limited his social contacts and policed his studying. Gradually he adapted, his distress disappeared and he was able to expand his activities and social contacts. When seen by us for the early adult follow-up at age 23 his temperamental rating was not in the difficult group.

Early Temperament and Later Disorders

Much of the research on temperament has a clinical focus and is concerned with the relationship between early temperament traits and later behavioral and emotional disorders, school problems and alcohol and drug abuse, and the possibilities of prevention and early intervention. Developmental psychopathology builds on the assumption that children's temperament can make it more difficult for them to adapt to the challenges of the environment and thereby contribute to the emergence of such disorders (Nigg, 2006). Studies have found small overall correlations between early temperament and later disorders, but children with very high or low scores on a particular temperament trait are more likely to develop disorders later. More often than other children, those with early inhibition show internalizing disorders later in life, whereas uninhibited children show more externalizing disorders. Children with early negative emotionality show both types of disorders (Rothbart & Bates, 2006).

It is never temperament alone that leads to later disorders, but an interaction between the child's temperament and the way in which children and parents adjust to one another. For example, studies have found that the combination of an inhibited temperament and a **permissive parenting** style (see Chapter 16, this volume) increases that risk for internalizing disorders (Williams et al., 2009). Parents who perceive their children as vulnerable sometimes try to protect them from difficult situations. This sort of overprotective behavior may exacerbate the effect of an inhibited temperament, because the children do not learn to deal with difficult situations, but rather learn to avoid them and withdraw (Coplan et al., 2008; Rubin et al., 2002; see also p. 50, this volume). Another study found that infants with difficult or more regular temperaments developed fewer behavioral problems when their mothers were sensitive, whereas the mother's sensitivity had little consequence for infants with an easier temperament. Maternal sensitivity thus had a different effect on children with different temperaments, and possibly with different alleles of certain genes as well (Bradley & Corwyn, 2008). In line with this, children with a difficult temperament (low inhibition, difficult to comfort, high level of frustration) showed the highest number of behavioral disorders when their mothers lacked sensitiveness and exercised a great deal of negative control (Kiff et al., 2011; van Aken et al., 2007). Children with an "exuberant" temperament and extremely positive reactions to unfamiliar people and things can develop a high degree of sociability, but can also show a lot of anger, as they often experience being prevented from reaching their goals (Degnan et al., 2011).

The studies illustrate that the consequences of children's early temperament are not given. The majority in all temperament groups do not develop disorders. Temperament only represents a starting point, and whether children with a particular temperament develop disorders will depend on the characteristics of their environment and the interactions they engage in.

Resilience and Protection

Research has mainly dealt with temperament as a vulnerability to developing disorders, but temperament traits can also be a source of resilience (Shiner, 2015). Children who are energetic and at the same time easily comforted cope better with a difficult family environment than children with other types of temperaments (Werner & Smith, 1982). An easy temperament can help children cope with stress and uncertainty in their surroundings, for example if the child's parents divorce (Davis & Suveg, 2014).

As pointed out earlier, some children with an inhibited temperament do not become shy and withdrawn because their environment supports the development of other behaviors. Children with a cautious temperament can react by withdrawing when they start in kindergarten, but sensitive and warm mothers seem to offer protection against a development path toward internalizing disorders (Early et al., 2002). Similarly, sensitive parenting can protect children with difficult temperaments from developing behavioral disorders (Bradley & Corwyn, 2008; see Box 12.1). Environments with high levels of stress can increase the risk of disorders in children with a very inhibited or uninhibited temperament, whereas environments in which adults adapt and help children regulate their emotions may not only prevent the development of disorders, but also take advantage of a child's temperament in a way that promotes a particularly positive development (Sameroff, 2009).

13

Personality

Nearly all theories of personality describe human qualities in terms of characteristic traits. Composite traits are sometimes combined into *personality types* such as "resilient," "over controlled" or "under controlled" (Robins et al., 1996). There is a close connection between the traits described by the various theories and their assumptions about how personality develops.

Personality Traits

Personality traits can be described in innumerable ways. Children, adolescents and adults are described as "kind," "malicious," "quick," "fun," "honest," "nice," "insecure" and so forth, and there are many ongoing efforts to reduce the number of descriptive traits to a relatively small collection of key dimensional characteristics. It is the position within each of these dimensions that together make up the description of an individual's personality.

Today, personality is commonly described in terms of the "Big Five," based on Goldberg's (1990) analysis of the terminology used to characterize human beings: "extraversion," "agreeableness," "conscientiousness," "neuroticism" (emotional lability) and "openness" (to experience). However, some researchers hold that five dimensions are insufficient to map the variation in human personality (Block, 1995), while others find that the three major traits – "extraversion," "conscientiousness" and "neuroticism" (emotional lability) – best describe the personality differences in the population (Eysenck, 1992; Rothbart & Bates, 2006). Costa and McCrae (1992) have assigned sub-characteristics to each of the Big Five for a total of 30 facets (Table 13.1).

Parents begin quite early to assess their child's personality along the same main dimensions as for adults. In one study across seven

DOI: 10.4324/9781003292531-15

Table 13.1 The Big Five and their 30 facets: the "Big Five" personality traits, the six facets describing each trait, and an adjective closely associated with each facet (Costa & McCrae, 1992, p. 49)

The Big Five	The thirty facets	Adjective
Extraversion versus **introversion**	Gregariousness Assertiveness Activity Excitement seeking Positive emotions Warmth	Sociable Forceful Energetic Adventurous Enthusiastic Outgoing
Agreeableness versus antagonism	Trust Straightforwardness Altruism Compliance Modesty Tender-mindedness (nurturance)	Forgiving Not demanding Warm Not stubborn Not a show-off Sympathetic
Conscientiousness versus lack of direction	Competence Order Dutifulness Achievement striving Self-discipline Deliberation	Efficient Organized Not careless Thorough Not lazy Not impulsive
Neuroticism versus emotional stability	Anxiety Angry hostility Depression Self-consciousness Impulsiveness Vulnerability	Tense Irritable Not contented Shy Moody Not self- confident
Openness versus closedness to experience	Ideas Fantasy Aesthetics Actions Feelings Values	Curious Imaginative Artistic Wide interests Excitable Unconventional

countries, parents of children aged 3–12 years were asked to describe what characterized their child. Three-quarters of the descriptions fell within the Big Five, with a larger percentage for the older than the younger children, but they also included some age-specific terms. The younger children were often referred to as "independent" and "mature for their age" (Kohnstamm et al., 1995, 1998). In order to provide an adequate description of younger children's personality,

Caspi (1998) suggests complementing the Big Five with "activity" and "irritability." With age, the parents' child-specific characteristics are gradually reduced in favor of traits used to describe adults.

General and Situation-Specific Traits

As a rule, personality traits aim to describe an individual's general ways of reacting, independent of the situation. In practice, however, there is often little agreement when several persons assess the personality of the same child. Parents and teachers, for example, can have very different views on a child's personality, degree of aggression, industriousness and sociability (Lewis, 2001a). This undermines the assumption of personality traits as general and situation-independent reaction tendencies.

Bandura (1999) and Mischel (1984) dismiss the notion that children develop general personality traits; a child's tendencies to react and act reflect adaptations to actual situations and, therefore, must be seen in light of the child's challenges and relationships. In their view, descriptions of personality traits should include traits that usually characterize the child's reactions and behaviors in specific situations, such as "aggressive during play," "introverted with strangers," "extraverted at home," and so on. These types of traits are illustrated by a study of children at a summer camp. Although the children showed

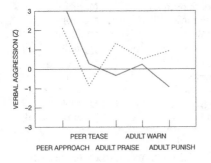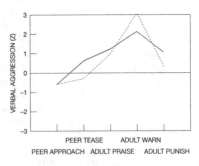

Figure 13.1 Different patterns of verbal aggression in two children.

A group of 7–13-year-old boys and girls were observed for 6 weeks at a summer camp. The figure shows the extent of verbal aggression by two children in relation to the group average in different situations and on two occasions. Most of Child A's aggressive statements occurred in connection with being approached by other peers, those of Child B when reprimanded by adults (based on Shoda et al., 1994, p. 678).

various types of responses that to some extent were consistent across situations, their reactions varied considerably from one situation to another. Those who showed the most aggression, happiness, sadness, and so on, were not always the same children (Shoda et al., 1994). Figure 13.1 shows observations of verbal aggression in two children who participated in the study. Both made approximately the same number of verbally aggressive statements, but the situations where they occurred differed. According to Shoda, children's reaction tendencies, or personalities, should include such situational variation and are best described by a *situation profile* or *behavioral signature*. Behavioral signatures thus redefine traits by taking into account the child's perception of the situation (Mischel & Shoda, 2008, 2010).

14

Theories of Personality Development

All theorists assume that an individual's reaction tendencies are affected by past experiences and search for mechanisms to explain the development of the adult personality. Freud formulated the first comprehensive theory of personality development. His **psychoanalytic theory** established the basis for **psychodynamic theories** and has had enormous influence on the understanding of personality development in general (Schultz & Schultz, 2016). Today, Freud's theory is largely of historical interest, as most modern psychodynamic theorists have disclaimed or reformulated many of Freud's most important ideas. If the theory is presented in some detail nonetheless, it is owing to its great significance and illustration of *psychodynamic thinking*. Theories about the development of children's relationships and self-development also incorporate assumptions about personality traits. They will be discussed in the following chapters.

Freud's Theory

In Freud's theory (see also Book 1, *Theory and Methodology*, Chapter 11), personality is a mental structure that derives from the interaction between innate drives common to all human beings and the child's unique experiences (Westen et al., 2008). **Libido** and **Thanatos** represent the basic forces behind all human actions, and the discharge of these drives must be adapted to the physical, social and cultural environment during development. As part of this adaptive process, children form a tripartite mental structure consisting of **id**, **ego** and **superego**). According to Freud, it is the interactions between these three parts, the way in which the drives are dealt with and internal conflicts during the three **psychosexual phases** that impact the traits that eventually characterize an adult's personality (Freud, 1905).

DOI: 10.4324/9781003292531-16

Table 14.1 The psychosexual phases and their potential impact on personality development if the conflicts in a phase remain unresolved (Pervin & John, 1997, p. 123)

Stage	Personality traits
Oral	Demanding, impatient, envious, covetous, jealous, rageful, depressed (feels empty), mistrustful, pessimistic
Anal	Rigid, striving for power and control, concerned with should and ought, pleasure and possessions, anxiety over waste and loss of control, concern with whether to submit or rebel
Phallic	Male: exhibitionistic, competitive, striving for success, emphasis on being masculine – macho – potentFemale: naive, seductive, exhibitionistic, flirtatious

In the **oral phase** (0–1 years), children explore the environment with their mouth, and drives are reduced by the consumption of food. When mental energy becomes fixated during the oral period, the individual may become talkative or feel "hunger" for others' attention as an adult. Smoking and excessive eating and drinking are also considered expressions of personality traits originating in this phase, according to Freud (Table 14.1).

Conflicts in the **anal phase** (2–3 years) are particularly linked to control over feces (expelling and withholding) and increasing demands for cleanliness. Overly strict toilet training, for example, can lead to excessive cleanliness in adulthood. The emphasis on cleanliness in this phase leads to the first conflict between the child's desires and the expectations of culture. This is an important aspect of Freud's theory, as it implies that children are not socially oriented to begin with. Enculturation is not a positive experience for children, but spawns discomfort as it limits the free reign of children's drives.

Conflicts in the **phallic phase** (4–5 years) revolve around children's discovery of their own and others' genitalia. The **Oedipus conflict** and the **Electra conflict** are central to the formation of personality. These conflicts are based on the notion that boys are sexually attracted to their mother and experience their father as competing for the mother's attention, while girls are attracted to their father. According to the theory, a developmentally favorable solution to this inner conflict is for boys to identify with their father and girls with their mother, an **identification** that leads to the **internalization** of the parents' social and cultural attitudes and values and the formation

Sigmund Freud.

of the superego. The absence of such identification can result in inadequate moral development.

Following the phallic phase, children enter a **latency phase** that lasts until the age of 13 years, with less sexual drive and without focus on new body zones. With the onset of puberty, sexual instincts awaken once again, as well as attraction to the parent of the opposite sex. According to Freud, this forms the basis for generational conflicts in adolescence.

According to Freud, the psychosexual phases give rise to individual differences in personality, as well as to mental health problems. Unresolved inner conflicts from these phases are maintained and become central and permanent elements of the individual's personality. Each phase can be seen as a form of **critical period** that depends on specific stimulation (see Book 2 *Genes, Fetal Development and Early Neurological Development*, Chapter 16). The various phases are characterized by personality traits that may emerge to a greater or lesser degree, a development that largely terminates with the Oedipus and Electra conflicts. This means that, in Freud's theory, the adult personality is more or less shaped by the age of 5.

Another central element in Freud's personality theory is the idea that the conflicts between the impulses of the id and the limitations of the superego lead to anxiety and use of **defense mechanisms** to reduce the anxiety (see Book 1, *Theory and Methodology*, Chapter 11). These defense mechanisms enable children to adapt to the demands of their surroundings, but their use can also form the basis for developing particular personality traits. Fanaticism, for example, can be the result of strong, unacceptable impulses, such as abstinence due to a craving for alcohol. Defense mechanisms can furthermore lead to pathological conditions. This happens when impulses become so strong and the use of defense mechanisms so extensive that the individual is unable to cope with everyday challenges (Freud, 1895).

The Status of the Theory

Freud's theory has been criticized by theorists both within and outside the psychodynamic group. An internal criticism of the theory is its predominant focus on the development of boys, while it is vague and unclear on a number of points regarding the development of girls (Simanowitz & Pearce, 2003). Although none of today's psychodynamic theorists completely endorse Freud's theory of personality development in its original form, psychodynamic developmental psychology has no alternative major theory to offer (Westen et al., 2008). Although Freud's explanations use different terminology and models than what is common today, they contain many of the elements of modern developmental theories, such as the emphasis on parent–child relations, self-regulation (ego function) and emotional regulation (defense mechanisms) in the development of personality (Luborsky & Barrett, 2006). Key elements of Freud's theory are being further elaborated by modern **psychodynamic psychology**. This applies above all to Freud's assumptions about **unconscious** processes and "psychodynamics" (see also Book 1, *Theory and Methodology*, Chapter 11). Early experiences remain important for the development of personality, but are less crucial than in Freud's theory. Defense mechanisms continue to have a central position as well, and it is assumed that the individual in the course of childhood and adolescence develops a stable *defensive style* to cope with anxiety and external threats. Positive early experiences lead to the development of flexible and adaptive defense mechanisms such as *sublimation* and *intellectualization*, while negative experiences lead to less mature and effective mechanisms such as *repression* and *projection* (Bornstein, 2006; Gilmore, 2008; Rice & Hoffman, 2014). Maternal and paternal relationships, as well as different interpretations of the Oedipus/Electra complexes as organizing elements in personality development, maintain a prominent place in psychodynamic theories (Balsam, 2015; Hindle & Smith, 1999; Westen et al., 2008).

A common criticism raised by other theories is the dearth of studies involving children. Instead, psychoanalytic developmental theory builds on clinical interpretations of adult patients – the psychosexual phases, for example, are based on assumptions about the causes of personality traits and mental disorders in adulthood. No studies exist to support the hypotheses about psychosexual phases or the Oedipus and Electra conflicts. Many critics point out that the theory's assertions, based on clinical interpretations of children's and adults' actions, have such a vague basis that they cannot be refuted in practice. Much research continues to focus on the development of personality disorders in studies of adult patients (Shiner, 2009).

Erikson's Theory

Erik Homburger Erikson (1963, 1968) belongs to the psychodynamic tradition, but offers a rather different view of development than Freud's description of children driven by **instincts**. His theory represents **ego psychology**, which emphasizes the regulatory and **adaptive functions** of the ego, the development of social relations, identity, autonomy, self-regulation and coping in a social world (see Book 1, *Theory and Methodology*, Chapter 11).

Erikson, too, describes biologically determined phases in development in which personality is shaped by experience, but does not share Freud's view that personality traits are formed by conflicts linked to drive impulses. According to Erikson, human beings go through eight psychosocial phases, each associated with social relations and *social crises*. Like in Freud's theory, personality is determined by the way in which each phase is traversed (Table 14.2). In the first phase, children learn to trust that their parents or other caregivers will provide them with food, care and love. The way in which this trust develops

Table 14.2 The psychosocial phases (based on Erikson, 1963)

Phase	Psychosocial crisis	Basic strengths
1 0–12 months	Trust versus mistrust	Energy and hope
2 13–24 months	Autonomy versus doubt and shame	Self-control and willpower
3 2–4 years	Initiative versus guilt	Direction and purpose
4 5 years to puberty	Industriousness versus inferiority	Method and competence
5 Adolescence	Identity versus role confusion	Devotion and fidelity
6 Early adulthood	Intimacy versus isolation	Friendship and love
7 Middle adulthood	Generativity versus stagnation	Productivity and care
8 Old age	Ego integrity versus despair	Moderation and wisdom

Erik H. Erikson.

impacts the development of autonomy in the second phase. Overprotection during this phase will lead children to doubt their own abilities and opportunities. Experiences in the third phase are important for the development of initiative and guilt. The basis of personality is thus formed by social and emotional conflicts.

Erikson's psychosocial phases incorporate a broader age span than Freud's psychosexual phases. The first five phases cover the period up to adolescence, and the last three include the remainder of the life cycle. Unlike Freud, Erikson does not believe personality to be fully formed by the end of the preschool period, and he considers adolescence to be of particular importance for the development of personality because adolescents actively define their self and establish their identity (see Book 7, *Social Relations, Self-awareness and Identity*, Chapter 24).

The Status of the Theory

Erikson's elaboration of Freud's theory continues to exert a major influence on descriptions of personality development, particularly for adolescence and adulthood. Some of the criticism of Freud's theory is also relevant for this theory. Like Freud, Erikson wrote most about the personality development of males. Additionally, his phases are somewhat old-fashioned and do not reflect more recent developments in education and the workplace. Although many of the **concepts** of ego psychology correspond to modern assumptions about self-regulation, little research exists to document any possible links between events in the various phases and personality traits in adulthood.

McCrae and Costa's Five-Factor Model

McCrae and Costa (1995, 2008) describe the development of personality traits based on temperament and general principles of development. The theory is based on Goldberg's **Big Five personality traits** (see p. 77, this volume), which McCrae and Costa believe to reflect basic personal characteristics formed by evolution. In their theory, there is a continuous development from children's earliest temperament traits to the personality characteristics typical of adults. Development is universal and identical in all cultures. Maturation and other biological processes form the basis for personality traits, especially in the first third of life, but development continues throughout the life span. Individual differences are mainly genetic in origin, but can also be affected by other biological factors, such as disease or brain injury. According to McCrae and Costa, individual experience plays only a minor role: "The course of personality development is determined by biological maturation, not by life experiences" (2008, p. 167).

McCrae and Costa's five-factor model differs fundamentally from other theories, in that personality traits are not the result of adaptations, but instead form the basis for the child's adaptation. Personality traits represent dispositions that contribute *causally* to a child's feelings, thoughts and actions in different situations. In McCrae and Costa's *model of the person*, personality traits interact with life events and other external factors to determine how the individual adapts in terms of roles, relationships, aspirations and attitudes that in turn affect the individual's **self-concept** (Figure 14.1). Unlike personality traits, these adaptations change with culture, family conditions and life-course development.

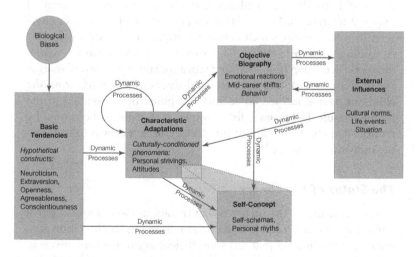

Figure 14.1 McCrae and Costa's model of the person.

The Big Five represent individual characteristics with origins in genetic and non-genetic biological factors, including maternal health, use of alcohol and narcotic substances, and illness during pregnancy. Personality traits affect the individual's self-concept and personal history, as well as adaptations, aspirations and attitudes (based on McCrae & Costa, 1995, p. 237. With permission from © John Wiley & Sons Ltd.).

The Status of the Theory

It is generally agreed that the Big Five describe important aspects of the personality, and McCrae and Costa's theory has considerable influence, although the centrality of these aspects is disputed (see p. 78, this volume). McCrae and Costa focus on the relationship between temperament traits and personality traits throughout the life span, and their theory has been criticized for failing to explain the mechanisms behind development, how personality traits are formed and how individual differences arise (Caspi, 1998; Caspi et al., 2005). The assumption that personality is rooted in biology alone, and that the Big Five represent a universal description of personality across cultural boundaries, has also been subject to criticism (Piekkola, 2011).

Behaviorism

In **behaviorism**, personality is the organization and quality of characteristic action tendencies that an individual has acquired through learning (Novak & Peláez, 2004). There is no inherent mental structure nor a specific set of phases that underlie the development of response tendencies. Personality does not consist of the child's characteristics, as children's inclinations are governed by external factors. According to Skinner (1971), "a person does not act upon the world, the world acts upon him." Skinner sees anomalous personality traits as "wrong" or maladaptive responses and reactions that result from the child not having learned an adequate response or responding to the wrong stimuli. Depression, for example, is thought to be caused by reduced activity due to lack of **positive reinforcements** to maintain the individual's activity level.

The Status of the Theory

A main criticism of the theory is that the assumptions about external control and human actions based on conditioning and imitation represent a simplification that takes insufficient account of the diversity of children's minds and the complex transaction chain that underlies children's emotional and social development and adaptation (Bandura, 2006; Pervin et al., 2005). All the same, much child-rearing advice to parents is based on the idea that children's personalities are learned, formed by reward and punishment, including television programs such as *Supernanny* (Rydland, 2007).

Cognitive Behavior Theory

Personality development from the perspective of cognitive behavior theory (or **social learning theory**) differs from traditional behaviorism on a number of important points (see Book 1, *Theory and Methodology*, Chapter 12). In cognitive behavior theory, children's reactions and behaviors are related to their self-image and expectations, especially their perceptions of themselves as *agents*, individuals acting in a social world (Bandura, 1986, 2006). Their behavior is not shaped by the environment, as Skinner argues, but by the children's own active exploration – how they perceive their surroundings and their goals, intentions and conscious self-regulation.

Bandura is skeptical of the idea of general personality traits, as they represent an **abstraction** of children's and adolescent's action strategies and intentions away from the situations in which they are functional (see p. 78, this volume). A child may, for example, be shy in the classroom, but extraverted on the soccer field. It is the specific environment that determines the degree to which an action strategy is functional, making it necessary to identify the situations in which children are extraverted and introverted. Thus, Bandura disagrees with both psychodynamic theories, which view children's personality traits as the result of internal dynamics and independent of the child's situation, and with McCrae and Costa's (2008) evolution-based trait theory.

As the name indicates, cognitive processes are central in this theory. Personality emerges as a result of how children interpret the reactions of the environment to their own and other people's actions. According to Bandura, a description of personality that fails to take children's reflections and intentions into account portrays them as automatons without subjectivity, conscious regulation and personal identity. There are two main ways in which children acquire action tendencies: either by experiencing the consequences of their own actions, or by observing others, including direct social models and models in mass media such as film and television (see Book 1, *Theory and Methodology*, Chapter 12). Seeing others succeed in achieving a goal or being rewarded can motivate children to try to reach a similar goal; seeing others fail or being punished can have the opposite effect. This was demonstrated in a classic experiment where preschool children first witnessed a man behaving aggressively toward a doll and receiving different reactions to his behavior. When the children played with the same doll afterwards, their actions reflected both the man's behavior and the other people's reactions (Box 14.1). Moreover, in cognitive behavior theory, the child's ability to imagine what *might* happen is important for developing sound action strategies. Children form *expectations* about themselves and their surroundings and establish a standard for their own behavior by internalizing the reactions and valuations of others. The family's reactions are extremely important for younger children, whereas the attitudes and reactions of peers and adults outside the family become more important with age. This becomes evident in the change of **reference groups** during childhood and adolescence, that is groups that children and adolescents use as a yardstick for desirable and appropriate behavior. Children with autism spectrum disorders are both impaired in their ability to form expectations and very insecure when they lack concrete expectations. For example, if they are going to the cinema, they need to know all the details about the film itself, the cinema and the schedule, and a change in one of these elements may lead to strong emotional reactions. This is an impairment that can make their everyday life extremely stressful (Martinsen et al., 2015).

Box 14.1   Learning from Observing Consequences of Aggression (Bandura, 1965).

Preschool children aged 3;6–5;11 years were shown a video where a man acted aggressively toward a doll called Bobo. Sometimes the man was rewarded after beating Bobo, other times he was punished or received no response. When the children were allowed to play with Bobo afterwards, they all performed similarly aggressive actions. The children who had seen the man being punished, however, showed fewer aggressive actions, especially the girls. When the children were encouraged to be aggressive toward Bobo, the children in each of the three groups showed approximately the same amount of aggressive behavior. The children's actions thus reflected both the consequences of the man's actions for himself and other people's attitudes about the action. This shows that adults can affect children's behavior by what they encourage them to do and not to do, and by letting them know what they think of different events and actions children encounter, for example on television.

A key element of the theory is that children's action tendencies are not determined by standards as such, but rather by how children perceive their own ability to meet these standards, their **self-efficacy** (Bandura, 1997). This affects the goals children set for themselves and how they act in different situations. For example, children will only read up on homework if they believe it will have an influence on their achievement. Some children believe their own efforts have little influence and therefore find it useless to invest any resources. This is where Bandura's theory differs most radically from traditional behaviorism. Children's behaviors are not simply a matter of actual competence and external consequences, but also of internal interpretation and processing. Nor does children's self-regulation merely rely on negative feedback and experienced failure, but equally on positive feedback and sense of mastery. According to Bandura, it is precisely this sense of mastering a skill or knowledge that gives children the motivation to set themselves new goals.

The Status of the Theory

Bandura's cognitive theory is very influential. Although it is usually placed within the behavioral tradition, the focus on inner mental processes makes it similar to psychodynamic theories. Cognition is a core aspect of the theory but it has been criticized for not integrating knowledge about general cognitive development and children's way of managing social information at different ages. It is also criticized for not taking sufficient account of changes due to physical maturation, for example in regard to sexuality, and for lacking an adequate explanation of motivational processes, such as conflicts involving incompatible or contradictory motives for action. Bandura's theory is the basis of *cognitive behavior therapy* and *cognitive developmental therapy*, which are used much in school psychology and treatment of children and adolescents. These therapies aim at influencing the child's or adolescent's thought **schemas**, self-awareness, self-esteem and self-efficacy, and thereby changing the cognitive basis of maladaptive action tendencies (Benjamin et al., 2011; Creed et al., 2016).

15

The Emergence of Personality

Temperament is generally regarded to be one of the cornerstones of adult personality – even if most researchers do not agree with Costa and McCrae's theory (Chen & Schmidt, 2015). The temperament traits *sociability*, *effortful control* and *negative emotionality* are mirrored in the personality traits *extraversion*, **conscientiousness** and **neuroticism** (emotional lability). However, although they overlap, personality traits describe individual differences that are not captured by temperament (Herzhoff et al., 2017).

Studies of early temperament and later personality traits suggest a certain continuity. The Dunedin study has followed up more than 1,000 children born in 1972 and 1973. Caspi (2000) found limited connection between temperament measures at the age of 3 and personality traits at 18 and 21 years in general. However, 10 percent of the children had the temperament type *under-controlled* at 3 years, and they appeared more reckless and aggressive at 21 years than the other children and had a tendency to feel mistreated and deceived by others. Another 8 percent of the children had the temperament type *inhibited* at the age of 3. They tended to become cautious, showed little aggression, avoided physically dangerous activities and disliked guiding or influencing others. At 21 years, other people characterized them as lacking in warmth and confidence. Other studies, too, have found that children who seem extremely inhibited in infancy tend to become introverted as adults (Asendorpf, 2010; Kagan & Snidman, 2004). Shyness is such a prominent part of a child's behavior that others tend to define the child in terms of this characteristic, and this may contribute to maintaining the shyness.

Kagan (1998) points out that the assumption of early personality formation contradicts the view that personality is the result of

DOI: 10.4324/9781003292531-17

adaptation. Although children's early reaction and action tendencies reflect their temperament, children are also part of a dynamic social context that contributes to regulating their reactions and behaviors (Chen & Schmidt, 2015). The extent to which temperament traits prove stable over time will therefore depend on how well they fit with other people and the cultural practices of the environment (Wachs, 1994). Early differences in temperament confirm that children make their own unique contribution to the transactional process. Temperament alone cannot explain the development of personality, but theories about the role of temperament still offer alternative or supplementary viewpoints to other theories.

Personality in Childhood

The transition to preschool age (3–4 years) is considered a developmental milestone in the sense that a number of person characteristics begin to be observable at this age, but, even when based on the Big Five, descriptions of children's personality traits differ from descriptions of those of adults (see p. 76, this volume). As children grow older, they show a broader and more complex set of individual differences. At the same time as new differences between children come to the surface, children's personalities become increasingly stable (Shiner, 2006, 2015).

Children who score *high* on *neuroticism* in the Big Five are described as anxious, vulnerable and tense. They have difficulties coping with stress, easily feel guilty, have a low frustration threshold and feel insecure in social relations. Emotionally, they are characterized by fear, anxiety and sadness. Anxiety and fear can be impediments to social relationships and to adapting in school and at work. Children who score *low* on this trait are typically stable and relaxed, adapt to new situations and quickly recover from negative events.

Parents describe their children as *conscientious* rarely before the age of 3, but often after the age of 6. Children who score *high* on this trait are attentive, responsible and have high standards. They plan, think before they act and persevere. Children with *low* scores are typically described as irresponsible, unreliable, careless and distractible and easily give up. Conscientiousness is generally associated with adaptability and a prosocial, positive development at school and in children's personal lives.

Children who score *high* on **agreeableness** are described as considerate, empathic, generous, protective and kind. They are compliant and easy to interact with. Agreeableness, too, is associated with positive development, good peer relations, positive progress in school and at work, and a low probability of externalizing problems and criminal behavior. Children who score *low* on this trait are described as aggressive, rude, stubborn, bossy and manipulative. They are often rejected by their peers and are more likely to do poorly at school and in the workplace and experience conflictual partner relationships.

Children who score high on **openness to experience** are described as eager and quick to learn, clever, knowledgeable, curious and original. This trait first shows up in parents' descriptions when children are about 6–7 years old and is typically associated with good achievements at school.

However, the picture is not as clear-cut as this brief summary may suggest. The various traits interact, and the presence of a positive trait does not always imply a positive development. A trait such as *compliance*, for example, is generally considered positive but can also involve a risk for abuse. Nor is a negative trait destiny; the developmental outcome depends on the social context of the child.

Stability and Change

Children's personality traits vary in stability. Some children show high stability, whereas the personality development of others is marked by change (Asendorpf, 1992). When children are compared at intervals of 1–2 years, stability is generally high, with correlations around 0.5–0.8. With a wider age span, stability decreases. One study found correlations of about 0.2 between the Big Five measured at 2 and 15 years of age (Lamb et al., 2002). The stability of personality traits lies within a range of 0.4–0.5 for a 3-year period in childhood and increases throughout the life span to over 0.7 within a 10-year period after the age of 50 (Ibáñez et al., 2016; Roberts & DelVecchio, 2000). Low to moderate correlations indicate considerable variation in the development of children with similar early traits. Moreover, participant attrition is a problem in most longitudinal studies. Families may move or tire of participating in observations and completing research forms (e.g. Magnus et al., 2016; Schreuder & Alsaker, 2014). Children who remain in these types of studies have therefore mostly grown up under stable conditions, which also may contribute to the stability of their personal characteristics.

Stability does not mean that the child does not change, as the behavior that forms the basis for assessing personality traits changes with age.

Children can change behavior while at the same time maintaining their position relative to their peers. In the longitudinal study from 2 to 15 years, the children on average became slightly less extraverted and somewhat more agreeable and conscientious (Lamb et al., 2002).

Children with frequent outbursts of anger at the age of 2 have usually learned to control their behavior by the age of 10. Although outbursts have become rare, they may still be perceived as quick-tempered compared with their peers. Thus, assessments of personality traits must account for what is typical at a given age (Caspi & Roberts, 2001).

Personality Development in Adolescence

Adolescence is a transitional and formative period during which instability in general is more prominent than stability. Stability in individual traits as well as in personality profile seems higher than in childhood, especially in late adolescence, and lower than in adulthood, but the degree of stability varies between studies (Hill & Edmonds, 2017; Klimstra et al., 2009). Adolescents tend to become more agreeable with age, but many of those who scored low on agreeableness when they were younger continue to do so, although they, too, become more agreeable over time. This indicates that the rank order to some extent is preserved over time. Stability may partly be due to the fact that adolescents seek out activities to fit their personality and thereby reinforce their existing traits. However, it depends on life events: a stable life situation contributes to stability, whereas parental divorce and other negative life events affect later personality, adaptability, reactions and behaviors (Caspi et al., 2005; Lewis, 2001b; Roberts et al., 2006).

The variation in development of personality in adolescence illustrates the continuous interaction between stability and change that characterizes development in most areas. An individual does not maintain exactly the same personality, but constantly changes from the characteristics developed before. Additionally, there seem to be individual differences in the tendency to change. Some children and adolescents change more than others, underlining the fact that the mature personality is not determined in childhood (Roberts et al., 2006).

16

Factors That Affect Personality Development

Genetic factors, aspects of the general environment and specific life events contribute to individual differences in personality.

Heritability

Genes have been found to influence personality development. A large meta-study found that roughly half of the variance in personality could be attributed to genes and half to the environment, indicating that genes and environment play equal roles in the development of personality (Briley & Tucker-Drob, 2014). However, heritability estimates (see Book 2, *Genes, Fetal Development and Early Neurological Development*, Chapter 6) for personality traits also vary with the age of the twins (Shiner, 2015). Both identical and fraternal twins growing up separately tend to become more dissimilar with age (McCartney et al., 1990). Viken and colleagues (1994) found that heritability estimates for *extraversion* and *neuroticism* declined from childhood to early adulthood and subsequently stabilized, whereas heritability of *inhibition* remained more stable. The notion that the influence of genes diminishes with age runs contrary to Scarr and McCartney's (1983) claim that individuals create their own environment (see also Book 2, *Genes, Fetal Development and Early Neurological Development*, Chapter 7). Based on their theory, similarities between identical twins should increase compared with fraternal twins as the biological basis is "freer" and less bound by their parents' lifestyle.

Genes are not independent: stressful life events can affect the relative impact of genes. One study found less overlap in personality traits among 29-year-old twins who had experienced stressful life events between the ages of 6 and 15 years than among twins

DOI: 10.4324/9781003292531-18

without similar experiences during the same period, especially for the traits agreeableness, conscientiousness and openness to experience (Torgersen & Janson, 2002). Moreover, it is likely that parents and others treat identical twins as more alike than fraternal twins because they resemble each other more in appearance (Joseph, 2013). Twins with parents who know or assume they are identical are often considered more similar than they actually are (**assimilation** effect). Even when they resemble each other strongly, fraternal twins are often attributed complementary characteristics such as "quick" and "sedate," or "happy" and "grumpy" (contrast effect). They are compared with one another rather than with a general **norm** (Neale & Stevenson, 1989; Plomin et al., 1997).

Recent years have seen the discovery of genes that seem to affect the way in which children respond to positive and negative experiences. Alleles of the genes MAO-A and 5-HTTP, for example, appear to be related to children's temperament and reactions to novelty and, in turn, impact their susceptibility to particular parenting styles. The effects of some genetic differences only seem to emerge during development when children have experienced neglect, abuse and similarly serious incidents. Genes do not cause such events, but may affect how the individual copes with them when they do occur (Meaney, 2010; Moffitt et al., 2006; Rutter, 2004). Consequently, it is not particular personality traits that distinguish individuals with different genetic makeups, but rather differences in flexibility and sensitivity to the characteristics of their social surroundings that may influence personality development.

Childhood Environment

The social environment is the other major source of individual differences in personality. In most societies, the family represents the main social environment in childhood and adolescence. Parents are an important resource for children's psychological growth, for instance by engaging in conversations about the child herself and others (Dunn et al., 1987; Pomerantz & Thompson, 2008). Parents' personality and their sense of competence and self-efficacy affect their parenting style. Parents who score high on extraversion and agreeableness and perceive themselves as competent parents do not overreact as often and have a warmer parenting style than parents who score lower on these two traits and perceive themselves as less competent (de Haan et al.,

2009). Depression and other mental health problems may also have an impact on perceived self-competence and parenting style in both mothers and fathers (Berg-Nielsen et al., 2002; Peláez et al., 2008; Wilson & Durbin, 2010).

Several theoretical perspectives imply that children should become similar to their parents. From a cognitive behavioral view, parents affect their children by being role models (see Book 1, *Theory and Methodology*, Chapter 6). According to Freud's theory, personality is partly shaped by children's identification with their parents (see p. 81, this volume). Research, however, has not found strong similarities between the personality traits of parents and their children. For *extraversion*, the correlation is 0.15; for *neuroticism*, it is 0.16 between children and their biological parents, and 0.10 and 0.05 between adopted children and their adoptive parents. The personalities of siblings growing up in the same family can be quite different. Although parenting style shows considerable stability (Dallaire & Weinraub, 2005), this does not mean that parents treat their children equally all the time. The entire family goes through transactional change over time, and parents adjust to their children's age and development.

The differences between siblings and the relative dissimilarity between children and parents have led to discussions about the amount of influence parents actually have on their child's personality. Scarr (1992) concludes that it is pointless for parents to try to influence their children's personalities, but many studies show that parental attitudes and parenting practices have **significance** for children's personality. In a classic study, Baldwin (1949) found that children of parents with a *democratic* parenting style tended to be active and social and could speak for themselves. Children with *controlling* parents were more obedient, fearful and withdrawn. Other studies have found that children and adolescents with controlling parents tend to be dependent and lacking in sociability, whereas those with *positive authoritative* parents (decisive, rational and loving) were more independent and socially competent (Baumrind, 1967, 2013). Many adult patients with personality disorders say that their parents did not understand them in childhood, that they were over-controlled, and that they did not get the love they needed (Cramer et al., 2007).

This small selection of studies demonstrates that the family impacts children's development in different ways. Children observe their parents' actions and reactions, and parents control, stimulate and challenge their children, encouraging, refusing and helping them to become autonomous and solve the challenges they face on their own. Their influence does not always lead to a personality that resembles their own – the family environment can contribute to both similarity and dissimilarity (Pomerantz & Thompson, 2008). Children growing up in the same family do not necessarily have identical environments. Even when they have a consistent parenting style, parents treat their children differently, and their adaptation to the children's temperament and other individual traits can result in very different environments for siblings. Contrast effects, too, have an impact on siblings: if parents found their first child to be difficult, they often perceive their next child to be easy, and vice versa (Rodgers et al., 1994). Moreover, studies also show that children with different gene variants (alleles) can be differentially susceptible to parent sensitivity and parenting (Pluess & Belsky, 2010). Knowledge of kinship and the parents' living situation is not enough to map the environmental factors that may contribute to children's similarities and differences: the interaction between parenting style and children's characteristics results in a relative influence rather than an absolute one (Collins et al., 2000; Torgersen & Janson, 2002). This means that all children are affected by their home environment, but on different premises and in different ways.

Parents do not only represent their own experiences or personalities. Social norms and cultural values contribute to forming the actions of children and adults, how their emotions are expressed, the relationships between them and so on. Cultures vary in how much they emphasize control, obedience, cooperation and autonomy (Chen & French, 2008; Rodríguez et al., 2009; Selin, 2014). In **collectivist cultures** such as China, parents stress the importance of the child's contribution to society's goals, whereas parents in **individualistic cultures** such as the United States emphasize competition and the child's own well-being (Kwan & Herrmann, 2015). Additionally, parenting style is influenced by the immediate surroundings. Parents living in violent or stressful neighborhoods tend to be more controlling and restrictive than parents who live in quieter areas (Furstenberg & Hughes, 1997; Gewirtz & Zamir, 2014).

Once children reach school age, peers become more important, and friends gain increasing influence (see Book 7, *Social Relations, Self-awareness and Identity*, Chapter 12). They represent a benchmark when children gain more knowledge about themselves and others. In late adolescence and adulthood, personality development is more influenced by forces outside the family, and positive **authoritative parenting** has greatest effect when the parents of the children's friends have the same upbringing style (Fletcher et al., 1995).

The Significance of Early Experiences

Both classical and modern theorists consider early childhood to be a particularly important period that sets the developmental course. Studies have especially focused on the consequences of serious neglect, maltreatment and abuse, and how change and improvement in the rearing environment affect children's social adjustment and personality development (Clarke & Clarke, 2000; Fox & Rutter, 2010). Negative experiences early in life seem to contribute to a *vigilance* that increases vulnerability to stressful events or to the development of behavioral tendencies that increase the likelihood of stress or personal problems later in life and may leave relatively permanent traces on the individual's personality (see McCrory & Viding, 2015). Early identification of limited family resources and timely intervention are therefore important priorities in a society (Guralnick, 2011; Herskind et al., 2015).

Early Neglect

Studies of infant monkeys have lent important insight into the possible consequences of early neglect (see also Book 7, *Social Relations, Self-awareness and Identity*, Chapter 2). A classic study demonstrates the importance of early active interaction. Harlow (1963) isolated infant monkeys so they could see other monkeys, but not have physical contact with them in the first few months of life. Observations showed that they developed neither playing skills nor ordinary social skills. When they later were brought together with non-isolated monkeys, they had significant problems interacting with them. As adolescents and adults, they were often aggressive and had difficulty engaging in normal sexual activities. Many of the female monkeys developed into incompetent mothers, and some abused their young. Problems were greatest with their firstborns, whereas later-born infants often were given better care. Individual differences were significant, however, and a third of the mothers in this group showed normal care for their infant (Suomi, 1991).

In this study, the monkeys were directly placed together with the rest of the group after isolation. In another study, similarly isolated infant monkeys were slowly exposed to social stimulation, initially in the company of a non-isolated 3-month-old monkey for 1 hour a day. Gradually, they improved at playing and socializing with others, but the other monkeys continued to be the only ones to take initiative. After a few weeks, they, too, started to initiate play and interaction. As adolescents and adults, they generally behaved normally, but new and stressful situations initially caused them to respond with rocking movements and other forms of stereotyped behaviors they had shown during their early isolation. They also reacted with strong emotions and by acting out when placed in isolation once again (Novak & Harlow, 1975; Suomi, 1991). The reaction patterns caused by their early isolation thus never completely disappeared, even though they only emerged under similar conditions.

Corresponding reactions have been observed in studies of children exposed to severe neglect in orphanages or in the home. Especially in countries at war, but also in other contexts, many children grow up in orphanages without adequate physical and emotional care. Several studies found a significantly higher **prevalence** of internalizing disorders in children and adolescents who had been victims of neglect than in children who had not experienced neglect (Gallo et al., 2017; Sadowski et al., 1999; Zeanah et al., 2009). Studies found a higher prevalence of suicide attempts, more antisocial personality disorders and alcohol abuse in individuals who had been neglected or abused in childhood (Sachs-Ericsson et al., 2017; Widom, 2000). In a follow-up study of children who had been taken from their parents owing to neglect or abuse and placed in orphanages, one-third showed poor adaptation as adults. A comparison group with normal upbringing showed a similar development for 10 percent of the males and none of the females. The difficulties experienced by the follow-up group were not only the result of early neglect, but also of having been separated from their families and growing up in institutions, with a continuous chain of risk factors (Rutter, 1991a).

Still, early neglect is not destiny. Many children are resilient to growing up under such negative conditions (Cicchetti, 2013; Luthar et al., 2014). A number of studies show that the negative consequences of poor childhood conditions are reduced when children are adopted into better home environments. Their age at adoption and the length of time children have spent in orphanages have major significance (Julian, 2013). Children from Romanian orphanages of low quality who were adopted between the ages of 6 and 24 months had somewhat poorer adaptation at the age of 6 years than children adopted before the age of 6 months. This was not only owing to the shorter amount of time the children had spent under normal child-hood conditions; the advantages of early adoption were also evident when comparing groups that had been adopted equally long. The developmental trajectory seems more difficult to change when a child has spent a longer time adapting to neglect – the longer time indicates to the child that the aversive features of the environment are stable and, hence, will continue (Chisholm, 1998; Rutter et al., 2010). Other studies have found poorer social cognitive and play skills in 4-year-old Romanian adoptees than in British adoptees, with greater differences for Romanian children adopted between the ages of 6 and 24 months than for those who had been younger at the time of adop-tion. Ten percent of the children had severe social cognitive problems reminiscent of autism spectrum disorder, including communication and social impairment, trouble understanding other people's thoughts and feelings, narrow interests and stereotyped repetitive movements. However, they took far more initiative in social interaction than children with autism spectrum disorder usually do, and the problems were significantly reduced when the children were 11–12 years old (Kreppner et al., 1999; Rutter et al., 2007).

Early intervention is important, but a number of studies show a positive development also in children who were adopted into stable environments at a relatively late age and offered appropriate treat-ment after many years in different foster homes (Dumaret et al., 1997). Moskowitz (1985) observed a small group of children who had been interned in German concentration camps during World War II. The children had managed to adapt and had not developed irreparable psy-chological damage. Although adoption studies show that it takes time for children to get over negative experiences, they also give reason to believe that the differences to their peers gradually dissipate once they get older and have lived under positive and stable conditions for longer periods.

Maltreatment and Sexual Abuse

Maltreatment and sexual abuse shatter the very foundation of chil-dren's life – that somebody cares for them. They affect children's per-ception of themselves and others (see also Book 7, *Social Relations,*

Self-awareness and Identity, Chapter 23) and can have profound consequences for the development of their personality and mental health.
A longitudinal study of physically abused 2-year-olds found that they
showed more anger and were less obedient to their mothers than
other children. A little more than a year later, they showed poor self-
regulation and a negative self-image. In kindergarten, they were negative, angry, disobedient and antagonistic toward their peers. They had
learned that the world is a hostile place in which they had to defend
themselves. Children who had been sexually abused before the age of
5 were exceptionally anxious and dependent on adults, while at the
same time exhibiting wide mood swings from extreme aggressiveness
to strong dependence and passivity (Erickson et al., 1989). Around
6 years of age, children who had been maltreated scored lower on
the traits agreeableness, conscientiousness and openness to experience,
and higher on neuroticism involving high negative emotionality and
low emotion regulation. This personality pattern was maintained at
9 years (Rogosch & Cicchetti, 2004).

Children who have been maltreated or abused often show poor
development, but their developmental trajectories vary. A strong
sense of shame (see p. 34, this volume), depression and a tendency
to perceive other people as a threat (see p. 50, this volume) are common reactions. Some react with hostility and aggression toward their
peers, whereas others tend to withdraw from them. Some children
alternate between aggression and withdrawal, incorporating the
actions of both perpetrator and victim in interacting with other children. At school age, some children develop delusions of grandeur,
seemingly as a protection against the negative image they perceive
others to have of them. In adolescence and early adulthood, some
of them develop dissociative personality disorder with disruptions in
identity and sense of being a person (Cicchetti, 2016; Cicchetti &
Toth, 2015).

Many parents who maltreat or abuse their children have themselves
grown up under difficult circumstances and were subjected to abuse
in childhood. As they received little help in regulating their own temperament, they may not have learned to deal with the kind of irritation
that a crying or nagging child can provoke. The use of violent strategies to resolve conflicts in childhood may further have led to a lower
threshold for these types of abusive actions (see p. 45, this volume).
Adults who have abused children outside their own family have often
experienced prolonged separation from their parents or grown up in
institutions, but less than half have been sexually abused themselves

(Waterhouse et al., 1994). These studies demonstrate the importance of the conditions under which children grow up, but also that the underlying causes of child abuse and maltreatment are complex, and that they cannot easily be explained (Clarke & Clarke, 2000).

Divorce and Death

Among all the single events involving major changes in children's lives, divorce is the most common, and for many children entails less contact with one of their parents, usually the father (Kalmijn, 2015). Numerous studies have shown that divorce can reduce children's confidence, cause them to blame themselves and cope poorly at school, as well as become more dependent on their teachers and the parent they live with. Adolescents can become anxious, depressed and disruptive, with girls reacting more strongly than boys (Størksen et al., 2005). Parental divorce may even influence well-being in adult life (Huurre et al., 2006). Studies that include information on the child *before* it was known whether the parents would divorce have found that domestic conditions were different for children whose parents divorced than for those who did not divorce, factors that were important for children's reactions following the divorce (Strohschein, 2005). Some studies show long-term effects, but the direct impact of divorce is usually short-lived. Most children show a **typical development**, and any long-term effects on their personality development are related to the new type of relationship they establish with their parents (Hetherington, 2003; Wallerstein & Lewis, 2004).

Losing a parent is always a dramatic experience for children and adolescents and brings with it the risk of internalizing disorders and problems at school (Dyregrov et al., 2015; Stikkelbroek et al., 2016). The strongest grief reactions generally do not last very long. After 1 year, they are usually significantly reduced, but depression in the surviving parent, including inadequate care and reduced parent–child interaction, can intensify and prolong these reactions (Pianta & Nimetz, 1992). Loss of a parent in childhood increases the likelihood of anxiety and depression as an adult, but also depends on the child's vulnerability and other life events (Brent et al., 2012; Howell et al., 2015). Vulnerability is highest when parents die of external causes, such as accidents, murder and suicide, early in children's lives (Berg et al., 2016). Although the majority of children in most countries do not lose one or both of their parents in childhood or adolescence, it is a common experience for children in countries at war, and many young refugees have lost one or both parents (Shaw, 2003; Werner, 2012). Also, in countries with poor health care and high rates of HIV and AIDS, many children lose their parents (Case et al., 2004).

The Developmental Consequences of Early Experiences

The studies presented here show that early negative experiences involve a risk of aberrant and delayed development, but also that even severe forms of neglect and abuse can be overcome. Children are often resilient to individual experiences, which rarely have a profound and lasting impact. It is the experience of repeated negative events and continuous neglect or abuse by the surroundings that can affect children's personality development in the long term (Wachs & Gruen, 1982; Sameroff, 2009).

17

Personality Development and Later Disorders

A personality disorder is a pattern of inner experiences and behavior that deviates from cultural norms. In DSM-5, this diagnosis is not usually given before the age of 18 on the grounds that an individual's personality is not sufficiently stable before that age (American Psychiatric Association, 2013). However, some claim that personality disorders are observable in childhood and adolescence, and it is a common assumption that they are rooted in childhood. Both child characteristics and environmental conditions appear to be related to later personality disorders (Shiner, 2009; Tackett, et al., 2009; van den Akker et al., 2016). Klein and associates (2014) hypothesize that maladaptive child development across the self and interpersonal **domains** plays an important role in the genesis of later personality pathology. Harsh parenting as well as physical, emotional and sexual abuse in childhood and adolescence seem to represent increased risk of developing borderline personality disorder. Still, symptoms of personality disorder may be difficult to distinguish from the normal emergence of personality traits in adolescence, and such symptoms are more unstable than in adulthood (Klein et al., 2014).

Studies show that children's early personality affects how they later adapt to and shape their own social surroundings. A comprehensive British study found a generally low incidence of emotional disorders in adults, but the incidence was several times higher in those who had shown significant behavioral problems and emotional disorders in childhood (Rutter, 1991b). Children who are social, secure and independent have a lower probability of developing internalizing disorders. In the Dunedin study (see p. 92, this volume), children who were under-controlled at the age of 3 years had more externalizing disorders at school age and in adolescence than other children.

DOI: 10.4324/9781003292531-19

At 21 years, they had committed more crimes than their peers, had relatively many conflicts in their relationships, and were often considered unreliable and untrustworthy by others. Over-controlled or inhibited children showed a tendency to develop internalizing disorders in the course of adolescence. At age 21, they had smaller social networks and less social support than children who had not been inhibited at the age of 3 (Caspi, 2000). Another study found that under-controlled children had a higher incidence of drug problems in adolescence than better regulated children (Shedler & Block, 1990). Some personality disorders in adolescence and adulthood are considered to be maladaptive variants of the Big Five (Shiner, 2009). Psychopathy (see p. 141, this volume) is considered a personality disorder, and adolescents may show symptoms of psychopathy similarly to adults (Lynam & Widiger, 2007).

Although early disorders entail greater vulnerability for later disorders, it is not always the same children who suffer from disorders at all age levels. In a follow-up study of children who had been referred to a psychiatric clinic for anxiety and emotional disorders, only 3 of 28 who had been referred before the age of 9 years received psychiatric treatment as young adults. A quarter of the children referred between the ages of 10 and 14 years and half of those referred between 15 and 19 years received psychiatric treatment when they were 20–24 years old (von Knorring et al., 1987). This indicates that most children with relatively early disorders eventually outgrow them, and that disorders later in childhood and adolescence are more indicative of disorders in adulthood.

18

Personality Development Is a Transactional Process

Children's tendency to feel, think, react and act in particular ways is formed by the possibilities and limitations of their surroundings, as well as by their previous development, while at the same time they contribute to shaping their own environment. Children's personality reflects their development history, their goals and values, and the characteristics of the people in their surroundings. The same event can have different meanings for children with differing backgrounds, interests and goals. Children's individual tendencies to act and react represent a *preparedness* that reflects their individual temperament and understanding of the world. Contrary to Scarr's (1992) claim, children can only create their own environment to a limited extent. They *affect* their parents, but do not create them. The parents' own temperament and established behaviors determine how they initially meet the child's actions and reactions. An insecure father living under difficult conditions can become more secure by experiencing himself as a successful parent of a temperamentally easy child, or become more insecure if the child has a difficult temperament. In that case, the father's insecurity is not caused by the child alone, however. Children born into unstable or war-torn areas are powerless to create peace for their parents. Most children have an important, albeit limited, impact on their caregivers and surroundings in general. A basic personality trait may be the ability to act in different ways and to choose action strategies based on the demands of the situation. The most important differences between children do not have to do with how they react in familiar situations, but how they deal with *new* situations (Kagan & Snidman, 2004; Masten, 2014). Sroufe and colleagues (1993) describe *developmental lines* not characterized by fixed behavior patterns, but rather by how consistently children meet and adapt to new contexts. It is this consistency the authors believe best represents what is known as personality.

DOI: 10.4324/9781003292531-20

Summary of Part II

1   Children differ with respect to emotionality, irritability, activity level and how they handle emotional situations, novelty and changes. Traditional temperament types include *easy*, *difficult* and *slow to warm up*. More recent categories include *sociability*, *positive* and *negative emotionality*, *extraversion*, *effortful control of attention and distractions*, *endurance*, *likeability* and *adaptability*. *Reaction to novelty* is an especially important trait that indicates whether children are cautious and timid or approach when they meet strangers and new situations. Temperament can be assessed through *physiological measures*, *questionnaires*, *parent interviews* and *observations*.

2   Temperament heritability ranges from 0.2 to 0.6, changes with age and shows greater stability over shorter than longer periods. There is generally a moderate continuity of temperament, but more for children with a pronounced trait.

3   Children's temperaments affect the way in which they are treated by their parents, whose reactions change with the child's age and can both strengthen or weaken the effect of the child's temperament. The "goodness of fit" of parents' and children's temperaments differs. A generally positive parental trait is *sensitivity* and the ability to adapt to the child's temperament.

4   Children's temperament can entail both vulnerability to *internalizing* and *externalizing* disorders and *resilience* to such disorders. Positive environmental characteristics and children's interactions with other people can protect children with a difficult temperament from developing problems. Temperament can contribute to both vulnerability and protection against disorders.

5   *Personality* is the tendency to feel, think and act in certain ways.
     The "Big Five" personality traits include *extraversion, agreeable-
     ness, conscientiousness, neuroticism* (emotional lability) and *openness
     to experience,* each consisting of six sub-facets. Younger children
     are typically described as *active, irritable, independent* and *mature for
     their age.* According to Bandura and Mischel, children's tendencies
     to act and react in certain ways are adaptations to actual situations
     that variously characterize a child in different situations, like a
     behavioral signature.

6   The main elements of Freud's *psychodynamic* theory of personality
     development are *id, ego* and *superego, the psychosexual phases* and
     the defense mechanisms. Many modern theorists build on Freud's
     basic ideas but have changed major parts of his theory. Erikson
     represents *ego psychology.* Each of eight life-span phases is associ-
     ated with a *social crisis,* and together they form the basis for an
     individual's personality. The theory has been criticized for being
     too male-oriented and poorly suited to modern society, but is still
     widely used.

7   McCrae and Costa's theory is based on evolutionary principles
     and the hypothesis that the Big Five and their 30 facets are uni-
     versal and develop through maturation. Personality is not the
     result of individual adaptation, but instead forms the basis for
     adaptation. The theory has been criticized for failing to explain
     the mechanisms underlying personality development.

8   *Behaviorism* describes personality in terms of *response tenden-
     cies* acquired through conditioning and imitation like all other
     behavior. The theory has been criticized for taking insufficient
     account of the diversity of children's minds and the complexity
     of development. In *cognitive behavior theory,* children's reactions
     and behaviors are the result of environmental adaptation related
     to children's self-esteem and expectations, and especially their
     perception of themselves as *agents* in a social world. They learn
     from the consequences of their own actions and by observing
     the consequences of others' actions. Cognitive behavior therapy,
     based on Bandura's theory, is very influential in clinical child and
     adolescent psychology, but he has been criticized for not integrat-
     ing knowledge of general cognitive development.

9   Early temperament and later personality are partially related.
     Descriptions of children's personality traits differ from descriptions

of adults'. New personal characteristics appear at preschool age, and toward adolescence personality is increasingly described with the same personality traits as for adults.

10 Personality traits are stable over shorter time spans and show low to moderate stability over longer time spans. Some children have a *stable* personality development, while others are more characterized by *change*. Although early *disorders* involve a greater risk of later disorders, it is generally not the same children who show disorders at all age levels.

11 Heritability varies for each trait, with estimates rarely exceeding 0.4–0.5, indicating that the genes and environment play equal roles. The influence of genes seems to decrease with age. Some genes have an impact on how vulnerable children are to neglect, parenting style and other environmental factors.

12 The personality traits of parents and their children generally show low correlations. Family affects the development of children's personalities, but not always in such a way that they come to resemble their parents or siblings. Parenting style and behavior reflect parents' experiences, personality and any possible disorders, as well as influences from their children. Children of parents with a *democratic parenting style* tend to be active, social and able to speak up for themselves. Children with *controlling* parents are obedient, fearful and withdrawn. *Friends and activities outside the home* gain increasing influence on the development of personality. Social and cultural factors affect parenting style and thereby contribute to shaping children's personalities.

13 Early childhood is often viewed as a developmentally **sensitive period** that leads to *vigilance*, with increased *vulnerability* or *resilience* to stress and problems later in life. Children who have been subjected to severe neglect usually show poor adaptation, but the risk of developing mental health problems can be reduced by improved domestic conditions or by adoption into stable rearing environments. Maltreatment and sexual abuse increase children's vulnerability and can have a profound and lasting impact on their development. They affect children's perception of their surroundings, and some children react by withdrawing from their peers, others by showing aggression and hostility. Divorce involves sudden and major changes in children's lives, but the effects are relatively short-lived.

14 Some children are *resilient* and manage to cope with relatively serious early neglect without apparent damage. It is continuous exposure to an environment of neglect or abuse, rather than isolated incidents, that can impact the development of children's personality in the long term.

15 The diagnosis "personality disorder" is not usually given before the age of 18, but many claim that such disorders may be observable in adolescence, and it is a common assumption that they are rooted in the individual's experiences in childhood and maladaptive variants of personality traits.

16 Personality development is an adaptive transactional process. The environment can either hinder or promote children's ability to self-regulate and adapt, and is in turn affected by the child's self-regulating mechanisms. One of the most basic personality traits is the ability to choose appropriate action strategies in new situations. *Developmental lines* represent the consistency in children's ability to meet and adapt to new contexts.

Core Issues

- The relationship between temperament and disorders.
- The measurement of temperament.
- The bases of personality traits.
- The importance of early experiences.
- The presence of personality disorders in childhood and adolescence.

Suggestions for Further Reading

Bandura, A. (2006). Toward a psychology of human agency. *Perspectives on Psychological Science*, *1*, 164–180.

Davis, M., & Suveg, C. (2014). Focusing on the positive: A review of the role of child positive affect in developmental psychopathology. *Clinical Child and Family Psychology Review*, *17*, 97–124.

Erikson, E. H. (1963). *Childhood and society*. New York, NY: W. W. Norton.

Guralnick, M. J. (2011). Why early intervention works: A systems perspective. *Infants and Young Children*, *24*, 6–28.

Kagan, J., & Snidman, N. C. (2004). *The long shadow of temperament*. Cambridge, MA: Belknap Press.

Kongerslev, M. T., et al. (2015). Personality disorder in childhood and adolescence comes of age: A review of the current evidence and prospects for future research. *Scandinavian Journal of Child and Adolescent Psychiatry and Psychology, 3*, 31–48.

Rothbart, M. K. (2007). Temperament, development, and personality. *Current Directions in Psychological Science, 16*, 207–212.

Widom, C. S., Czaja, S. J., & Dutton, M. A. (2008). Childhood victimization and lifetime revictimization. *Child Abuse and Neglect, 32*, 785–796.

Part III

Moral Development

Understanding of Right and Wrong

Morality is the ability to tell right from wrong and forms the basis for judging whether one's own actions and those of others are just, caring and to the benefit of other people, or unjust, harmful and selfish. Morality is socially oriented, and moral norms and values, as well as the development of **conscience**, are crucial to human interaction and coexistence within societies. Thus, moral development is a process of enculturation and social functioning in a broader social and societal context. This chapter is about the biological and social bases of moral development and offers theoretical explanations of the emergence of **moral reasoning**, how children and adolescents reason about the morality of actions, based on their consequences and intentions, and resolve **moral dilemmas**. Moral development is related to prosocial and antisocial development, which is the topic of Part IV.

DOI: 10.4324/9781003329253I-22

Theoretical Perspectives

Most major theories have a view on moral development and offer widely differing explanations. Some theories emphasize children's cognitive abilities as a basis for moral reasoning, while others see morality as primarily motivational and driven by emotions. Earlier theories of moral development were concerned with the *transmission* of norms and values and the internalization of norms imposed by authorities, while constructivist theories assume that children develop moral understandings in interaction with their surroundings (Dahl, 2014; Turiel, 2014). Three main perspectives are included here: logical constructivism, evolutionary theory and social domain theory.

Logical Constructivism

Logical constructivism is primarily concerned with the cognitive processes underlying moral reasoning, and it is children's ability to reason that determines their moral views.

Piaget's Theory

According to Piaget (1932), moral development is a process of differentiation whereby children gradually learn to distinguish actions based on reciprocity and fairness from actions based on ready-made rules by an authority. Early moral judgments reflect children's interaction with adults, while social conflicts with *peers* have greater significance for moral development in later childhood. Piaget examined, for example, how children develop an understanding of rules through marbles and other games. As no adult authority can provide the correct answer, children are forced to compare their own views with those of other

DOI: 10.4324/9781003292531-23

children. The resulting cognitive conflict (see Book 4, *Cognition, Intelligence and Learning*, Chapter 3) in each individual child is the driving force behind moral development.

Piaget describes three stages of moral development with approximate age levels. Until the age of 4–5 years, children are in the *pre-moral* stage. They have a poor understanding of the general rules of right and wrong and follow personal rules without a fixed system, based on their own desires. They like to play marbles but have little understanding of the rules of the game and may well call the marbles "mummy ball" and "baby balls."

The second stage, **moral realism**, begins around the age of 5. Although children are able to follow rules, they can only do so literally, with little willingness to adapt or change. Children now try to win at marbles, but the rules to them are defined by an inviolable authority rather than being something everyone has agreed on. An important characteristic of this age is children's emphasis on the consequences of an action rather than its intent. Piaget asked children who was naughtier – Jean, who accidentally broke 12 cups because he did not know that the cups stood behind a door he opened, or Henri, who broke one cup when he was about to steal some jam and

Piaget considered children's participation in games an experiential basis for moral development.

therefore intended to do something wrong. Here, Piaget talks with 6-year-old Geo (1932, pp. 120–121).

P: *Have you understood these stories?*
G: *Yes.*
P: *What did the first boy do?*
G: *He broke eleven cups.*
P: *And the second one?*
G: *He broke a cup by moving roughly.*
P: *Why did the first one break the cups?*
G: *Because the door knocked him.*
P: *And the other?*
G: *He was clumsy. When he was getting the jam the cup fell down.*
P: *Is one of the boys naughtier than the other?*
G: *The first is because he knocked over twelve cups.*
P: *If you were the daddy, which one would you punish more?*
G: *The one who broke twelve cups.*
P: *Why did he break them?*
G: *The door shut too hard and knocked them. He didn't do it on purpose.*
P: *And why did the other boy break a cup?*
G: *He wanted to get jam. He moved too far. The cup got broken.*
P: *Why did he want to get the jam?*
G: *Because he was all alone. His mother wasn't there.*
P: *Have you got a brother?*
G: *No, a little sister.*
P: *Well, if it was you who had broken the twelve cups when you went into the room and your little sister had broken one cup while she was trying to get the jam, which of you would be punished most severely?*
G: *Me, because I broke more than one cup.*

The children understood the intention behind the actions and gave many replies such as: *It wasn't his fault, he didn't do it on purpose,* but did not take these insights into account. Their reasoning was solely based on adults saying it is wrong to break cups.

The third stage, **moral subjectivism**, begins around the age of 9–10 years. Children now understand that rules are *conventions,* that is, **social constructs** based on agreement, and that it is possible to change them if one agrees on it. They consider the *intention* behind an action and, faced with the broken-cup dilemma, they reply that Henri is naughtiest because he intended to do something wrong. This inclusion of intention in moral evaluation is a significant qualitative step in their moral reasoning.

Later studies have found that children show moral understanding considerably earlier than Piaget had found. Preschool children, for example, seem to distinguish between social conventions and moral dictates. Critics point out that Piaget's studies are biased in favor of language skills, and that his stories are too long and complex for younger children. It is the complexity of the tasks, rather than their moral dilemmas, which makes them difficult for the children. Studies have shown that, if the extent of damage caused is equal, younger children make greater allowances for the intent behind the action. When children are told that two children have broken the same number of cups, they say that the naughtier child is the one who did it on purpose (Imamoglu, 1975).

Kohlberg's Theory

Kohlberg (1969, 1976) extends Piaget's theoretical framework, adding stages for adolescence and adulthood, and introduces the *moral judgment interview*, a predetermined set of stories consisting of moral dilemmas. The best known among these is about Heinz (Kohlberg, 1963, pp. 18–19):

> *In Europe, a woman was near death from a special kind of cancer. There was one drug that the doctors thought might save her. It was a form of radium that a druggist in the same town had recently discovered. The drug was expensive to make, but the druggist was charging ten times what the drug cost him to make. He paid $200 for the radium and charged $2,000 for a small dose of the drug. The sick woman's husband, Heinz, went to everyone he knew to borrow the money, but he could only get together about $1,000 which is half of what it cost. He told the druggist that his wife was dying and asked him to sell it cheaper or let him pay later. But the druggist said: "No, I discovered the drug and I'm going to make money from it." So Heinz got desperate and broke into the man's store to steal the drug for his wife. Should the husband have done that?*

The answers to the interview dilemmas are ranked according to the *reasons* given, rather than whether the actions were considered right or wrong. Kohlberg describes three main levels of moral development, each consisting of two stages and characterized by a specific line of reasoning (Box 20.1). At Level I, **pre-conventional morality**, the authority decides. This stage usually lasts until the age of 10, but pre-conventional moral reasoning can also be found among many adolescents. At Stage 1, actions are judged according to their consequences, and Heinz's dilemma is justified based on the likelihood of ending up in prison. At Stage 2, any action is judged by the extent to which it meets one's own needs. From this point of view, the solution to Heinz's dilemma can be to steal the drug.

Box 20.1   Kohlberg's Stages of Moral Development (adapted from Kohlberg, 1971; Kohlberg & Hersh, 1977)

I   Pre-Conventional Level

Stage 1   The Punishment and Obedience Orientation

The physical consequences of an action determine how good or bad it is, for example expectations of punishment. The reason for doing right is to avoid punishment from the superior power of authorities who decide the rules. Motive for moral action: obey the rules to avoid punishment.

Stage 2   The Instrumental Relativist Orientation

Right action consists of what instrumentally satisfies one's own needs and occasionally the needs of others. It is necessary to recognize that other people have their interests, and elements of fairness, reciprocity and equal sharing are present. Motive for moral action: conform to obtain rewards, have favors returned and so on.

II   Conventional Level

Stage 3   The Interpersonal Concordance or "Good Boy–Nice Girl" Orientation

Good behavior is what pleases or helps others and is approved by them. Behavior is frequently judged by intention – "he means well" becomes important for the first time. One earns approval by being "nice." Motive for moral action: conform to avoid disapproval and dislike from others.

Stage 4   The "Law and Order" Orientation

Right behavior consists in doing one's duty, showing respect for authority, maintaining the given social order for its own sake and avoiding breakdown of the system. Motive for moral action: conform to avoid censure by legitimate authorities and resultant guilt.

III   Post-Conventional, Autonomous or Principled Level

Stage 5   The Social-Contract Legalistic Orientation, Generally with Utilitarian Overtones

Right action tends to be defined in terms of general individual rights and standards that have been critically examined and agreed upon by the whole society. Aside from what is constitutionally and democratically agreed upon, right is a matter of personal values and opinion. Laws may be changed after rational considerations of social utility. Motive for moral action: conform to maintain the respect of the impartial spectator judging in terms of community welfare.

Stage 6   The Universal Ethical-Principle Orientation

Right is defined by the decision of conscience in accord with self-chosen abstract ethical principles that appeal to logical comprehensiveness, **universality** and consistency, such as the Golden Rule or the categorical imperative. At heart, these are universal principles of justice, of the reciprocity and equality of human rights, and of respect for the dignity of human beings as individual persons. Motive for moral action: conform to avoid self-condemnation.

Level II is **conventional morality**. Most children reach Stage 3 around the age of 13, and adolescents are able to incorporate the perspectives and intentions behind other people's actions. "Nobody will think badly about you if you steal the medicine, and your family will think you are inhuman if you don't." Stage 4 also includes orientation toward social order and one's duty as a citizen. "It is natural that Heinz wishes to save his wife's life, but it is always wrong to steal."

Level III, **post-conventional morality**, requires the capacity for **formal-operational reasoning** (see Book 4, *Cognition, Intelligence and Learning*, Chapter 3). At Stage 5, the rights of the individual and the values of society become increasingly important. Rules are still not fixed, however, but remain relative. "One cannot let people steal because they are desperate. The goal may be good but does not justify the means." At Stage 6, the individual reasons are based on abstract moral principles. What is morally right depends on the individual's conscience, guided by universal moral principles rather than the laws of a particular society. "If you don't steal the medicine and let your wife die you will condemn yourself afterwards. You will not live up to the standard of your own conscience." According to Kohlberg, only 10 percent of adults reach this stage.

In a longitudinal study, Kohlberg followed the development of moral reasoning in a group of boys from the age of 10–16 until they were 36 years old (Colby et al., 1983). Their answers to the dilemmas did not only follow their age: reasoning associated with different stages existed side by side in their development. Pre-conventional moral reasoning was found even in adults, albeit rarely, and none of the answers belonged to Stage 6. Nonetheless, the group of boys largely followed Kohlberg's stages. None of them skipped over a stage, and **regression** to an earlier stage was rare. Their reasoning also remained consistent within one or two adjacent stages. Later studies support these findings but take issue with the fact that the stages are not entirely distinct and that Stage 6 lacks responses (Boom et al., 2007; Lourenço, 2003). All the boys in Colby et al.'s study had normal cognitive development as adults and should therefore have been capable of post-conventional moral reasoning. When some of them did not show such reasoning, it indicates that general cognitive skills are *necessary* but not *sufficient* for advanced moral reasoning. The question is: what other conditions have to be met for an individual to develop the ability to make difficult moral judgments?

Lawrence Kohlberg.

Cultural Factors

According to Kohlberg (1981), the stages of moral development are universal, and children and adolescents in different countries largely show the same development. Stages 5 and 6, however, appear less structured and integrated in **cross-cultural** comparisons than the other stages. Many people from rural cultures, for example, do not present arguments belonging to the two most advanced stages, although this does not necessarily reflect a lower level of moral or cognitive competence (Snarey, 1985). Furthermore, most studies have used Kohlberg's stories and therefore do not reflect the particular moral dilemmas children and adolescents may face in their own social and cultural context. The reasoning demanded by these types of dilemmas is also affected by practical factors, such as the interests of one's own family and a sense of intuition and of having found a good solution (Snarey, 1985). Some studies have therefore tried to pose ethical questions more relevant to children's or adolescents' daily lives, such as: "Think of a time you made a promise to someone.

How important is it that people keep their promises?" or "Think of a time you helped your parents. How important is it for children to help their parents?" (Gibbs et al., 2007b). Also, religious rules can be perceived as natural and inevitable and determine the outcome of a moral dilemma. Some forms of moral reasoning among non-Western cultures are difficult to incorporate into Kohlberg's stages. Nor are arguments based on notions such as non-violence and social harmony easily reconciled with the assumption of fairness and justice as overriding moral goals (Walker & Hennig, 1997). However, Gibbs and associates (2007b) conclude: "Our review bolsters the conclusion that Kohlberg was in principle correct regarding the universality of basic moral judgment development, moral values, and related social perspective-taking processes across cultures" (p. 491).

Justice and Caring

Another objection to Kohlberg's theory is that it fails to account for differences between male and female reasoning. Carol Gilligan (1982) argues that male morality is oriented toward justice and female morality toward care and describes three stages in the development of women's morality. The first stage focuses on caring for oneself, the second stage on caring for other people, while the third stage integrates care for oneself and others. The challenge for women is to find a balance between their own needs and those of others in connection with moral dilemmas.

According to Gilligan, these differences in moral reasoning are not the result of biological factors. Women's upbringing teaches them to be more aware of how their actions affect other people's feelings, whereas men's upbringing focuses more on independence, self-awareness and result-oriented thinking. Therefore, women approach moral dilemmas from the perspective of caring and taking responsibility for others, whereas men's reasoning is based on a sense of justice. As fairness and justice are central to Kohlberg's stages and the dilemmas he presents, Gilligan believes women will inevitably achieve lower scores on Kohlberg's moral judgment interviews, thus underestimating their moral sense. However, Walker (1984) compared the results of a large number of studies and found no systematic differences between the scores of boys and girls on Kohlberg's interview, indicating that any differences in moral reasoning do not affect the scores. One of these differences is that girls seem to provide more arguments based on empathy and care than boys do. This is contrary to Kohlberg's (1981) own assumption that morality is about a sense of justice.

In one study, 80 children were asked to judge both hypothetical moral dilemmas and dilemmas they had experienced in their own daily lives. Gender differences were minor, and only a few subjects reasoned consistently based on either justice or care. The majority showed both types of reasoning, including those who achieved the highest scores on Kohlberg's interview (Walker et al., 1987). This is contrary to Gilligan's assumption that boys and girls develop different forms of morality. Both girls and boys reasoned based on care and justice when this was required by a moral dilemma. No doubt there are differences in how boys and girls are enculturated (see Book 7, *Social Relations, Self-awareness and Identity*, Part IV), but these differences do not seem to lead to radically different ways of reasoning about moral issues. Instead, studies suggest that care and justice are important elements in the morality of both boys and girls. Gilligan's views can thus be seen as an extension rather than an alternative to Kohlberg's theory (Jorgensen, 2006).

Evolutionary Theory

The key assumption of evolutionary theories is that the basis of morality is formed by evolution, and that human beings have an innate tendency to regard certain actions as right, good and deserving of reward, and others as wrong, bad and deserving of punishment (Hamlin, 2013). According to Hauser (2006), children are fundamentally moral at birth, they react in an intuitively moral way to certain events, and altruism, fairness and care have their basis in human nature. The innate mechanism underlying moral development is a *universal moral grammar* that defines the possibilities and limitations of moral development, similar to the way Chomsky's **universal grammar** is assumed to impose restrictions on language development (see Book 5, *Communication and Language Development*, Chapter 6). This universal moral grammar contains a set of abstract moral rules, and children's social experiences tell them which of these rules apply in their society. In practice, this happens when children expect other people to act morally and react emotionally when their expectations are broken. In this way, children's moral sense is formed by the rules of culture, thus allowing for differences in morality across cultures. However, the theory raises the question of why some members of the human species act in immoral ways.

Ethical intuitionism is a related theory arguing that morality is an immediate, unconscious, irrational and intuitive appraisal of something experienced as wrong and is not subject to reasoning. Moral judgments are driven by emotions such as disgust and contempt. According to the theory, moral reasoning is a post hoc construction, generated *after* a moral judgment has been reached, even if such reasoning can sometimes lead to a change in attitude so that the individual's action is not always determined by intuitive judgment (Haidt, 2001, 2008, 2013). Innate intuitions are compared to a set of "moral taste buds" that are biologically conditioned to react to certain stimulation, while the sensitivity of their receptors and the trigger for individual intuitions are modulated by cultural input (Rottman & Young, 2015).

Critics of this theory point out that moral judgments are not always immediate and irrational, but just as often intentional and well considered. Moreover, malicious actions are not necessarily judged immoral, for example in war, and also children judge physically harmful acts differently depending on whether they consist of an unprovoked attack or a retaliation to such an attack (Nucci & Turiel, 2009). Assumptions about an innate intuitive morality meet the same criticism as many other assumptions about specific innate characteristics, that development is unnecessary. The child only needs a certain amount of experience to implement what already exists. Besides, the theory remains an assumption: there is no evidence that moral judgments are automatic and intuitive or that children's moral development actually has its basis in an innate predisposition that specific. Instead, results suggest that children's (and adults') judgments of right and wrong are complex, and that cognitive, emotional and social factors contribute to moral development (Turiel, 2014).

Social Domain Theory

Social domain theory is partly based on Piaget's and Kohlberg's model but considers the development of moral reasoning to be **domain-specific** rather than an expression of general cognitive development (Smetana et al., 2014; Turiel, 2014). It sees morality as one of three forms of social knowledge (the other two are societal and psychological knowledge) – actions may have consequences for the welfare, just treatment and rights of other people. The three domains develop in parallel, but younger children have a better understanding of other people's welfare than of justice. Social domain theory also emphasizes the emotional basis for the development of moral

Elliot Turiel.

concepts. Children use information about positive and negative emotions – both their own and those of others – in judging whether something is right or wrong. Social domain theory differs from evolutionary theory in that emotions do not govern moral judgments, and the assumption of a dichotomy between emotions and reasoning is seen as a fallacy. Additionally, the theory emphasizes experiences with positive emotions (Dunn, 2014; Smetana et al., 2014). Critics point to the lack of a clear distinction between social conventions as part of social order and moral norms related to the welfare of others (Rottman & Young, 2015), but moral judgments of older children and adolescents can incorporate both conflicting moral norms and conventional norms, such as when children lie in order not to hurt someone.

Morality is about doing good or bad to others and, hence, is fundamentally social. Many theorists underline the importance of children's social relations in moral development (Carpendale et al., 2013; Dunn, 1988, 2014). Children gradually become more sensitive to moral issues through social interaction within and outside the family. As family life provides many opportunities for conflicts involving moral issues, Dunn (1988) views children's interaction within the family as a window to their moral understanding, sensitivity and acquisition of moral norms. Values and norms are not simply transferred but acquired through a *process of collaboration*: children observe, interpret and internalize different aspects of parental behavior, sometimes disagreeing with their parents on what is fair and just, and in turn affect parents by externalizing their own beliefs and attitudes – it is a **dialectical** and transactional process (Kuczynski & Knafo, 2014).

The Development of Moral Understanding

The extent to which young children judge actions from a moral perspective in their first 2 years of life is subject to considerable disagreement (e.g., Hamlin, 2015; Killen & Dahl, 2018). There is little doubt that children show *morally relevant* reactions and actions early on. Infants react with unease when they hear other infants cry, for example (see p. 23, this volume). In their second year of life, children often help others as long as they understand how to do so (Vaish & Tomasello, 2014). A number of studies in which infants were shown two puppets – one puppet helping and the other preventing a third puppet from reaching a goal such as opening a box – found that more children reached for the helping puppet than the hindering puppet or looked at them for different lengths of time (Hamlin, 2015; Hamlin & Wynn, 2011). Other studies, however, have not found corresponding reactions (Salvadori et al., 2015), and some have questioned the results (Killen & Dahl, 2018). Nativist researchers interpret early social actions as an expression of a nascent concern for others, rooted in innate moral concepts (Wynn & Bloom, 2014; Hamlin, 2015). However, other researchers point out that children at this age see and perform many actions that are unfair or potentially harmful to others, but these are not interpreted as reflecting an innate tendency to carry out immoral actions (Killen & Dahl, 2018).

Toddlers show better understanding of the consequences actions may have, for example, whether they can cause harm, and what is and is not allowed in the family. They also begin to justify their actions (Dunn, 2014; Killen & Smetana, 2014). They also seem to start to become aware of the difference between conventional rules, for example that it is wrong to throw clothes on the floor instead of hanging them up, and moral "truths," such as the importance of sharing with others and not hitting other children. In one study, 3-year-olds

DOI: 10.4324/9781003292531-24

intervened when they saw a puppet destroying a clay figure made by another puppet (Box 22.2). Dunn (1988) observed that toddlers often denied having done something wrong, even when it was obvious that they were responsible for the action. This shows that the children had acquired a certain understanding that the action was wrong and had expectations about the likely reaction of others.

Box 22.2 Three-Year-Olds React to the Transgressions of Others (Vaish et al., 2011)

Thirty-two 3-year-olds were randomly assigned to a harm condition and a control condition. Together with a child, there were two hand puppets (cow and elephant). One puppet brought four clays pieces, leaving the extra one on the side. One puppet created a clay snail, the other a flower, and the child whatever he wanted. Each puppet happily showed off her sculpture twice, and both puppets took an active interest in the child's sculpture. Then, one of the puppets left the room. In the harm condition, the actor said in a neutral but firm manner, "Well, I don't like the cow's/elephant's flower/snail. I'm going to tear/break it now." In the control condition, she said in the same manner, "Well, I don't like the ball of clay. I'm going to tear/break it now." In both conditions, she then moved towards the target object and repeated, "Yes, I'm going to break it now." Picking up the object, she returned to her position, said, "Yes, I'm going to break it now," then destroyed the object and threw the pieces into a bin. The actor's intention was repeated, and her actions were presented in this stepwise manner to provide children with ample occasions to protest.

After the object was destroyed, the recipient reentered, looked into the bin and neutrally said "Hmm" to show that she had noticed something there. She looked at the remaining objects on the table, again said "Hmm" neutrally and looked back into the bin. In the Harm condition, the recipient then said, in a somewhat surprised and sad tone, "Oh, that was my flower/snail," waited about 6 s, said "Oh well" mildly despondently and returned to her seat. In the control condition, the puppet behaved the same way except that she noted in a neutral tone that the object in the bin had been the extra clay.

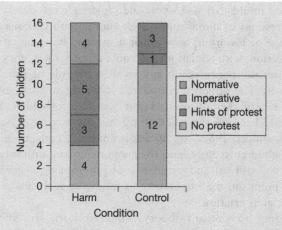

The children protested in three different ways: (a) normative (No, you're not supposed to do that), (b) imperative (No! Don't destroy it), and (c) hints of protest (Hey! Why are you doing that?). The figure shows that the 12 of 16 children protested when one puppet destroyed the sculpture of the other puppet. When the puppet destroyed the extra clay ball, only four children protested. The results demonstrate that the 3-year-olds can understand and act on moral aspects of situations.

Throughout preschool age, and in agreement with domain theory, children begin to distinguish more clearly between events in the moral, social and personal domain (Killen & Smetana, 2014; Turiel, 2015). Studies of preschool-age children from different cultures have found that the children regard moral transgressions that cause harm to another person, such as pushing someone off a swing, as more serious than transgressions that only affect the one breaking the rule, for example when a boy gets hurt falling off a chair he was not allowed to climb on (Dunn, 1995; Yau & Smetana, 2003). The distinction is not absolute, however: some events can represent a combination of moral issues and conventions (Dahl et al., 2011; Killen & Smetana, 2014). At this age, children also begin to take more account of the intent behind actions (Smetana et al., 2014).

Although both younger and older school-age children say that moral transgressions are wrong because they hurt others, older children also begin to include arguments related to equality and justice.

One study found that 6–13-year-old children were quick to react to transgressions of moral norms, responding with comments about the damage or loss itself, how unfair it was and how the victim felt. In connection with violations of conventional rules, they merely pointed out the transgression and recalled the rule or ridiculed the transgressor. The children considered it wrong to steal, even in a country where they were told this was not forbidden, but had no qualms changing the rules of a game if everyone agreed on it (Nucci & Nucci, 1982a, b). When it comes to conventional rules, younger children mainly base their arguments on authority figures (the teacher said so) and avoidance of punishment, whereas older children point out the importance of following such rules for regulating social interaction.

According to domain theory, children learn to differentiate between domains by the types of emotional reactions and comments they are met with in different domains (Killen & Smetana, 2014; Turiel, 2015). Even younger children are aware that they feel pain when someone hits them or that they become upset and cry when someone makes fun of them. When children violate moral rules, adults usually stress the experience and welfare of the person being subjected to the action. For example, mothers respond by intercepting physically and by reasoning with their children about the consequences (Dahl & Campos, 2013). Children's own justifications seem to reflect the situations in which moral aspects are commented by adults. When children break conventional rules, adults typically react by asking them to stop what they are doing and telling them how disruptive their actions are to social order. Seven-year-olds react with ridicule and similarly demeaning responses when other children violate such rules (Smetana, 1993). Children aged 4–5 and 10–12 years and their mothers were presented with small stories about prudential transgressions such as lighting matches and opening a bottle of poison, moral transgressions such as hitting a friend and stealing money, or social convention transgressions such as eating lunch with the fingers and staying up past bedtime. Both the younger and older children and their mothers said the prudential and moral transgressions were more serious. The older children and the mothers were also more willing to accept corporal punishment (spanking) for acts that would harm others (prudential and moral) than for transgressions of social rules (conventions), whereas the younger children said all three transgressions should be punished (Catron & Masters, 1993).

With age, discussions with peers outside the family gain increasing importance in the development of morality. In peer discussions, 8-year-old children are engaged and active whereas, with their mothers, they are more passive and contribute little to the discussion (Kruger, 1992). This supports the assumption that negotiations are particularly conducive to moral understanding when there is a certain equality between the parts, as Piaget claims.

With age, children are able to consider an increasing number of factors, and in adolescence their moral reasoning becomes more complex. In one study, children between the ages of 7 and 16 years agreed that it was important to help those in need, avoid causing harm to others and respect the right to property, as long as there were no competing considerations. When situations became more complex, such as when helping one person could indirectly harm another, differences in ages became more pronounced. The youngest children responded directly based on moral rules, whereas the 14-year-olds, and particularly the 16-year-olds, tried to balance different considerations (Nucci & Turiel, 2009).

The development of morality is related to relevant experiences, but morality does not reflect actions in the environment in any simple sense. Children and adolescents growing up with war and violence develop an understanding of what is morally right and wrong. However, there can be a large gap between actions they consider to be right and how they expect themselves and others to act (Posada & Wainryb, 2008; Wainryb & Pasupathi, 2010).

22

Morality and Emotions

Most theorists believe emotions play a decisive role in moral development, and self-evaluative emotions such as pride, guilt and shame are often referred to as "moral emotions" (Malti & Ongley, 2014). Sensitivity to other people's feelings is therefore central in evaluating emotions, in particular the aspect of care in connection with morality (Dunn, 2014).

Some theorists emphasize the role of negative emotions. Freud (1916, 1930) relates conscience and morality to anxiety and discomfort. Hoffman (2000) describes *empathy-related guilt*, a self-directed negative emotion of distress and remorse rooted in something the child has done that causes another person to be upset. In order to escape this feeling, the child has to avoid performing similarly hurtful actions or try to do something to repair the damage that has been done. Thus, feelings of guilt become a motive for moral action. It is the task of parents and other adults to direct the child's attention to the harm or suffering inflicted on the other person and to induce *other-oriented* responses in the child.

Others argue that morality springs from a broader emotional spectrum than guilt and fear (Turiel & Killen, 2010). Dahl and colleagues (2011) stress the importance of *social joy* and parents' positive emotional expressions to young children's helping behavior. Dunn (2014) describes how social interactions with positive emotional content can have an important influence on the development of moral understanding. Children respond empathically to the distress and joy of others, show interest in others' feelings and discover that right and wrong can be linked to different emotions. They can show anger as the result of their moral judgment, for example when seeing others humiliated or treated unjustly, but also joy and pleasure at transgressing something forbidden.

DOI: 10.4324/9781003292531-25

Parents influence children by how they talk with them about moral issues, and the family's emotional climate determines how children react to rules. Dunn and colleagues (1995) found that even 2-year-olds were able to follow simple rules and negotiate about rules in emotionally warm families. The parents who supported a dialogue based on equality seemed to have the most positive influence. Their conversations centered not only on restrictions and punishment, but equally on sharing happiness and giving comfort. When children show shame and guilt, this demonstrates that they take into account other people's judgments (see p. 34, this volume). These emotions, too, have an impact on children's moral interactions, but Dunn considers close and positive relationships with parents and siblings an important basis for children's moral development, rather than guilt or the wish for **conformity**. Studies show that children whose parents engaged in dialogues about moral issues with their children offered emotional support, helped them ask questions and reformulated what they said had a more positive moral development than children whose parents merely criticized their wrongdoings and told them what was right. Also humor, listening responses and praise promoted moral development, whereas hostility, sarcasm and threats had an inhibiting effect (Walker & Taylor, 1991).

Adolescence is an emotional period (see p. 38, this volume), and, for adolescents, their own and other people's emotions are central to their making sense of events in the social world and evaluating their own and other people's actions. They can report strong feelings of guilt in connection with having hurt a friend or otherwise acted wrongly in a social context (Wainryb & Recchia, 2012).

Understanding the Relationship between Morality and Emotions

Children's own understanding of the relationship between moral transgressions and experienced emotions evolves gradually. Even when they say that an action, such as stealing, is wrong, they have problems relating the agents' feelings and moral judgment (Krettenauer et al., 2013). Nearly all 4-year-olds say that both the giver and the receiver will be happy when children share something, and that a child will be upset when something is stolen from him (Arsenio & Lover, 1995). At this age, children argue that the person who has stolen something from someone else will feel happy as long as he or she is not found out, termed "happy victimizers." Seventy-four percent of 4-year-olds, 40 percent of 6-year-olds and 10 percent of 8-year-olds thought that someone stealing candy without being discovered would feel happy. In addition, 57 percent of 4-year-olds, 71 percent of 6-year-olds and 41 percent of 8-year-olds said that someone who resisted the temptation to steal the candy would feel upset (Arsenio & Lover, 1995). Thus, younger preschoolers seem to focus on the outcome of the victimizer's action. Although they judged the action wrong, it did not change their belief that the thief would feel happy. Not until school age did children begin to ascribe mixed feelings to the thief based on both personal gain and consequences for the victim. It is possible that young children have difficulty attributing simultaneous, conflicting emotions to another person, and that the positive emotion associated with the consequences takes precedence over any possible feelings of guilt, which children usually begin to show around the age of 3–5 (see p. 32, this volume). Another related explanation is that younger children focus on the actual experience, whereas older children increasingly consider how the thief *ought* to feel (Arsenio et al., 2006). Adolescents become increasingly aware of everyday moral conflicts and their complexities, leading to more subtle feelings and reasoning skills (Malti et al., 2012).

23

Conscience

Conscience is an inner regulatory system characterized by negative self-evaluations and feelings of *guilt* in connection with something one has done or failed to do. It is based on an internal standard and an internalization of cultural attitudes that enable children to resist temptations in the absence of adults. The development of conscience begins in early childhood and continues throughout adolescence (Kochanska et al., 2010; Laible et al., 2008).

Although most theorists emphasize the importance of other people's negative reactions for the development of conscience, there are several **developmental pathways** to conscience. Which path a child follows may depend on the child's temperament, parental reactions to the child's actions and the relationship between child and parents (Kochanska, 1997). Children with a positive relationship to their parents, for example, show *committed compliance*, a willing, eager stance to go along with parental directives, and an implicit internalization of the rules laid out by the parent. Parental warmth and reciprocity are important incentives for moral compliance, but also contribute to feelings of guilt when the child's action is not in agreement with the moral directive (Kochanska & Aksan, 2004, 2006).

The best parental strategy is one that suits the child's characteristics. In anxious children, the development of conscience seems best promoted by parental strategies based not on force but on explanations and warmth. Such strategies are less effective with impulsive children, as they find it more difficult to internalize imposed rules (Kochanska, 1997, 2002). This is not to say that impulsive children necessarily have particular difficulty developing a conscience, but rather that they have problems acquiring social skills. Many impulsive children with little self-control develop poor social understanding and inadequate interaction strategies, and thus they end up in the **unpopular children** group. For them, positive directives

DOI: 10.4324/9781003292531-26

that lead to compliance may be an effective developmental pathway to conscience (Cornell & Frick, 2007; Kochanska, 1997).

The ability to arrive at a negative emotional evaluation of one's own actions is considered an important characteristic of the mature individual and member of society. It is crucial for both society at large and for the individual's mental health that conscience and guilt develop without major complications. However, conscience shows significant individual variation. Some children and adolescents have too little conscience, while others suffer from strong feelings of guilt (Thompson et al., 2006).

24

Callous-Unemotional Traits and Psychopathy

Atypical developmental pathways provide insight into the importance of emotions for morality and conscience. Some children and adolescents appear callous and unemotional, showing a lack of guilt and remorse, as well as manipulative behavior, impulsiveness and irresponsibility (Marsee & Frick, 2010). As these traits also lie at the core of psychopathy, the terms *psychopathic traits* and *callous-unemotional traits* are often used interchangeably (Viding & McCrory, 2015).

Studies show a relation between behavioral disorders and emotional understanding. Children 8–10 years old who had been referred to a psychiatric clinic for behavioral disorders (aggression, vandalism, shoplifting and the like) attributed less fear to both a person acting contrary to moral rules and the victim of the action than children of the same age without behavioral disorders. The children with behavioral disorders were also less concerned with the negative consequences for the victim than with the positive consequences for the victimizer. Moreover, their descriptions of negative consequences revolved more around material issues, such as losing a toy, than emotional consequences, such as pain and grief. In addition, they used a single set of conceptual terms for their experienced emotions (happy, sad), whereas the other children gave more varied emotional descriptions (Arsenio, 1988).

Such results suggest that some children with behavioral disorders lack insight into the emotional consequences of immoral actions for both the victimizers and the victims of these actions. They do not recognize sadness and fear as readily as others, either in facial or vocal expressions, whereas their perception of joy, surprise, disgust and anger does not differ from that of other people. Conscience is the very ability to direct negative emotions toward something one has done to others and requires an understanding of both one's own

DOI: 10.4324/9781003292531-27

and the other person's feelings. From a developmental psychopathology perspective (see Book 1, *Theory and Methodology*, Chapter 9), Frick and colleagues (2014) explain atypical conscience development in children with callous–unemotional traits by their reduced ability to experience negative emotional arousal, fearful inhibition and empathy. They can tell right from wrong, but with little emotion attached to their judgment. Attention to positive consequences and lack of attention to negative emotions and punishment lie at the core of these children's inadequate conscience development and their increased risk of developing antisocial behavior (see p. 165, this volume).

Studies have found some degree of heritability of callous–unemotional traits, as well as links to early neglect. A genetic basis is most prominent in the children who develop antisocial behavior (Viding et al., 2012). Studies of early neglect include children who have spent their early childhood in orphanages with little stimulation and developed callous–unemotional traits, but often without the presence of behavioral disorders (Bowlby, 1946; Kumsta et al., 2012). In line with this, studies also show that positive and warm parenting strategies reduce the risk of developing callous–unemotional traits and behavioral disorders in children showing signs of such traits (Pasalich et al., 2016; Wall et al., 2016). Children and adolescents with callous–unemotional traits are aware of rewards and other positive aspects but less so of any potential punishment. Consequently, parenting strategies and interventions based on punishment and negative sanctions are less effective, whereas initiatives based on reward show more positive changes in these children and adolescents (Viding & McCrory, 2015).

Children with autism spectrum disorder have social impairments and can also appear callous and unemotional, but without any strong connection to conduct disorders and criminal behavior. Unlike children with autism spectrum disorder, children with callous–unemotional traits have no problem understanding other people's thoughts and intentions. They have problems processing emotional information, whereas children with autism spectrum disorder can become emotionally aroused at seeing others in pain (Leno et al., 2015; Viding & McCrory, 2015).

Summary of Part III

1   Morality is the understanding of right and wrong. *Moral reasoning* involves reflection on the correctness of one's own and others' actions.

2   *Logical constructivism* associates morality with cognitive development. Piaget divides moral development into three stages, arguing that social conflicts between peers give rise to cognitive conflicts that drive the development from *premoral reasoning* to *moral realism* and *moral subjectivism*. Critics point out that children show moral understanding earlier than Piaget claims.

3   Kohlberg extends Piaget's stage theory and methodology by introducing the *moral judgment interview*. *Pre-conventional morality* is determined by what others say is good or bad, *conventional morality* is linked to the group's views on morally right actions, and *post-conventional morality* is determined by the values of society. In adulthood, morality is tied to the individual's conscience and universal moral principles. Although children in different countries largely show the same development in moral reasoning, this applies to a lesser extent to post-conventional morality.

4   Gilligan distinguishes between *justice-oriented* male morality and *care-oriented* female morality and describes three stages in the development of women's morality: (1) caring for oneself, (2) caring for other people, (3) integrated care of oneself and others. Both men and women reason based on care and justice, but women are more concerned with relationships and therefore reason more often based on a morality of care.

5   Hauser believes humans have an innate *universal moral grammar* that sets the parameters for moral development. According to the theory of *ethical intuitionism*, moral judgments are immediate, unconscious and intuitive, and moral reasoning only justifies an action *after* a situation has been evaluated.

6   *Social domain theory* views morality as one of three forms of social understanding. The development of norms and values is a collaborative process, and children gradually become more sensitive to moral issues through their experiences with social interaction within and outside the family.

7   Children show different reactions to violations of moral norms and social conventions early on, both in regard to themselves and others, and with increasing age distinguish more clearly between actions belonging to the moral, social and personal domain. With age, they also improve at taking into account several factors at the same time.

8   Most theorists believe emotions to be central to moral development and an understanding of others' feelings. According to Hoffman, *empathy-related guilt* leads children to avoid hurtful actions or try to repair the damage that has been done. Dunn, Campos and Dahl emphasize the importance of *social joy* and parents' positive emotional expressions when young children help others. Children's understanding of the relationship between moral violations and experienced emotions undergoes a gradual development. Children with behavioral disorders have a more immature understanding of transgressions of moral rules and norms.

9   *Conscience* is characterized by negative self-evaluations and feelings of *guilt* directed at one's own actions. Different developmental pathways can lead to a sense of conscience, depending on the child's temperament, the parents' way of meeting the child's actions and the child–parent relationship.

10 Some children with *callous-unemotional* traits may have an atypical conscience development and show signs of *psychopathy*.

Core Issues

•   The evolutionary origin of moral reasoning.
•   The cognitive and emotional bases of moral development.
•   Emergence of early morality.
•   The role of positive and negative emotion in development of conscience.

Suggestions for Further Reading

Flom, M., & Saudino, K. J. (2017). Callous-unemotional behaviors in early childhood: Genetic and environmental contributions to stability and change. *Development and Psychopathology, 29*, 1227–1234.

Gibbs, J. C., Basinger, K. S., Grime, R. L., & Snary, J. R. (2007). Moral judgment development across cultures: Revisiting Kohlberg's universality claims. *Developmental Review, 27*, 443–500.

Gilligan, C. (1982). *In a different voice: Psychological theory and women's development.* Cambridge, MA: Harvard University Press.

Hamlin, J. K. (2013). Moral judgment and action in preverbal infants and toddlers: Evidence for an innate moral core. *Current Directions in Psychological Science, 22*, 186–193.

Kochanska, G. (1997). Multiple pathways to conscience for children with different temperaments: From toddlerhood to age 5. *Developmental Psychology, 33*, 228–240.

Kohlberg, L. (1981). *The philosophy of moral development: Moral stages and the idea of justice.* New York, NY: Harper & Row.

Nucci, L., & Turiel, E. (2009). Capturing the complexity of moral development and education. *Mind, Brain, and Education, 3*, 151–159.

Piaget, J. (1965). *The moral judgment of the child.* New York, NY: Free Press.

Part IV

Prosocial and Antisocial Development

Doing Good and Harm

In all human societies, people share with others and help each other, and such prosocial actions are necessary for societies to function. However, antisocial actions are also part of social life in most societies, both among children and adults. These behaviors are defined according to their functions in social interaction. The intention of prosocial actions is to benefit others, whereas antisocial actions aim to inflict physical or psychological harm on others. Children are social and gradually learn what is and is not appropriate and approved behavior when interacting with others in their society. Their social orientation can lead to both prosocial and antisocial actions, but these behaviors show opposing developmental trajectories (Padilla-Walker et al., 2017). This chapter describes the emergence of understanding and production of prosocial and antisocial behavior in children, and how parenting styles and other conditions may influence this development.

DOI: 10.4324/9781003292531-29

Prosocial Behavior

Prosocial action is defined by an intention of doing well for others and having "costs" and no benefits for the actor, such as helping, caring or sharing (Dunfield, 2014; Paulus & Moore, 2012). It is a requirement that the actions are voluntary; actions resulting from external pressure or requirements, such as putting on boots when it rains or when the father says so, are not considered prosocial. Thus, actions motivated by *obedience* are not prosocial as such, but they are often seen as behavioral precursors to prosocial actions (Eisenberg et al., 2015).

Development in Childhood

Typical prosocial actions consist of (a) helping someone, such as picking up something a person has dropped or carrying something for another person; (b) giving something to someone, such as sharing a toy with another child; or (c) comforting someone who is upset, for example a child who has been injured (Dunfield, 2014; Paulus & Moore, 2012). Such actions require a certain degree of empathy and sympathy. Children must be able to understand and react to the "negative" state of another person, such as someone failing to reach a goal or obtain something or experiencing grief or discomfort, and be motivated to change the negative state. Many factors may influence children's prosocial actions and contribute to individual differences, including **mind understanding**, motivation and earlier experience with performing and observing prosocial actions, and the three main types of prosocial actions show somewhat different developmental trajectories (Paulus, 2014). The social norms of the society will influence the development of **prosocial behavior** (House, 2018), and parents guide their children toward actions that are considered prosocial in

DOI: 10.4324/9781003329253-30

the culture; both parental expectations and their strategies to promote prosocial behavior in children change throughout childhood (Dahl, 2015; Pettygrove et al., 2013). Younger children require unambiguous situations to understand the needs of another person and show prosocial behavior, whereas older children understand others' needs in more complex situations (Dunfield, 2014).

Helping

Offering help to someone who has lost something or fails to manage a task can be observed from the age of 1 year and shows a rapid development. At around 18 months, children spontaneously help adults without having been asked to do so, as long as the child is able to understand the goal of the action (Warneken & Tomasello, 2007, 2009). Helping becomes common around the age of 2 and does not substantially increase in scope throughout preschool age (Eisenberg et al., 2015).

Children's early help is influenced by their parents' style. In one study, 18–24-month-old children with mothers who encouraged and supported their children's active participation in clearing up toys and the like were helping more often than children whose mothers did not

Children share with others from an early age.

support and encourage their participation to the same degree (Hammond & Carpendale, 2015). It is notable, however, that children's early help seems to be intrinsically rather than extrinsically motivated (Martin & Olson, 2015). When 20-month-olds were given a small toy in reward for picking up something an adult had lost, they were *less* helpful afterwards than when the adult praised them or simply took the object and continued what she was doing (Warneken & Tomasello, 2008). In another study of 4-year-olds, those who were not praised by their mother for helping offered spontaneous help most often (Grusec, 1991). These studies, showing that rewards decreased rather than increased helping, have been used to argue for an inborn tendency to help (Hay, 2009; Warneken & Tomasello, 2008). However, Dahl (2015) argues that the results also can be explained by children's tendency to take part in adult activities and parental reactions to the child in these activities. He found that parental praise and thanks were associated with an increase in helping in the second year of life. When children are older, they are more often encouraged to help because adults see more opportunities for them to help and get less praise because their ability to help is well established and help is therefore expected (Dahl, 2015). Praise may not lead to increased helping because children perceive praise as reflecting a low evaluation of their competence (see Book 7, *Social Relations, Self-awareness and Identity*, Chapter 21).

Children's early tendency to help is general and relatively independent of the characteristics of the person receiving help, but, around 2 years of age, helping begins to become more selective: children prefer to help someone they perceive as helpful and kind or with whom they have made music, rather than someone who seems little helpful and unkind (Dahl et al., 2013; Dunfield & Kuhlmeier, 2010; Kirschner & Tomasello, 2010). Thus, whatever the motive is for children's early helping, it is still influenced by the behavior of possible recipients of the helping behavior. Moreover, appropriate help depends on the understanding of another person's need for help. Five-year-olds were better at evaluating the situation and provided more help when it was needed, whereas 3-year-olds gave the same amount of help, whether it was needed or not (Paulus & Moore, 2011).

Sharing

Sharing requires children to discover that another person has less than they do and be motivated to change this. Eighteen-month-olds are able to share, but only if an adult both expresses a wish for something the child has *and* asks directly for it; thus, early sharing is related to compliance. Two-year-olds will share with an adult if the adult expresses a desire for something the child has, but sharing of objects is rare throughout toddler age (Brownell et al., 2009, 2013; Dunfield & Kuhlmeier, 2013).

Principles of reciprocity and fairness have an early influence on sharing. In one study, children aged 2–3 years were placed in pairs on either side of a low fence. Only one side had toys, and so the child on that side had to give toys to the other child so that child, too, would have something to play with. After a while, the roles were switched. The child who originally had been toy-deprived now had the toys and generally shared toys with the other child only if that child, too, had shared. When the child who first had the toys did not share, the other child did not share either (Levitt et al., 1985). Similarly, children aged 4–5 years gave less to another child when they themselves had received less than the others in a group of children than when they had received as much as the others (Masters, 1971). In another study, 5-year-olds shared more with an adult when they were in a reciprocal situation where they expected to be a recipient of the adult's sharing later (Xiong et al., 2016). Children are also positively influenced by peer behavior. Seven-year-olds gave more when a same-age peer began to give more (Messer et al., 2017).

The principle of fairness is not fully established until early school age, however, and sharing depends on costs. In one study, children from 4 to 7 years of age accepted that another child got less, but not that they themselves did. The 8-year-olds accepted no disadvantageous inequity (Blake & McAuliffe, 2011). Another study found that sharing steadily increased from 3 to 14 years in all of six different cultures as long as it did not "cost" the child anything: the child got the same amount of food independent of his sharing. However, sharing decreased from 3 to 7–9 years if the child himself got less food when he shared; it then rose again toward the age of 14 years. Early development was similar across cultures, but, in middle childhood, cultural differences emerged for actions that had a cost to children, and the 14-year-olds approached the typical adult-level of sharing within their society (House et al., 2013).

One might have assumed that, because of their social difficulties and problems with mind understanding, young children with autism spectrum disorder would show less prosocial behavior than other children. However, a study found that 3–6-year-olds with autism spectrum

disorder both gave more of their part to others and helped spontaneously more often than children with typical development (Paulus &
Rosal-Grifoll, 2017).

Comforting

Giving comfort also emerges early. It requires children to understand
another person's emotional state. Toddlers have a certain understanding of how they can hurt and comfort others, but less than half of
17-month-olds comfort someone who is hurt or sick. Below is a
mother telling about her son comforting a peer (Zahn-Waxler et al.,
1979, pp. 321–322):

> John [92 weeks] had a friend over, Jerry. Today Jerry was kind of cranky;
> he just started completely bawling and he wouldn't stop. John kept coming
> over and handing Jerry toys, trying to cheer him up so to speak. He'd say
> things like, "Here Jerry," and I said to John, "Jerry's sad; he doesn't feel
> good; he had a shot today." John would look at me with his eyebrows
> kind of wrinkled together, like he really understood that Jerry was crying
> because he was unhappy, not that he was just being a crybaby. He went
> over and rubbed Jerry's arm and said, "Nice Jerry," and continued to
> give him toys.

At 29 months, 70–80 percent offer comfort, at least occasionally
(Baillargeon et al., 2011). Three-year-olds will comfort a doll whose
drawings or playthings have been damaged (Vaish et al., 2011). Such
actions are relatively rare in early childhood, however. Both child
temperament and the social environment, including the warmth
and behavior of parents and preschool teachers, have an impact on
how much comfort children give in preschool age (Paulus & Moore,
2012).

Children's comments about prosocial actions change as well. When
4–5-year-old children who have spontaneously helped, encouraged or
shared with someone are asked why they did it, many children give
standard replies such as "it's nice to help" or justify their action based
on others' needs or practical aspects. Occasionally, they mention their
own benefits. From 5 to 11 years, children increasingly say that prosocial behavior makes them happy. At this age, they also include more
prosocial traits in descriptions of other children (Eisenberg, 1982;
Eisenberg-Berg & Neal, 1979).

Development in Adolescence

Overall, studies show that preschoolers on average perform about twice as many prosocial actions as toddlers, school-age children about twice as many as preschoolers, and adolescents 50 percent more than school-age children. These changes are related to improved cognitive and social-cognitive skills, emotional development and enculturation in general. Adolescents are more aware of social expectations and are better at evaluating social situations. In addition, they show increasing differentiation, with more prosocial behavior directed toward friends than others. Peers are therefore an important mediator of prosocial behavior in adolescence (Güroğlu et al., 2014).

However, not all prosocial behavior increases in adolescence – the outcome varies depending on the type of behavior and situation. Some studies show that adolescents share more with their peers, but not with adults, and that they do not help others more than children do. Helping victims of aggression is actually on the decline, a fact that may be related to young people not wanting to get involved and risk subjecting themselves to aggression (Eisenberg et al., 2006, 2015). One study found a decline in prosocial behavior, but not in sympathy, from 13 to 17 years, with a subsequent increase until the age of 21. Girls showed somewhat more prosocial behavior than boys, but both showed the same pattern of development (Luengo Kanacri et al., 2013).

Antisocial Behavior

Antisocial actions are defined by an intention to inflict physical or psychological harm, or to acquire or damage objects belonging to others. Some antisocial actions involve violations of the law. Aggression is the most studied form of antisocial behavior and will be treated in more detail here as well. Disobedience, vandalism, crime and drug abuse are also commonly referred to as antisocial behaviors (Séguin & Tremblay, 2013).

Instrumental aggression refers to aggressive acts used to achieve something, such as when one child pushes another off a bike to get the bike for himself or threatens to take another child's money. **Hostile aggression** describes acts whose main objective is to harm someone else, such as when one child bullies another, and consists of two forms: **open aggression** involves acts that cause physical harm to someone, while **relational aggression** aims to harm the relationship between two people, such as backbiting or manipulating a friendship. Another important dividing line runs between reactive and proactive aggression. *Reactive aggression* is a spontaneous reaction to something and is often associated with anger. The experience of a friend who intends to inflict damage, for example, can quickly lead to aggressive retaliation. *Proactive aggression* is instrumental, such as threating to beat up another child to obtain something.

Aggression is part of the normal behavioral repertoire, and most children show occasional aggression without violating norms or moral rules. Some children show atypical development, with far more aggression than usual and in situations in which aggression is inappropriate. It is important to distinguish between children's normal aggression and aggressive behavior with an extent and severity that meet the criteria for diagnosing a behavioral disorder (see Book 1, *Theory and Methodology*, Chapter 33).

DOI: 10.4324/9781003292531-31

Prevalence of Antisocial Behavior

In their second year of life, most children show aggressive actions, which at this age are particularly common in connection with conflicts over toys. In line with the development of language, verbal aggression increases from 2 to 4 years of age and eventually stabilizes. Although early aggression is generally instrumental, it does not always revolve around access to a desired object – the argument itself seems to hold a certain attraction. Toddlers often argue over a toy even though an identical toy is available (Caplan et al., 1991).

Hitting and many other forms of physical aggression increase throughout early childhood and subsequently become less frequent. Seventy percent of all 2-year-olds hit other children, compared with 20 percent of 4–5-year-olds and 12 percent of 8–9-year-olds. This decline is the result of improved self-regulation but also of the fact that with age children gain a better understanding of how others experience being hit. Fighting is common among boys throughout childhood, but much of it is make-believe and part of **rough-and-tumble play** and play fighting. The number of openly aggressive acts continues to decline throughout childhood (Dodge et al., 2006). At school age, hostile aggression becomes more common, and relational aggression increases compared with open aggression. Other forms of antisocial behavior, such as lying, cheating and shoplifting, also become more prevalent (Loeber & Schmaling, 1985).

Adolescent aggression is a major topic of discussion in today's society, but aggressive acts are actually on the decline at this age, while the incidence of other antisocial acts rises, such as skipping school, shoplifting, oppositional behavior and more serious criminal conduct (Figure 27.1). This increase may be related to adolescents' separation from parents and the parents' reduced control over what their children are doing (Morgado & da Luz Vale-Dias, 2013). Some adolescents with a high degree of antisocial behavior are diagnosed with ADHD and behavioral disorders.

The age of 12–14 years is a typical age of onset for many criminal offenses across countries, but the majority are non-serious; more serious offenses such as assault or bicycle theft are rare in adolescence (Junger-Tas, 2012). The highest frequencies of criminal offenses occur at the end of adolescence, and the highest frequency of arrests occurs a little later for both boys and girls, but boys are charged by the police or arrested much more often than girls (Elonheimo et al., 2014; Loeber et al., 2012, 2017). Only a small group continues to show high levels

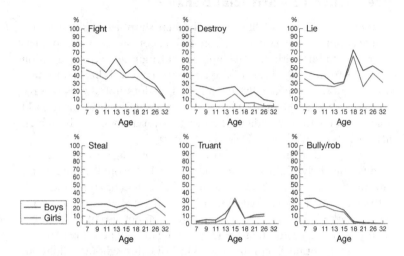

Figure 27.1 Antisocial conduct in females and males aged 7–32 years.

The percentage of females and males at different age levels who showed six different types of antisocial conduct problems: fighting, destroying, lying, stealing, truancy and bullying/robbery. The figures are based on reports from parents and teachers in childhood; parents, teachers and adolescents themselves in adolescence; and adults' self-reports in adulthood (based on data from Odgers et al., 2008).

of aggressiveness and criminal behavior in adulthood. They include adults who showed antisocial behavior early in life, as well as adults who began to veer onto an antisocial developmental pathway in adolescence (Odgers et al., 2008; Piquero et al., 2012).

Bullying

Bullying represents a significant share of the aggression among children and adolescent groups. Bullying typically consists of teasing and physical or verbal aggression and differs from other forms of aggression by being repeated over time and directed against one or more individuals or a group. Social media, e-mails and cell phone messages are used in cyberbullying (Navarro et al., 2016; see Book 7, *Social Relations, Self-awareness and Identity*, Chapter 38). Direct bullying consists of open attacks on the one being bullied, while indirect bullying entails social exclusion. It is rare for large groups of children to bully another child – usually, two or three students do the bullying, and a single student can be responsible for 35–40 percent of it. In a school environment, however, a certain contagion effect can occur and encourage many others to participate in the bullying (Olweus, 1993).

Bullying typically begins to show up in middle childhood, and its incidence declines with age. Bullying is a considerable problem in schools (Rosen et al., 2017). At the start of school, bullying can be part of the process of establishing dominance relations between children (see Hinde, 1974). In first grade, **popular children** often do the bullying, and aggressive children in particular become the target for their bullying (Humphreys & Smith, 1987). In one study, about 9 percent of 8–16-year-olds were bullied at school, 7 percent bullied others occasionally or regularly, and 1.6 percent bullied others and were bullied themselves. However, the numbers varied with the school climate and the school's preventive measures and interventions (Pellegrini & Long, 2002). The frequency of children reporting being bullied was found to vary considerably across 40 countries, from 5–6 percent in Sweden to around 40 percent in Lithuania, and involved more boys than girls (Craig et al., 2009). Although direct bullying is most common among boys, girls and boys are equally exposed to indirect bullying (Olweus, 1993).

Indirect bullying with gossiping may lead to feelings of loneliness and internalizing disorders.

Bullying declines over time, but some aspects of bullying show stability. Children who are bullied at early school age are at risk of being bullied at later age levels, and the same children largely do the bullying at different ages. In some cases, the relationship between bully and victim can last for several years. Among older children who bully, bullying increasingly becomes part of a broader pattern of antisocial behavior. A Swedish study of 14–15-year-olds found a link between bullying at school and violence and weapon carrying outside of school. The adolescents who bullied were also themselves subjected to violence outside of school (Andershed et al., 2001). In another study, 60 percent of boys who bullied in middle school had been convicted of at least one offense by the time they were 24 years old (Olweus, 1993).

Previously, it was commonly assumed that bullying behavior was rooted in insecurity and lack of social competence, but research does not support such a hypothesis. This group, too, shows variation, but, compared with their peers, bullies are generally confident and show unusually low levels of anxiety and insecurity (see also Book 7, *Social Relations, Self-awareness and Identity*, Chapter 23). Instead, it is the victims of bullying who often are socially insecure and isolated, without a single good friend (Olweus & Breivik, 2014). Children with intellectual disability, autism spectrum disorder and **attention deficit disorder** report being victims of bullying more often than other children (Twyman et al., 2010). Bullying involves an asymmetrical power balance, and Olweus (1993) suggests that bully and victim enter into complementary roles in the sense that the bully searches for someone who will not resist aggression. Moreover, children rarely bully when they are emotionally aroused. Thus, bullying is not part of children's and adolescents' ordinary conflicts and differences (Gasser & Keller, 2009). It is not uncommon for bullies to be popular among their peers. As a group, their popularity is slightly below average and decreases with age, but they are generally more popular with their peers than the victims of bullying (Humphreys & Smith, 1987). Moreover, the social capital of popularity may be one reason why anti-bullying programs appear ineffective with popular bullies compared with bullies who are less popular (Garandeau et al., 2014).

To the extent bullying is part of a general antisocial trajectory, other factors influencing development of antisocial behavior will also affect children's bullying. Poor social-cognitive skills can contribute to both bullying behavior and victimization (Shakoor et al., 2012).

Generally speaking, the risk of children bullying others is increased by negative attitudes from parents with little warmth and interest, together with parental indifference, lack of boundary setting and use of corporal punishment in childhood. This applies to both boys and girls. Bullying may have severe consequences: being a victim of bullying has been associated with mental health problems, including internalizing disorders, eating disorders and suicidal ideation and behavior (Gunn & Goldstein, 2017; Olweus & Breivik, 2014; Troop-Gordon, 2017). There are many intervention programs, and studies have demonstrated that it is possible to reduce bullying in schools, but the effects may vary with the age, gender and socioeconomic background of the children (Cantone et al., 2015; Farrington & Ttofi, 2009).

Individual Differences in Antisocial Behavior

Throughout childhood, the individual child's level of aggression shows considerable variation. At school age, the extent of aggressive behavior decreases, and differences between children gradually become more stable, also over longer periods. For some children, aggressiveness becomes a hallmark of their behavior and relationships, but children with low levels of aggression show the greatest stability. The correlations for assessed aggression at different age levels lie around 0.3–0.5 for 5-year periods at school age and in adolescence. These moderate correlations indicate both a certain stability and the fact that many children show changes in aggression over time (Dodge et al., 2006; Piquero et al., 2012).

Children with behavioral disorders are a heterogeneous group. Some may be callous–unemotional (see Chapter 24, this volume), while others show signs of self-regulation problems (Fanti et al., 2016; Frick, 2006). Studies have found much higher rates of callous–unemotional traits in children and adolescents with behavioral disorders (32–46 percent) than in the general population (3–7 percent), and there is clear evidence that such traits involve a vulnerability to severe and persistent behavioral disorders (Herpers et al., 2012; Klingzell et al., 2016). DSM-5 specifies the diagnosis of a small subset of conduct disorders with the label "with limited prosocial emotions" (American Psychiatric Association, 2013). Children with this disorder are particularly characterized by proactive and instrumental aggression but often show reactive aggression as well (Frick & Morris, 2004). Children with regulation disorders mainly show reactive aggression in response to experienced provocation and tend to perceive other people as threatening (see p. 55, this volume). Problems with attention and **hyperactivity** are an impediment to impulse control and regulation in the children, as well as help from adults in the environment (Moffitt, 1993). Social disorders and unpopularity are common among this group, whereas children and adolescents with proactive aggression can be popular and be perceived as leaders by their peers (Poulin & Boivin, 2000). However, they tend to have more contact with the police than adolescents with behavioral problems without such traits (Viding & McCrory, 2015). Children with autism spectrum disorder and intellectual disability are vulnerable for developing challenging behavior, especially those who have limited language and communication skills (Emerson & Einfeld, 2011).

Studies indicate a relatively strong genetic influence on the development of antisocial behavior in callous–unemotional children, but not on antisocial behavior without these traits (Hyde et al., 2016). Genes associated with behavioral problems are "susceptibility genes" that can contribute to different developmental trajectories and do not represent a vulnerability to a particular disorder (see Book 2, *Genes, Fetal Development and Early Neurological Development*, Chapter 6). For example, studies have shown that **neglected children** with a low-activity allele of the MAO-A gene were more likely to display antisocial behavior than children with other alleles of this gene. Without neglect, there were no differences in antisocial behavior (Caspi et al., 2002; Foley et al., 2004). This means that the environment is at least equally important for children's behavior (Caspi et al., 2010). A Swedish follow-up study of 862 adopted boys found that 12 percent of boys with criminal biological parents were arrested in connection with minor offenses as adults (not alcohol-related). The same was the case for 7 percent of the boys without criminal biological parents who had been adopted by parents with a criminal background, while 40 percent of those with both foster parents and biological parents with a criminal background were arrested for such offenses (Cloninger et al., 1982). The combined **interaction effect** of the genes and the environment was thus significantly higher than the effects of genes and the home environment added together.

Moreover, children's aggressive acts are not merely related to other people's reactions to their behavior. When children frequently see others in conflict involving anger and faces full of fear, they will become distressed and react in accordance with a dangerous world (see Part I, this volume). Children and adolescents who regularly experience violent conflict resolutions at home and in their local community can, over time, become desensitized to violence, increasing the likelihood that they, too, will commit violent acts (Mrug et al., 2016). Not everyone reacts this way, however. Some children growing up in families with high levels of anger and parental conflict show prosocial behavior toward their parents and siblings, but not toward their peers. It is possible they minimize their own negative emotions in order to reduce the conflict level at home, but without developing a corresponding degree of sympathy and prosocial behavior toward others (Eisenberg et al., 2006). One study found that, when physically abused children witnessed a female stranger showing anger toward their mother, they reacted by giving more comfort to the mother and reacting more negatively and aggressively toward the stranger than children without such a background (Cummings et al., 1994). Similarly, children can react with anger and aggression when child protective services come to remove them from difficult home circumstances.

Some children are witness to conflicts involving anger and violence in the home.

Mistreated children generally react with stronger emotions than other children, both when supporting their mother and showing aggression toward others (Maughan & Cicchetti, 2002).

There is a link, in other words, between antisocial behavior in children and parenting style (see below). Patterson and colleagues (1989) argue that behavioral problems are related to parents "rewarding" their children's antisocial behavior instead of punishing it. Studies show that a strict and inconsistent parenting style seems to increase the likelihood of antisocial behavior in children with callous traits, while an emotionally warm parenting style seems to reduce it (see p. 141, this volume). Children whose parents are cold, punitive and dismissive typically have a high level of aggression (Eisenberg & Fabes, 1994). These observations, however, say nothing about the causal relationship behind parent–child interaction; the children's behavior may have elicited negativity and contributed to stricter and more inconsistent parenting (Kimonis et al., 2013; Waller et al., 2014). Kochanska and colleagues (2017) describe a developmental cascade (see Book 1, *Theory and Methodology*, Chapter 7) from 4-year-olds' carefree transgression of rules, via parental attempts at enforcing strict discipline at the age of 8, to antisocial behavior at 10–12 years of age. The prosocial and antisocial behavior of parents themselves can be of importance as well. Increased presence of a prosocial father, for example, may lead to reduced aggression in children, whereas increased presence of an antisocial father may raise children's level of aggression (Jaffee et al., 2003).

With age, peers gain increasing importance for children's development, including their prosocial and antisocial behavior (Dishion & Tipsord, 2011). Aggressive, unpopular children often seek out peers with antisocial attitudes, sometimes because they are rejected by other children (Carlo et al., 2014; Murray & Farrington, 2010). Adolescents with aggressive and antisocial behavior join violent and criminal gangs more often than other adolescents (O'Brien et al., 2013). The influence of peers is also evidenced by a study in which high-risk adolescents' participation in group therapy led to more rather than less antisocial behavior, especially among the children with initial low levels of delinquency (Dishion et al., 1999; Poulin et al., 2001).

Differences in aggressiveness between boys and girls are relatively small, and it is only in preschool age that they become apparent. Boys are involved in more conflicts than girls and show more hostile as well as instrumental aggression (Ostrov & Crick, 2007). There is no gender difference in verbal aggression, but girls show somewhat more relational aggression in the form of gossip, group exclusion and the like (Underwood, 2003). Fighting and other forms of physical aggression are more accepted among boys than girls. As girls' aggressive actions are often less conspicuous, they are ignored by others, whereas boys' actions are to a greater extent met with resistance. Ignored behavior often disappears, whereas resistance leads to more fighting and prolongs the conflicts of boys (Fagot & Hagan, 1985). Gender differences increase in adolescence, mainly because girls' oppositional behavior declines earlier than that of boys (Dodge et al., 2006; Murray-Close et al., 2006).

When it comes to behavioral disorders, gender differences are significant. In the United States and Canada, the incidence of behavioral disorders at school age and in adolescence is estimated at 7–9 percent for boys and 2–3 percent for girls. Moreover, compared with girls, boys show far more involvement in all types of serious criminal activity beginning as early as childhood. These differences increase toward adulthood and are greatest for robbery and burglary (Odgers et al., 2008; Rutter et al., 1998).

Culture, too, affects the development of prosocial and antisocial behavior. Some cultures do not attach much importance to helpfulness and other forms of prosocial behavior, and children in these cultures largely take on the same values. One example of this is sharing behavior among the Ik people of Uganda. Sharing virtually disappeared at all age levels when the tribe lost much of its livelihood because its natural hunting and food-gathering grounds were converted into a nature reserve (Turnbull, 1972). Parent perspectives on aggression vary as well. US mothers show a higher tolerance for aggressive behavior in their children than mothers from Japan (Hess et al., 1980).

Antisocial behavior and behavioral disorders can be found in most countries, but their prevalence varies significantly, for example the prevalence for **oppositional defiant disorder** and conduct disorder is 1.2 percent in Italy, 5.3 percent in Britain and 7.1 percent in Yemen (Scott, 2015). In many countries, prevalence increased from 1970 until the turn of the century. Since then, it has leveled off and declined to some degree in a number of countries, but the reasons for these changes are uncertain (Collishaw, 2015).

Pathways to Antisocial Behavior

There is a relation between antisocial behavior in childhood and later adaptation, but following different developmental pathways

(Jennings & Reingle, 2012). The *early authority conflict* pathway develops from early stubbornness to avoiding authority, such as truancy. The *covert* pathway follows a trajectory of covert antisocial behavior such as lying and shoplifting to more serious forms of delinquency such as property damage, car theft, burglary and selling drugs. The *overt* pathway escalates from bullying and harassment of others to physical fighting and violence. According to Loeber and colleagues (1993), children with an overlap between all three pathways are most likely to develop serious forms of antisocial behavior.

Prosocial children have a high probability of peer acceptance and positive adaptation later in life, while children with little prosocial behavior risk being rejected by their peers. Children with high levels of antisocial behavior are often unpopular with their peers and are at greater risk of poor personal relationships and social maladjustment later in life, but only a small minority show persistent aggression and antisocial behavior (Séguin & Tremblay, 2013; Viding & Larsson, 2007). One US study found that children who were rated aggressive by their peers at 8 years of age were often perceived as aggressive at 18 years of age, with a correlation of 0.38 between peer evaluations at 8 and 18 years. At 30 years of age, they continued to be perceived as more aggressive by their peers, had more criminal convictions and a higher rate of spousal abuse, and punished their children more harshly than those who had not shown an aggressive style in childhood (Eron, 1987). Not everyone follows such a development, however. Many adults with antisocial behavior were affected by behavioral disorders in childhood, but well under half of all children with behavioral disorders developed these types of problems as adults (Odgers et al., 2008; Robins, 1978). Nor do adult criminals necessarily have a childhood with behavioral disorders. There is a subgroup of adolescents who transgress the liberal norms of behavior typical for their age and begin to participate in criminal activities. For most members of this group, however, such behavior is temporary (Moffitt, 1993; Odgers et al., 2008).

Correlations between early development and later antisocial behavior are often statistically significant, but generally low and occasionally moderate. Thus, early development does not determine the future. Many young children with more than usual aggressive behavior show good adaptation later in life, whereas some children with inconspicuous behavior in childhood show poor adaptation as adults. Maladaptation in adulthood, however, is more prevalent among children with aggression and behavioral problems than among children with early positive adaptation. This is a good argument for early intervention.

A Social-Cognitive Model

Traditionally, theories of antisocial behavior have focused on the underlying motives and external factors maintaining this type of behavior (Freud, 1927; Lorenz, 1963; Skinner, 1971). More recent theories reject the notion of drives or basic motives that make children "helpful" or "aggressive." Based on a model of social **information-processing**, Crick and Dodge (1994) describe six continuously recurring steps in children's social adaptation (Figure 27.2). The model incorporates cognitive and emotional processes and can be applied to all forms of behavior, but Crick and Dodge focus on the

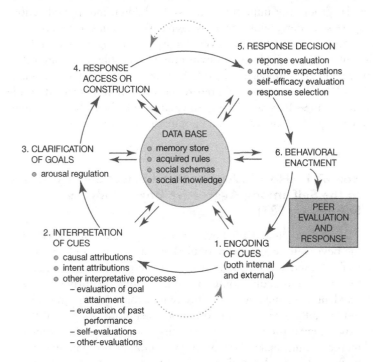

Figure 27.2 A social information-processing model of children's social adjustment.

The model consists of six continuously repeated steps. Children begin by interpreting internal and external situational cues, such as other people's facial expressions and their own arousal in the form of increased heart rate. They then use this information to ascribe intentions to others and make causal assumptions. The model also incorporates emotions. The outcomes of children's chosen goals and behavioral strategies are stored as knowledge that contributes to later interpretations of the environment and action strategies (based on Crick & Dodge, 1994, p. 76. With permission from the American Psychological Association ©).

development of aggressive behavior in particular. Aggressive children and adolescents have difficulty assuming the perspective of others, take into account fewer social cues and are more attentive to signs of aggression in others than nonaggressive children. Other people's intentions are often interpreted as hostile. A peer who tries to establish positive contact can therefore be perceived as aggressive, accidents can be perceived as intentional and so on. This reaction pattern has been found among aggressive children in different cultural settings (Dodge et al., 2015).

In one study, popular children and unpopular aggressive children were asked to describe a video of peers at play. More often than the popular group, the unpopular aggressive children interpreted actions as aggressive. Perceiving others as aggressive does not necessarily lead to aggressive behavior, however. Depressed nonaggressive children also interpret people in their environment as hostile more often than other children (Quiggle et al., 1992). Another study found that a fake "threat" led to an emotional preparedness and more perceived hostile intentions in 9–10-year-old aggressive unpopular boys than in a same-aged group of nonaggressive and popular boys (Box 27.1).

Box 27.1   Hostile Attributional Biases and Threats to the Self among Aggressive Boys (Dodge & Somberg, 1987)

The study included 65 boys aged 8–10 years. Thirty-two of the boys were rejected (unpopular) and aggressive, and 33 were well-adjusted and nonaggressive. Each were to watch 12 videos that showed someone doing something wrong on purpose or by accident (e.g., one boy assures his own victory in a painting contest by spilling paint on the other boy's painting). As part of the experimental procedure, after the first four videos, the experimenter would make a break to fetch another boy. The experimenter went to the back room and turned on a tape recorder with a prerecorded conversation that the boy heard through a loudspeaker. In this way, half of the boys would "incidentally" overhear the boy he was going to be together with having a conversation with the experimenter and saying things like "If I go in there, I'm just going to get into a fight with that boy." The experimenters hypothesized that such a "threat" would lead to emotional preparedness even though, after the "conversation," the experimenter returned to the front room and explained to the boy that he would soon have to do a task with another boy, but that the other boy was "in a bad mood," so they would have to wait a short while. In the meantime, the subject was to listen to the final eight stories. Thus, the other boy never really appeared.

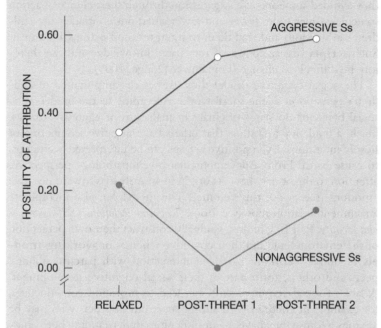

The results supported the hypothesis. The figure shows that, without a threat, there was only a small and non-significant difference in how the aggressive and nonaggressive children perceived the situations they watched on video. For the two first videos after hearing the threat (post-threat 1 and 2), the aggressive boys described more hostile intentions, whereas the nonaggressive children's perceptions of the videos did not change significantly. The emotional level thus had a negative effect on how the situation was perceived: the relaxed situation led to similar evaluations, whereas the threat situation elicited different responses in the two groups.

The model in Figure 27.2 is circular, illustrating that the steps repeat. Over time, the consequences of the child's chosen goals and behavioral strategies are embedded as *social scripts* (**generalized** expectations of specific social situations), in turn affecting the child's later interpretation of the environment and choice of strategies. For children who tend to interpret others as hostile, the process represents a vicious circle. Expectations of aggression are confirmed because the children themselves create aggression or interpret the situation to imply that they avoided someone else's aggression through their choice of action strategies. Over time, fewer and fewer situations contradict the children's evaluations and lead them to interpret most actions as a threat. Such **scripts** largely consist of automated knowledge and can therefore be difficult to change (Fontaine & Dodge, 2009).

The social–cognitive model thus stresses the importance of children's perception of the social world. According to the model, antisocial behavior does not originate in malicious or aggressive drives, but in a tendency to assume that others have negative, competing or hostile intentions. Even positive actions can be interpreted as attempts to cause harm. From a developmental psychopathology perspective, attention to threat may have its origin in an early bias toward negative emotions (see p. 50, this volume). The model can also incorporate attachment relationships (see Book 7, *Social Relations, Self-awareness and Identity*, Part I). Children gradually construct their own perception of the environment, and their cognitive schemas or **working models** of human relations, based on interaction with parents, siblings, peers and others, form part of their social-cognitive development. A lack of social-cognitive skills can lead to profound consequences, for example in children with autism spectrum disorder, who may be anxious because they have major difficulties understanding both emotions and intentions in others (see Book 1, *Theory and Methodology*, Chapter 32). Emotion perception and regulation, too, may have an impact on this development. Some children have been subjected to such severe neglect and abuse that their experiences have far-reaching consequences for their perception of others' attitudes and intentions (see p. 100, this volume). But for most children, social-cognitive schemas are the result of interaction between temperament, parental rearing style and experiences with relationships within and outside the family.

28

Parenting Influences

Parents are the core of children's social environment, and parental influence is important for the development of prosocial and antisocial behavior. Both presence and lack of prosocial behavior in situations in which prosocial behavior is expected usually lead to a response from adults (Dahl & Campos, 2013). In one study, mothers reported that they responded to over 90 percent of all incidents in which their 4–7-year-old children either showed or failed to show prosocial behavior. When the children were helpful, their mothers generally responded by smiling, thanking them, praising them and expressing appreciation. When their children failed to be helpful, they responded with moral exhortations, admonishments to do the right thing, questions about empathy, expressions of disapproval and direct interventions (Grusec, 1982).

Children's desires and parents' demands will inevitably lead to conflicts. Unambiguous rules and emotionally mediated explanations seem to promote prosocial behavior, whereas prohibitions without further explanations have the opposite effect. Toddlers whose mothers tended to respond to their child's distress with affective explanations more often showed prosocial behavior and comforted others than children whose mothers rarely offered affective explanations. The toddlers with mothers who often imposed unexplained prohibitions showed less altruistic behavior and gave less comfort than children whose mothers rarely imposed such prohibitions (Zahn-Waxler et al., 1979). Praise can promote prosocial behavior, but a study found that 4-year-olds whose prosocial actions usually were taken for granted and not commented upon by the parents were slightly more prosocial than children whose parents gave praise (Grusec, 1991). Praise can thus both undermine and increase children's intrinsic motivation, or have no effect on it (Dweck, 1999).

DOI: 10.4324/9781003329253-32

Baumrind (1997) describes four parenting styles that differ in emotional warmth and control. Parents with an **authoritarian parenting** style are demanding and emotionally unresponsive. Parents with an *authoritative* style set high standards for their children and show a high degree of responsiveness. A *permissive* style means that parents are responsive but make few demands. Parents with an *uninvolved* style are neither demanding nor responsive. According to Baumrind and associates (2010), it is authoritative parenting, with both high demands and high responsiveness, that best promotes prosocial behavior.

Parental control is part of raising a child and can be important for preventing or reducing antisocial behavior and norm-violating activities in adolescence (Galambos et al., 2003). Disagreements with parents about parenting issues can furthermore teach older children and adolescents how to negotiate as well as to comply (Baumrind, 1997; Eisenberg et al., 2006). Thus, it is not control as such that is decisive, but how parents exert it – parents can monitor their children both too little and too much. Authoritative parenting is characterized by emotional warmth, moderate or high levels of control, and negotiation. Authoritarian upbringing consists of a high level of control, little warmth and few negotiations and, when based on asserting power and demanding (involuntarily) obedience, will impede rather than promote the child's prosocial development. Longitudinal studies have found a relation between strict early upbringing and corporal punishment and later antisocial behavior, and between strict and callous disciplinary upbringing at school age and later acting-out behavior and criminal activities (Bornstein, 2015; Dodge et al., 2006).

Rearing styles reflect the characteristics of both parents and child, and the relationship between children and parents in general. Children who know that their parents are physically and emotionally available perceive disturbing events as less threatening than children with less sensitive and more unavailable parents. When responding slowly and inconsistently, parents increase their children's distress (Grusec, 2011), and, more dramatically, abuse in early childhood often leads to less prosocial and more antisocial behavior in later childhood and adulthood. (Lansford et al., 2002; Luntz & Widom, 1994). Thus, research clearly indicates that assertion of power should not be a key element in children's upbringing; strategies that promote children's empathy, sympathy and understanding of themselves and others show far better outcomes. However, in many countries, corporal punishment remains relatively common (Lansford et al., 2010). One US study found that 28 percent of 1-year-olds had been spanked by their mother, 7 percent twice or more a week. At 3 years of age, the numbers were

57 percent and 13 percent, respectively. Additionally, the results suggest a transactional effect: maternal physical punishment led to an increased incidence of behavioral disorders, and children's behavioral problems in turn led to an increased incidence of corporal punishment (MacKenzie et al., 2015). As corporal punishment is common, it alone is unable to explain some children's antisocial development and depends on the context in which punishment takes place. Occasional use of force need not have a negative effect if it is exercised by parents who are generally supportive; it is the cumulative effect of repeated physical punishment that leads to antisocial behavior in childhood and adolescence (Fréchette, 2016).

The relation between corporal punishment and behavioral disorders is also affected by cultural differences (Lansford, 2010). In countries in which corporal punishment is rare, children subjected to such punishment develop behavioral disorders. In countries in which it is more common, the developmental outcome more often consists of anxiety and aggression (Lansford et al., 2005). Nor is there a clear connection between what would be considered prosocial behavior in Western cultures and a warm, affectionate parenting style. The Waorani people of Amazonian Ecuador are highly belligerent and constantly at war with neighboring tribes, and their basic philosophy is extremely individual-oriented. If the tribe is attacked, everyone takes responsibility for themselves only, regardless of what happens to family and friends. The Semai people of Malaysia represent the very opposite type of culture, putting extreme emphasis on cooperation, and especially solidarity and support within the family. At the same time, both tribes show themselves to be loving and caring toward their children, with little use of punishment (Robarchek & Robarchek, 1992). These studies show that a loving parenting style promotes collective cultural values, no matter what those values may be. A culture that encourages individuality will promote individual-oriented behavior, while encouragement of cultural unity will lead to traditional prosocial behavior. Similarly, there is an increased likelihood that children from societies with many conflicts will develop poor social skills and manipulative relationships (Trevarthen & Logotheti, 1989). The acquisition of society's values is part of children's adaptation to the society they live in.

29

Society and Prevention

Violence and other forms of antisocial behavior are a serious problem in many countries. There are prevention and intervention programs with documented effects in reducing aggression and other forms of antisocial behavior and increasing non-violent conflict resolution, such as *The Incredible Years* (Webster-Stratton, 2006) and *Triple P Programmed* (Sanders, 1999; Sanders et al., 2000). There are also programs directed at children and adolescents with developmental disorders who exhibit challenging behavior (Brosnan & Healy, 2011; McIntyre, 2013; von Tetzchner, 2004). Worries about violence can have a major impact on mental health in children attending schools with a violent school climate. Interventions that focus on educational and social support of students and their sense of belonging to the school may counteract a violent school climate (Eisenbraun, 2007; Gavine et al., 2014).

Theory and research on prosocial and antisocial behavior provide guidelines for how parents and society can promote prosocial behavior and prevent antisocial development. Reducing poverty and preventing child neglect and abuse will contribute to preventing antisocial behavior (Daro & Benedetti, 2014; Gavine et al., 2014). However, it is important to focus not only on reducing risk factors but also on factors that may support positive child development and well-being (Daro & Benedetti, 2014; Sameroff, 2009). Problems that may start in early childhood and escalate transactionally into later antisocial behavior are an argument for early intervention: both children's behavior and parental strategies may be more easily changed while children are young (MacKenzie et al., 2015). Additionally, parents have to change strategies as their children grow older; strategies that are effective for toddlers may be ineffective in later childhood and adolescence (Bornstein, 2015).

DOI: 10.4324/9781003292531-33

Although individual intervention is useful, the goal of society is to implement preventive measures aimed at larger groups or entire populations. There are a number of more general or community-wide programs to promote sensitive and positive parenting (Brock & Kochanska, 2016; Enebrink et al., 2015; Skar et al., 2015). Legislation is an important tool for cultural change. In 2015, corporal punishment of children was only prohibited by a minority of the world's countries (46), most of them European (Heilmann et al., 2015). The resources used by society to rehabilitate adolescents and adults are considerable in most countries. In the United States, antisocial behavior costs over a trillion dollars every year, making prevention an important priority in terms of human and economic factors (Dodge, 2009).

Summary of Part IV

1   Typical prosocial actions are helping, sharing and comforting. Around 1 year of age, children begin to show helping behavior, followed a little later by sharing with and comforting others. Children differ in the development of social skills and disposition for prosocial behavior, and parents differ in how they guide their children toward such behavior. Extrinsic rewards have little effect, whereas warm and supportive parenting promotes children's prosocial actions. A sense of justice, regardless of self-interest, is established at school age. In adolescence, various forms of prosocial behavior develop in slightly different ways and depend on the particular situation.

2   The most common form of *antisocial behavior* is *aggression*, and children begin to show aggressive actions in their second year. With age, there is a reduction in openly aggressive acts, whereas relational aggression increases. Other forms of antisocial behavior, such as lying, cheating and shoplifting, increase during school age. Following adolescence, there is a general decrease in antisocial behavior, but a small group continues to show such behavior.

3   *Bullying* consists of repeated *negative actions* such as teasing and physical or verbal aggression directed at one or more particular individuals over time. Bullying typically begins to show up in middle childhood, and its prevalence declines with age. Boys bully more than girls. Children who are bullied at an early school age are at risk of being bullied at later ages. Individuals who bully have a higher probability of developing criminal behavior and alcohol abuse in adulthood, especially adolescents who bully. Bullying relationships can last for many years.

4   Children with behavioral disorders and callous-unemotional traits are characterized by proactive aggression, whereas children with emotion-regulation problems show more reactive aggression

and perceive the environment as threatening. Both genes and the environment are contributing factors. Children whose parents are cold, punitive and dismissive typically show high levels of aggression, which in turn can trigger negative parental reactions. Children are affected by the way in which conflicts are resolved at home and in their local community. With age, peers gain more importance. Antisocial children commonly seek out each other because they are rejected by other children; as adolescents, they are more often involved with violent and criminal gangs than others.

5   Gender differences are generally small. Boys show more hostile and instrumental aggression in both physical and verbal behavior and are more involved in all types of criminal activity. There is no gender difference in verbal aggression, but girls show somewhat more relational aggression in the form of gossip, group exclusion and the like. The incidence of behavioral disorders shows significant gender differences.

6   The relation between antisocial behavior in childhood and later adaptation can follow different developmental pathways. Children with low levels of prosocial behavior risk being rejected by their peers. Children with high levels of antisocial behavior are often unpopular among their peers and have an increased likelihood of poor personal relationships and social maladjustment later in life, but only a small minority show persistent aggression and antisocial behavior. The connections between early development and later antisocial behavior are often statistically significant, but correlations are generally low and occasionally moderate.

7   The model based on social information processing emphasizes children's interpretation of external and internal situational cues and how they use them to ascribe intentions to others and make causal assumptions. Aggressive children are more attentive to signs of aggression in others than nonaggressive children, and their *social scripts* tend to incorporate more hostile elements and can be difficult to change.

8   Parenting styles can both promote and inhibit prosocial and antisocial behavior. Baumrind describes four different *parenting styles*: *authoritarian, authoritative, permissive* and *uninvolved*. Authoritative parenting best promotes prosocial behavior, whereas an authoritarian style with high demands on obedience and a low degree of emotional responsiveness has the opposite effect. There is a link between strict and callous disciplinary upbringing at school age and later acting-out behavior and criminal activities.

9 The relationship between corporal punishment and behavioral problems is affected by cultural differences and depends on how common such punishment is in a given culture. There is no clear link between the way in which cultural values are conveyed and the specific underlying values. A loving parenting style promotes collective cultural values, no matter what those values may be.

10 Today's knowledge provides guidelines for promoting prosocial and preventing antisocial behavior, and community-wide parenting programs and legislation against corporal punishment can bring about both human and economic gains.

Core Issues

- The biological and social bases of prosocial behavior.
- Factors influencing children who bully.
- The cognitive and emotional bases of antisocial behavior.
- Parenting style and development of prosocial and antisocial behavior.
- Strategies for preventing antisocial behavior in society.

Suggestions for Further Reading

Crick, N. R., & Dodge, K. A. (1994). A review and reformulation of social information-processing mechanisms in children's social adjustment. *Psychological Bulletin, 115*, 74–101.

Dahl, A. (2015). The developing social context of infant helping in two US samples. *Child Development, 86*, 1080–1093.

Dishion, T. J., et al. (1999). When interventions harm: Peer groups and problem behavior. *American Psychologist, 54*, 755–764.

Dodge, K. A., et al. (2015). Hostile attributional bias and aggressive behavior in global context. *Proceedings of the National Academy of Sciences of the United States of America, 112*, 9310–9315.

House, B. R. (2017). Diverse ontogenies of reciprocal and prosocial behavior: Cooperative development in Fiji and the United States. *Developmental Science, 20 (6)*, e12466.

Loeber, R., et al. (2017). *Female delinquency from childhood to young adulthood: Recent results from the Pittsburgh Girls Study*. Cham, Switzerland: Springer.

Olweus, D. (2013). School bullying: Development and some important challenges. *Annual Review of Clinical Psychology, 9*, 751–780.

Glossary

See subject index to find the terms in the text

Abstraction   A cognitive process that gives rise to a generalized category of something concrete, such as people, objects and events that are associated with less detailed features, aspects or similarities.

Activity   A stable and complex system of goal-oriented activities or interactions that are related to each other by theme or situation and have taken place over a long period of time.

Adaptation   Changes that increase the ability of a species or an individual to survive and cope with the environment.

Adaptive behavior   Behavior that enables an individual to survive and cope with the physical, social and cultural challenges of the environment.

Adaptive function   Behavioral consequences that contribute to an individual's survival.

Adolescence   The period between *childhood* and adulthood, age 12–18.

Affect attunement   See *emotional attunement*.

Aggression   Behavior intended to harm living beings, objects or materials; see *hostile aggression, instrumental aggression, open aggression* and *relational aggression*.

Agreeableness   One of the *Big Five personality traits*.

Allele   One of several variants of the same gene at the same location on a *chromosome*, and controlling the same genetic characteristics.

Anal phase   According to *psychoanalytic theory*, the second stage in *psychosexual development*, in which the area around the anus becomes a source of pleasure; age 2–3 years; see *latency phase, oral phase* and *phallic phase*.

Antisocial behavior   Behavior that shows little concern for other people's feelings and needs, and violates the common social and ethical norms of a culture; see *prosocial behavior*.

Assessment (in clinical work)   The mapping of an individual's strengths and weaknesses, competencies and problem areas.

Assimilation   The adaptation, integration or interpretation of external influences in relation to existing cognitive *schemas*.

Attachment   A *behavioral system* that includes various forms of *attachment behavior*; the system is activated when a child finds herself at a shorter or a longer distance from the person she is attached to, and experiences emotions such as pain, fear, stress, uncertainty or anxiety; the term is also used to describe emotional attachment to a caregiver; Attachment can be secure, insecure and disorganized; see *exploration*.

Attachment behavior   According to Bowlby, any behavior that enables a person to achieve or maintain closeness with another, clearly identified person who is perceived to be better able to cope with the environment; includes signal behavior and approach behavior.

Attention deficit disorder; ADD   Characterized by impulsivity, low ability to concentrate on a task, and little sustained attention, may experience problems with emotional regulation, motor coordination, working memory, spatial perception and executive function.

Atypical development   Course of development that differs significantly from the development of the majority of a *population*; see *individual differences* and *typical development*.

Authoritarian parenting   Parenting style that places high demands on the child and in which parents show a large degree of control and *responsivity*; see *authoritative parenting* and *permissive parenting*.

Authoritative parenting   Parenting style that places high demands on the child and in which parents show a large degree of warmth and *responsivity*; see *authoritarian parenting* and *permissive parenting*.

Autism spectrum disorder   Neurodevelopmental disorder that appears in the first years of life; characterized by persistent deficits in social skills, communication and language, and by repetitive behavior and restricted interests.

Autonomy   Independence, self-determination. Ability to make independent decisions related to life's everyday tasks; an important element in the formation of *identity* in *adolescence*.

Babbling Speech-like vocalization; usually occurs at 6–7 months of age.

Basic emotions A set of *emotions* related to the evaluation of an entire situation or its individual aspects; includes joy, grief, fear and anger; also called primary emotions; see *self-referential emotions*.

Behavioral disorder All forms of behavior that are socially unacceptable in one way or another, such as running away from home, screaming, cursing, messy eating manners, bed-wetting, ritual behavior, excessive dependency, poor *emotion regulation*, *aggression*, fighting and *bullying*.

Behaviorism; Behavior analysis Group of psychological theories that emphasize the influence of the environment to explain developmental changes.

Big Five personality traits Five traits frequently used to describe *personality*: *agreeableness, conscientiousness, extraversion, neuroticism* (emotional lability) and *openness to experience*.

Bullying Negative actions, such as teasing and physical or verbal *aggression*, that are repeated over time and directed toward one or several individuals; direct bullying consists of open attacks on the person being bullied, while indirect bullying entails social exclusion.

Childhood Age 1–12 years.

Classical conditioning See *conditioning*.

Cognition Thinking or understanding; includes some type of perception of the world, storage in the form of mental *representation*, different ways of managing or processing new and stored experiences, and action strategies.

Cognitive behavior theory School within the behavioral tradition built on the basic premise that development is a cumulative learning process, and that learning forms the basis for most individual differences between children; also emphasizes the importance of models and *observational learning*, and cognitive processing and regulation of own behavior; also known as social learning theory.

Collectivist culture; collectivist society Emphasize social values and the individual's responsibility and place in society; see *individualistic culture*.

Communication Intentional conveyance of thoughts, stories, desires, ideas, emotions, etc., to one or more persons.

Concept Mental *representation* of a category of objects, events, persons, ideas, etc.; see *extension (of a concept)*.

Conditioning   The learning of a specific reaction in response to specific stimuli; includes classical and operant conditioning. In *classical conditioning*, a neutral stimulus is associated with an unlearned or *unconditioned stimulus* that elicits an unlearned or *unconditioned response*, eventually transforming the neutral stimulus into a conditioned stimulus that elicits a conditioned response similar to the unconditioned response. In *operant conditioning*, an action is followed by an event that increases or reduces the probability that the action will be repeated under similar circumstances; see *reinforcement*.

Conformity   The adoption of other people's attitudes and behavior due to actual or perceived pressure from them.

Conscience   Emotional evaluation of one's own actions, often involving feelings of having done something wrong; closely related to shame and guilt.

Conscientiousness   One of the *Big Five personality traits*; see *agreeableness, extraversion, neuroticism* and *openness to experience*.

Constructivism   Psychological theories based on the notion that an individual constructs his or her understanding of the outside world; see *logical constructivism*.

Continuity (in development)   Development in which later ways of functioning build directly on previous functions and can be predicted based on them.

Conventional morality   According to Kohlberg, the second of three main stages of moral development, in which children emphasize other people's values, attitudes and possible reactions to an action being considered; see *post-conventional morality* and *pre-conventional morality*.

Correlation   Measure of the degree of covariation between two variables, ranging from −1.00 to +1.00; values close to 0.00 show a low degree of correlation; a positive correlation (+) means that a high score on one variable is associated with high score on the other; a negative correlation (−) indicates that a high score on one variable is associated with a low score on the other.

Correspondence (cognitive)   In Piaget's New Theory, the perception of structural similarity that provides a basis for comparing people, objects, events, actions, etc.

Critical period   Limited time period in which an individual is especially susceptible to specific forms of positive or negative stimulation and experience; if the stimulation or experience fails to take place during this period, a similar stimulation or experience later in life will neither benefit nor harm the individual to any appreciable extent; see *sensitive period*.

Cross-cultural developmental study Study comparing children who grow up in different cultures in order to map the importance of genetic and environmental impacts in the broadest sense.

Culture The particular activities, tools, attitudes, beliefs, values, norms, etc., that characterize a group or a community.

Defense mechanism In *psychodynamic theory*, unconscious mental strategies for dealing with inner psychological conflicts and reducing anxiety that follows the drives and impulses of the *id* and threatens control by the *ego*.

Dependent variable The outcome, conditions resulting from variation in the *independent variable*.

Development Changes over time in the structure and functioning of human beings and animals as a result of interaction between biological and environmental factors.

Developmental disorder Disorder that is congenital or appears in *infancy* or *childhood* without the presence of external injuries or similar.

Developmental pathway One of several possible courses of development within the same area or domain.

Developmental psychopathology Multidisciplinary tradition among researchers and practitioners with a basis in developmental psychology; attempts to identify and influence the processes that underlie various psychological disorders, founded on assumptions about vulnerability and resilience in children, and risk and protection in the childhood environment.

Dialectical reasoning The process of basing decisions and conclusions on dialectical reflection or argumentation.

Difficult temperament According to Thomas and Chess, temperament characterized by a tendency to withdraw in new situations, general negativity, strong emotional reactions and highly irregular sleeping and eating patterns; see *slow-to-warm-up* and *easy temperament*.

Disability The difference between an individual's abilities and the demands of the environment.

Discriminate Distinguish between, react differentially; see *generalize*.

Domain A delimited sphere of knowledge; an area in which something is active or manifests itself.

Domain-specific   Abilities and skills within a specific domain of knowledge.

Dynamic system (in development)   A system of nonlinear *self-organizing* and *self-regulating* processes in which qualitatively new functions occur as an *integrated* result of interaction between sub-systems that may have different developmental rates.

Easy temperament   According to Thomas and Chess, tempera-ment characterized by an overall good mood, regular sleeping and eating patterns, easy adaptation to new situations, a positive attitude toward strangers, and moderate emotional reactions; easy to calm down when agitated; see *difficult temperament* and *slow-to-warm-up*.

Ego   In *psychoanalytic theory*, one of the three parts of the human psyche; its purpose is to regulate the drives and impulses of the *id* in relation to the realities of the world and the limitations of the *superego*.

Ego psychology   Branch of *psychodynamic psychology* that empha-sizes the autonomous role of the *ego* in the development of per-sonality, independent of drives.

Electra conflict   According to psychoanalytic theory, a geneti-cally based psychological conflict rooted in the idea that girls are sexually attracted to their father, and experience the mother as a competitor for the father's affection; equivalent to the *Oedipus conflict* for boys.

Emotion   A state caused by an event important to the person and characterized by the presence of feelings; involves physiological reactions, conscious inner experience, directed action and out-ward expression.

Emotion regulation   Implicit and explicit strategies to adapt one's own emotional reactions and those of others in line with social and cultural conventions, especially in regard to the expression, intensity, duration and contexts in which they arise.

Emotional attunement; Affect attunement   A state in which a person is *sensitive* and *responsive* to the emotional state of another. Accord ing to Stern, a process by which the caregiver "mirrors" the experiences of the child without using language and allows the child to understand how he or she is perceived.

Emotional competence   The ability to understand one's own and others' feelings, and to make use of and regulate the expression of one's own emotions in problem solving and social interaction.

Emotionality The mood of an individual; the amount and intensity of positive and negative emotions.

Empathy Feel with someone; emotional reaction similar to the emotion another person is perceived to experience; see *sympathy*.

Enculturation Acquisition of a culture's practices, customs, norms, values, and the like; the first foundation in this process is children's innate social orientation.

Experiment Method to test a hypothesis on specific causal relationships or connections. One or several conditions are systematically altered, and the effect is recorded. As many conditions as possible are kept constant in order not to affect the outcome, increasing the probability that the results are solely related to the conditions being studied.

Exploration According to Bowlby, a behavioral system whose function is to provide information about the environment and enable the individual to better adapt to it; activated by unfamiliar and/or complex objects; deactivated once the objects have been examined and become familiar to the individual; see *attachment*.

Extension (of a concept) All actual and possible exemplars encompassed by a concept.

Extraversion One of the *Big Five personality traits*; the opposite of *introversion*; see *agreeableness, conscientiousness, neuroticism* and *openness to experience*.

Formal operational thinking According to Piaget, the highest form of cognitive functioning, where thinking is completely free of specific objects and experiences.

Fraternal twins; dizygotic twins Twins resulting from two separate fertilized eggs and sharing 50 percent of each other's genes; see *identical twins (monozygotic twins)*.

Gender difference; Sex difference Characteristic, ability or behavior pattern that differs between the two sexes.

Generalize To perceive and react in the same way to events that are similar in some respects; see *discriminate*.

Gesture Distinct movement primarily used as a means of communication and interpreted consistently within a social system.

Goodness of fit A measure of how well something fits together with something else; often used to describe the degree to which the *temperaments* of parents and children coincide.

Grammar Rules that describe how sentences are formed in a language.

Habituation   Gradual reduction in the intensity of a reaction or response following repeated stimulation; allows an individual to ignore familiar objects and direct attention at new ones.

Heritability estimate   Calculation of heritability based on the difference between the correlations of fraternal and identical twins.

Hostile aggression   Actions whose main objective is to harm someone else, such as when a child bullies another; see *instrumental aggression*, *open aggression* and *relational aggression*.

Hyperactivity   Unusually high activity level that is difficult for an individual to control.

Id   In *psychoanalytic theory*, one of the three parts of the human psyche, consisting of drives that seek to find an outlet; see *ego* and *superego*.

Identical twins; monozygotic twins   Twins resulting from the splitting of the same fertilized egg, sharing 100 percent of each other's genes; see *fraternal twins (dizygotic twins)*.

Identification   Process characterized by a tendency to mimic behavior and assume someone else's points of view.

Identity   An individual's sense of who he or she is, as well as of affiliation with larger and smaller social groups and communities.

Imitation   The deliberate execution of an action to create a correspondence between what oneself does and what someone else does.

Incidence   The appearance of new occurrences of a trait, disease or similar in a particular *population* during a particular time span, often expressed as the number of incidences per 1,000 individuals per year; see *prevalence*.

Individual differences   Variation in skills and characteristics between the individuals in a *population*; see *atypical development* and *typical development*.

Individualistic culture; individualistic society   Society where values emphasize on the uniqueness of each individual; see *collectivist culture*.

Infancy   The first year of life.

Information processing (theory)   Psychological theories based on the assumption that all mental phenomena can be described and explained by models in which the flow of information is processed by one or more systems.

Inhibition   Shyness and withdrawal from social challenges.

Instinct   Species-specific behavior with a genetic basis, such as nest-building among birds.

Instrumental aggression The use of aggressive actions to achieve a goal, such as when one child pushes another off a bike in order to ride the bike themselves; see *hostile aggression, open aggression* and *relational aggression.*

Instrumental communication Communicative action aimed at getting someone else to do something specific.

Intellectual disability; Learning disability; Mental retardation Significant problems learning and adjusting that affect most areas of functioning; graded mild (IQ 70–50), moderate (IQ 49–35), severe (IQ 34–20) and profound (IQ below 20); in clinical contexts, a significant reduction in social adjustment is an additional criterion.

Interaction effect An influence by one or several other factors.

Internalization Process whereby external processes are reconstructed to become internal processes, such as when children independently adopt problem-solving strategies they have previously used in interaction with others, or adopt the attitudes, characteristics and standards of others as their own.

Internalizing disorder Negative emotions directed at oneself, anxiety, depression; often involving a negative self-image, shyness and seclusion; see *externalizing disorder.*

Introversion *Personality trait* characterized by shyness, anxiousness and withdrawal from social situations, as opposed to *extraversion.*

Irritability (temperament) Tendency of an individual to become easily agitated and lack patience and tolerance.

Joint attention Two or more individuals share a common focus of attention, while at the same time being aware that the same focus of attention is shared by the other person(s).

Latency phase According to *psychoanalytic theory*, a period of reduced sexual drive without focus on a new area of the body; lasts from the end of the phallic phase until puberty (approx. age 6–13); see *anal phase, oral phase* and *phallic phase.*

Learning Relatively permanent change in understanding and behavior as the result of experience; see *development* and *maturation.*

Libido Sexual or life drive; according to *psycho-analytic theory*, a source of energy aimed at reproduction, but among human beings also converted into other forms of expression. Motivates all action together with *Thanatos.*

Logical constructivism Psychological tradition that includes Piaget's theory and the theories of others that build on it; its main

principle is that children actively construct their own understanding of the outside world, and that *perception* and *cognition*
are affected by logical and conceptually driven processes; see
constructivism.

Longitudinal study   Research method that involves the observation of the same individuals at various age levels.

Maladaptation   *Mental disorder* or antisocial behavior with a basis
in an individual's lack of adaptability and difficulties adjusting to
the environment.

Maturation   Developmental change caused by genetically determined regulating mechanisms that are relatively independent of
the individual's specific experiences; see *development* and *learning*.

Mental disorder   Behavioral or psychological pattern that occurs
in an individual and leads to clinically significant distress or
impairment in one or more important areas of functioning.

Mind understanding   Understanding that other people have
internal states, such as knowledge, feelings and plans, that may be
different from one's own and may affect their actions.

Mirror neuron   Nerve cell that is activated both when an individual observes an action and when he or she performs the action.

Moral dilemma   Situation involving a conflict between two or
more solutions that may violate an individual's perception of
what is right and wrong.

Moral realism   According to Piaget, the second of three stages in
moral development, beginning at 5 years of age; characterized by
the child's ability to follow rules, but in an absolute way, i.e. with
little ability to adapt or change the rules; see *moral subjectivism*.

Moral reasoning   Reasoning about real or hypothetical moral
dilemmas.

Moral subjectivism   According to Piaget, the third and final stage
in moral development; begins at age 9–10; characterized by the
child's understanding that rules are conventional, *social construc-
tions* based on consensus, and that it is possible to change them if
consensus can be reached; see *moral realism*.

Neglected children (sociometry)   Children who are neither
accepted nor rejected by their peers; few features distinguish
them from other children, but they have less interaction with
others, and little attention is paid to them; they typically show
little aggressiveness and seem to try to avoid aggression to a
somewhat greater degree than other children, but do not appear

overly anxious or withdrawn; see *popular children* and *unpopular children*.

Neonatal period   The first month of life.

Neuroticism   One of the *Big Five personality traits*; see *agreeableness, conscientiousness, extraversion* and *openness to experience*.

Norm (in a test)   A standard or normative score for a certain age level, based on the results from a large number of individuals.

Oedipus conflict   According to *psychoanalytic theory*, a genetically determined psychological conflict rooted in the idea that boys are sexually attracted to their mother and experience the father as a competitor for the mother's affection; equivalent to the *Electra conflict* in girls.

Open aggression   A form of *hostile aggression*; actions whose purpose is to harm another person physically; see *hostile aggression, instrumental aggression* and *relational aggression*.

Openness to experience   One of the *Big Five personality traits*; see *agreeableness, conscientiousness, extraversion* and *neuroticism*.

Oppositional defiant disorder   Externalizing disorder characterized by hostility toward adults, reluctance to do what authorities say and to follow normal rules, and maliciousness and vindictiveness when met with resistance.

Oral phase   According to *psychoanalytic theory*, the first stage in *psychosexual development*, in which the area around the mouth becomes a source of pleasure; age 0–1 years; see *anal phase, latency phase* and *phallic phase*.

Over-controlled behavior   Inhibited and anxious behavior; see *under-controlled behavior*.

Over-regulation (in language development)   Application of a general grammatical rule beyond the particular cases it applies to, for example *goed* instead of *went*.

Parenting style   General description of how parents raise their children; see *authoritarian, authoritative* and *permissive parenting*.

Perception   Knowledge gained through the senses; discernment, selection and processing of sensory input.

Permissive parenting   Parenting style that places few demands on the child, but in which parents are *responsive*; see *authoritarian* and *authoritative parenting*.

Personality   An individual's characteristic tendency to feel, think and act in specific ways.

Personality traits   Summary description of an individual's *personality*.

Phallic phase   According to *psychoanalytic theory*, the third phase in *psychosexual development*, in which the genital area becomes a source of pleasure; age 4–5 years; see *anal phase*, *latency phase* and *oral phase*.

Popular children (sociometry)   Children who are actively accepted by other children. Often they are physically strong with an attractive appearance, but their willingness to share, ability to cooperate and other social skills are equally important for their acceptance and popularity among peers; see *neglected children* and *unpopular children*.

Positive reinforcement (in conditioning)   An event or other factor that, when injected into a situation, increases the likelihood of a particular action; for example, the likelihood of a child doing homework may increase when homework leads to good grades; see *reinforcement*.

Post-conventional morality   According to Kohlberg, the third and final of three main stages of moral development; characterized by abstract values that are valid under all circumstances and in every society; see *conventional morality* and *pre-conventional morality*.

Pre-conventional morality   According to Kohlberg, the first of three main stages of moral development; characterized by moral reasoning based on reward, punishment and authority; see *conventional morality* and *post-conventional morality*.

Preschool age   Age 3–6 years.

Prevalence   Relative presence of for example traits, diseases and syndromes in a particular population at a certain time; see *incidence*.

Primary emotions   See *basic emotions*.

Prosocial behavior   Behavior intended to help others and share objects or other benefits without advantage to the individual itself; see *antisocial behavior*.

Protection (in development)   Conditions that reduce the negative effects of *vulnerability* and *risk*.

Psychoanalytic psychology; psychoanalytic theory   Psychological theories based on Freud's theory and psychotherapeutic method (psychoanalysis); founded on the principle that an individual's thoughts and actions are determined by drives and impulses and their internal, often *unconscious*, regulation through interaction between the different parts of the human psyche; both *personality* and mental problems of children and adults are explained on the basis of unconscious processes and conflicts rooted in early childhood; see *ego*, *id*, *psychodynamic theory* and *superego*.

Psychodynamic psychology; psychodynamic theory Tradition that emphasizes the importance of feelings and needs for an individual's thoughts and actions; describes *personality* and its development based on the assumption that the human psyche involves mental forces that frequently are in conflict with each other, and have an important basis in early childhood; *psychoanalysis* belongs to this tradition.

Psychopathology Mental problems and disorders that make everyday functioning difficult.

Psychosexual phase According to *psychoanalytic theory*, a *critical period* in which a child's mental energy is directed toward a specific area of the body; the development of an individual's personality and sociocultural adaptation depends on certain stimuli and experiences and the resolution of mental conflicts during these periods; see *anal phase, latency phase, oral phase* and *phallic phase*.

Psychosocial crisis According to Erikson, a *critical period* of developmental challenges or tasks related to the formation of specific characteristics; the experience of a psychosocial crisis leaves a permanent mark on an individual's personal and social development, and has consequences for the course of future psychosocial crises.

Punishment In behavioral psychology, any event that reduces the probability of repeating an action under similar circumstances; see *reinforcement.*

Reaction to novelty Behavior characterized by shyness and uncertain reactions to new situations, objects and people.

Recognition The process of experiencing something in the moment that has been experienced before, such as when children consciously or nonconsciously show that they have seen a particular image before.

Reference group Group that forms the basis for an individual's values, norms, attitudes and behaviors.

Reflex Unlearned and involuntary response to an external stimulus.

Regression The relapse into earlier, more primitive or childish ways of functioning.

Reinforcement (in conditioning) In *classical conditioning*: presentation of an *unconditioned stimulus* and a *neutral stimulus* that becomes a *conditioned stimulus*, such that the *conditioned response* is triggered more consistently. In *operant conditioning*: events that follow the execution of an action and increase the likelihood of repeating the action under similar circumstances.

Relational aggression   A form of *hostile aggression*; actions whose main intent is to damage the relationship between two people, for example by speaking ill of them; see *hostile aggression, instrumental aggression* and *open aggression.*

Resilience   Attributes that lead to a positive development under difficult childhood conditions, such as children who are biologically or socially at *risk* of aberrant or delayed development; see *vulnerability.*

Responsivity (as a human trait)   The ability to provide a quick and appropriate response to an individual's *signals* and behavior; see *sensitivity.*

Rigidity   *Personality trait* characterized by poor social adaptability and lack of flexibility.

Risk   Increased likelihood of a negative developmental outcome; may be linked to biological and environmental factors.

Role   Expectations of certain action patterns and behaviors associated with an individual by virtue of their function or position in society, for example as a girl, teenager or boy scout.

Role-play   Form of *pretend play* in which the participants make-believe they are another person, an animal or a human-like figure.

Rough-and-tumble play   A type of *exercise play* in which children run after each other, push, tickle, play-fight and similar.

Schema   Mental *representation* that emerges when actions are generalized by means of repetition and transformed through mental processing, thus shaping the individual's perception of the environment.

School age   Age 6–12.

Screening test   Brief *test* that aims to identify individuals who should be examined using more thorough and time-consuming methods.

Script (cognition)   Generalized mental *representation* of a sequence of events that recur within the context of a specific situation; provides among other things the basis for an individual's expectations of how to behave in different situations, such as at school or at a restaurant.

Self   Personal awareness, perception or evaluation of oneself.

Self-concept   Awareness of having specific and independent traits.

Self-efficacy   The experience of acting and having control over one's own life; belief in one's own ability to deal with different situations and events.

Self-evaluation; Self-esteem   The assessment of one's own characteristics in relation to an inner standard that includes how and who one wishes to be; can also refer to questionnaires, surveys and the like about a person's characteristics.

Self-image   Positive or negative perception of oneself and one's own characteristics.

Self-referential emotions; Self-conscious emotions; Secondary emotions   Emotion associated with an individual's self-evaluation in relation to a standard based on personal emotional experiences and information provided by others; includes pride, shame, embarrassment, guilt and envy; see *basic emotions*.

Self-regulation   The ability to monitor and adapt one's own thoughts, feelings, reactions and actions in order to cope with the requirements, challenges and opportunities of the environment and be able to achieve one's goals; also referred to as self-control.

Sensitive period   Limited period of time when an individual is particularly susceptible to specific forms of positive or negative stimulation and experience; if the stimulation or experience does not take place during the given time period, the individual will still be able to take advantage of, or be impaired by, similar types of stimulation or experience later in life, but to a lesser extent; see *critical period*.

Sensitivity (of a caregiver)   Ability to understand a child's condition, respond quickly and adequately to the child's *signals* and behavior, and provide challenges the child is able to master; see *responsivity*.

Sex   See *gender*.

Signals (in early development)   Infant actions and expressions used by adults as an indication of the infant's interests, preferences and general well-being.

Significance (in statistics)   Indication of the likelihood that a statistical difference or relationship is based on pure coincidence.

Slow-to-warm-up (temperament)   According to Thomas and Chess, slow adaptation to new situations; includes irregularities in daily routines and a tendency to cry and feel restless, but with moderate reactions; may initially resemble *difficult temperament*, but mostly resembles *easy temperament* once the individual has warmed up.

Sociability (temperament)   Interest and enjoyment in being in the company of other people.

Social construct; social construction   Anything rooted in or created by means of social interaction.

Social learning theory   See *cognitive behavior theory*.

Social referencing   Using other people's emotional reactions to evaluate uncertain situations; see *emotion regulation*.

Stability (in development)   Describes the constancy of an individual's position in relation to peers with respect to a particular characteristic; the fact that individual differences in the execution of a skill are constant from one developmental stage to another.

Stage (in development)   Delimited period of time in which thoughts, feelings and behavior are organized in a way that is qualitatively different from the preceding or following periods.

Stage theory   Theory based on the assumption that development proceeds in distinct and qualitatively different *stages*.

Superego   In *psychoanalytic theory*, one of the three parts of the human psyche, consisting of internalized demands and expectations, primarily from parents, but also from other important persons in the child's environment; its function is to ensure that an individual's actions remain within the norms and values of culture; see *id* and *ego*.

Symbol   Something that represents something other than itself, such as a sign, a word, an image or the like.

Sympathy   Understanding why another person experiences the emotions that they express.

Temperament   A biologically determined pattern of emotional reactivity and regulation unique to an individual; includes the degree of *emotionality*, *irritability* and *activity level*, and reactions to and ability to cope with emotional situations, new impressions and changes; see *easy temperament*, *difficult temperament* and *slow-to-warm-up*.

Thanatos   According to *psychoanalytic theory*, the aggressive and destructive drive that together with *libido* motivates all human action.

Toddlerhood   Age 1–3.

Typical development   Course of development that characterizes the majority of a *population*; see *atypical development* and *individual differences*.

Unconditioned stimulus   See *conditioning*.

Unconscious   Not within the sphere of conscious attention; in *psychoanalytic theory*, an inaccessible part of consciousness where repressed, often anxiety-eliciting memories and desires are stored.

Under-controlled behavior   Impulsive, disruptive and aggressive behavior; see *over-controlled behavior*.

Universal grammar   In Chomsky's theory, an innate grammatical device that contains the grammars of all human languages.

Universality   General validity; phenomena that exist in all cultures, such as language.

Unpopular children (sociometry)   Children who are actively rejected by other children; some children in this group appear particularly aggressive and hostile, others are socially withdrawn and often submissive, while others yet are immature and childish compared with their peers; see *neglected children* and *popular children*.

Vulnerability   An individual's susceptibility to be adversely affected by particular conditions or circumstances in the environment; see *resilience* and *risk*.

Working model (in social relations)   Mental representation of an early relationship that forms the basis for expectations about the nature of social relationships, such as a caregiver's inclination to provide emotional support and be devoted and reliable.

Bibliography

American Psychiatric Association (2013). *Diagnostic and statistical manual of mental disorders, Fifth edition (DSM-5)*. Washington, DC: American Psychiatric Association.

Andershed, H., Kerr, M., & Stattin, H. (2001). Bullying in school and violence on the streets: Are the same people involved? *Journal of Scandinavian Studies in Criminology and Crime Prevention, 2*, 31–49.

Anisfeld, M. (2005). No compelling evidence to dispute Piaget's timetable of the development of representational imitation in infancy. In S. Hurley & N. Chater (Eds), *Perspectives on imitation: From neuroscience to social science, Volume 2: Imitation, human development, and culture* (pp. 107–131). Cambridge, MA: MIT Press.

Anticich, S. A., Barrett, P. M., Silverman, W., Lacherez, P., & Gillies, R. (2013). The prevention of childhood anxiety and promotion of resilience among preschool-aged children: A universal school based trial. *Advances in School Mental Health Promotion, 6*, 93–121.

Arsenio, W. F. (1988). Children's conceptions of the situational affective consequences of sociomoral events. *Child Development, 59*, 1611–1622.

Arsenio, W. F., & Lover, A. (1995). Children's conceptions of sociomoral affect: Happy victimizers, mixed emotions, and other expectancies. In M. Killen & D. Hart (Eds), *Morality in everyday life: Developmental perspectives* (pp. 87–128). Cambridge: Cambridge University Press.

Arsenio, W. F., Gold, J., & Adams, E. (2006). Children's conceptions and displays of moral emotions. In M. Killen & J. G. Smetana (Eds), *Handbook of moral development* (pp. 581–609). Mahwah, NJ: Erlbaum.

Asendorpf, J. B. (1992). Beyond stability: Predicting inter-individual differences in intra-individual change. *European Journal of Personality, 6*, 103–117.

Asendorpf, J. B. (2010). Long-term development of shyness: Looking forward and looking backward. In K. H. Rubin & R. J. Coplan (Eds), *The development of shyness and social withdrawal* (pp. 157–175). New York, NY: Guilford Press

Asher, S. R., & Parker, J. G. (1989). Significance of peer relationship problems in childhood. In B. H. Schneider, G. Attili, J. Nadel & R. P. Weissberg (Eds), *Social competence in developmental perspective* (pp. 5–23). Norwell, MA: Kluwer.

Baillargeon, R., Morisset, A., Keenanc, K., Normand, C. L., Jeyaganthe, S., Boivinf, M., & Tremblay, R. E. (2011). The development of prosocial behaviors in young children: A prospective population-based cohort study. *The Journal of Genetic Psychology: Research and Theory on Human Development*, *172*, 221–251.

Baldwin, A. L. (1949). The effect of home environment on nursery school behavior. *Child Development*, *20*, 49–62.

Balsam, R. H. (2015). Oedipus Rex: Where are we going, especially with females? *The Psychoanalytic Quarterly*, *84*, 555–588.

Bandura, A. (1965). Influence of models' reinforcement contingencies on the acquisition of imitative responses. *Journal of Personality and Social Psychology*, *1*, 589–595.

Bandura, A. (1986). *Social foundations of thought and action: A social cognitive theory.* Upper Saddle River, NJ: Prentice Hall.

Bandura, A. (1997). *Self-efficacy: The exercise of control.* New York, NY: W. H. Freeman.

Bandura, A. (1999). Self efficacy: Toward a unifying theory of behavioral change. In R. F. Baumeister (Ed.), *The self in social psychology* (pp. 285–298). London: Taylor and Francis.

Bandura, A. (2006). Toward a psychology of human agency. *Perspectives on Psychological Science*, *1*, 164–180.

Bar-Haim, Y. (2010). Research review: Attention bias modification (ABM): A novel treatment for anxiety disorders. *Journal of Child Psychology and Psychiatry*, *51*, 859–870.

Bar-Haim, Y., Morag, I., & Glickman, S. (2011). Training anxious children to disengage attention from threat: A randomized controlled trial. *Journal of Child Psychology and Psychiatry*, *52*, 861–869.

Barrett, K. C., & Campos, J. J. (1987). Perspectives on emotional development: II. A functionalist approach to emotions. In J. D. Osofsky (Ed.), *Handbook of infant development, Second edition* (pp. 555–578). New York, NY: Wiley.

Barrett, K. C., Zahn-Waxler, C., & Cole, P. M. (1993). Avoiders versus amenders–implication for the investigation of guilt and shame during toddlerhood? *Cognition and Emotion*, *7*, 481–505.

Barrett, P. M., & Turner, C. (2001). Prevention of anxiety symptoms in primary school children: Preliminary results from a universal school-based trial. *British Journal of Clinical Psychology*, *40*, 399–410.

Barrett, P. M., Cooper, M., & Guajardo, J. G. (2014). Using the FRIENDS programs to promote resilience in cross-cultural populations. In S. Prince-Embury & D. H. Saklofske (Eds), *Resilience interventions for youth in diverse populations* (pp. 85–108). New York, NY: Springer.

Barth, J. M., & Archibald, A. (2003). The relation between emotion production behavior and preschool social behavior: In the eye of the beholder. *Social Development, 12,* 67–90.

Bastounis, A., Callaghan, P., Banerjee, A., & Michail, M. (2016). The effectiveness of the Penn Resiliency Programme (PRP) and its adapted versions in reducing depression and anxiety and improving explanatory style: A systematic review and meta-analysis. *Journal of Adolescence, 52,* 37–48.

Bates, J. E., Schermerhorn, A. C., & Petersen, I. T. (2012). Temperament and parenting in developmental perspective. In M. Zentner & R. L. Shiner (Eds), *Handbook of temperament* (pp. 425–441). New York, NY: Guilford Press.

Baumrind, D. (1967). Child care and practices anteceding three patterns of preschool behavior. *Genetic Psychology Monographs, 75,* 43–88.

Baumrind, D. (1997). The disciplinary encounter: Contemporary issues. *Aggression and Violent Behavior, 2,* 321–335.

Baumrind, D. (2013). Authoritative parenting revisited: History and current status. In R. E. Larzelere, A. S. Morris & A. W. Harrist (Eds), *Authoritative parenting: Synthesizing nurturance and discipline for optimal child development* (pp. 11–34). Washington, DC: American Psychological Association.

Baumrind, D., Larzelere, R. E., & Owens, E. B. (2010). Effects of preschool parents' power assertive patterns and practices on adolescent development. *Parenting, 10,* 157–201.

Bechor, M., Pettit, J. W., Silverman, W. K., Bar-Haim, Y., Abend, R., Pine, D. S., Vasey, M. W., & Jaccard, J. (2014). Attention Bias Modification Treatment for children with anxiety disorders who do not respond to cognitive behavioral therapy: A case series. *Journal of Anxiety Disorders, 28,* 154–159.

Beer, J. S., & Keltner, D. (2004). What is unique about self-conscious emotions? *Psychological Inquiry, 15,* 126–128,

Bell, S. M., & Ainsworth, M. D. S. (1972). Infant crying and maternal responsiveness. *Child Development, 43,* 1171–1190.

Benjamin, C. L., Puleo, C. M., Settipani, C. A., Brodman, D. M., Edmunds, J. M., Cummings, C. M., & Kendall, P. C. (2011). History of cognitive-behavioral therapy in youth. *Child and Adolescent Psychiatric Clinics of North America, 20,* 179–189.

Berg, L., Rostila, M., & Hjern, A. (2016). Parental death during childhood and depression in young adults—a national cohort study. *Journal of Child Psychology and Psychiatry, 57,* 1092–1098.

Berg-Nielsen, T. S., Vikan, A., & Dahl, A. (2002). Parenting related to child and parental psychopathology: A descriptive review of the literature. *Clinical Child Psychology and Psychiatry, 7,* 529–552.

Blackford, J. U., & Walden, T. A. (1998). Individual differences in social referencing. *Infant Behavior and Development, 21,* 89–102.

Blake, P. R., & McAuliffe, K. (2011). "I had so much it didn't seem fair": Eight-year-olds reject two forms of inequity. *Cognition, 120 (2),* 215–224.

Block, J. (1995). A contrarian view of the five-factor approach to personality description. *Psychological Bulletin, 117,* 187–215.

Blurton-Jones, N. (1967). An ethological study of some aspects of social behaviour of children in a nursery school. In D. Morris (Ed.), *Primate ethology* (pp. 347–368). Chicago, IL: Aldine.

Boom, J., Wouters, H., & Keller, M. (2007). A cross-cultural validation of stage development: A Rasch re-analysis of longitudinal socio-moral reasoning data. *Cognitive Development, 22,* 213–229.

Bornstein, M. H. (2015). Children and their parents. In M. H. Bornstein & T. Leventhal (Eds), *Handbook of child psychology and developmental science, Seventh edition, Volume 4: Ecological settings and processes* (pp. 55–132). Hoboken, NJ: Wiley.

Bornstein, M. H., & Arterberry, M. E. (2003). Recognition, discrimination and categorization of smiling by 5-month-old infants. *Developmental Science, 6,* 585–599.

Bornstein, M. H., Putnick, D. L., Gartstein, M. A., Hahn, C. S., Auestad, N., & O'Connor, D. L. (2015). Infant temperament: Stability by age, gender, birth order, term status, and socioeconomic status. *Child Development, 86,* 844–863.

Bornstein, R. F. (2006). A Freudian construct lost and reclaimed: The psychodynamics of personality pathology. *Psychoanalytic Psychology, 23,* 339–353.

Bowlby, J. (1946). *Forty-four juvenile thieves; their characters and home-life.* Oxford: Bailliere, Tindall and Cox.

Bowlby, J. (1980). *Attachment and Loss: Volume 3. Loss: Sadness and depression.* New York, NY: Basic Books.

Bradley, R. H., & Corwyn, R. F. (2008). Infant temperament, parenting, and externalizing behavior in first grade: A test of the differential susceptibility hypothesis. *Journal of Child Psychology and Psychiatry, 49,* 124–131.

Brenner, E. M., & Salovey, P. (1997). Emotion regulation during childhood: Developmental, interpersonal and individual considerations. In P. Salovey & D. J. Sluyter (Eds), *Emotional development and emotional intelligence* (pp. 168–192). New York, NY: Basic Books.

Brent, D. A., Melhem, N. M., Masten, A. S., Porta, G., & Payne, M. W. (2012). Longitudinal effects of parental bereavement on adolescent developmental competence. *Journal of Clinical Child and Adolescent Psychology, 41,* 778–791.

Bretherton, I., Fritz, J., Zahn-Waxler, C., & Ridgeway, D. (1986). Learning to talk about emotions: A functionalist perspective. *Child Development, 57,* 529–548.

Bridges, L. J., & Grolnick, W. S. (1995). The development of emotional self regulation in infancy and early childhood. In N. Eisenberg (Ed.), *Social development* (pp. 185–211). Thousand Oaks, CA: Sage.

Briggs-Gowan, M. J., Pollak, S. D., Grasso, D., Voss, J., Mian, N. D., Zobel, E., McCarthy, K. J., Wakschlag, L. S., & Pine, D. S. (2015). Attention bias and anxiety in young children exposed to family violence. *Journal of Child Psychology and Psychiatry, 56,* 1194–1201.

Briley, D. A., & Tucker-Drob, E. M. (2014). Genetic and environmental continuity in personality development: A meta-analysis. *Psychological Bulletin, 140,* 1303–1331.

Britton, J. C., Lissek, S., Grillon, C., Norcross, M. A., & Pine, D. S. (2011). Development of anxiety: The role of threat appraisal and fear learning. *Depression and Anxiety*, *28*, 5–17.

Brock, R. L., & Kochanska, G. (2016). Toward a developmentally informed approach to parenting interventions: Seeking hidden effects. *Development and Psychopathology*, *28*, 583–593.

Brosnan, J., & Healy, O. (2011). A review of behavioral interventions for the treatment of aggression in individuals with developmental disabilities. *Research in Developmental Disabilities*, *32*, 437–446.

Brownell, C. A., Svetlova, M., & Nichols, S. (2009). To share or not to share: When do toddlers respond to another's needs? *Infancy*, *14*, 117–130.

Brownell, C. A., Iesue, S. S., Nichols, S. R., & Svetlova, M. (2013). Mine or yours? Development of sharing in toddlers in relation to ownership understanding. *Child Development*, *84*, 906–920.

Brunborg, G. S., Mentzoni R. A., & Frøyland L. R. (2014). Is video gaming, or video game addiction, associated with depression, academic achievement, heavy episodic drinking, or conduct problems? *Journal of Behavioral Addictions*, *3*, 27–32.

Burleson, B. R., & Kunkel, A. (2002). Parental and peer contributions to the emotional support skills of the child: From whom do children learn to express support? *Journal of Family Communication*, *2*, 81–97.

Buss, K. A., & McDoniel, M. E. (2016). Improving the prediction of risk for anxiety development in temperamentally fearful children. *Current Directions in Psychological Science*, *25*, 14–20.

Campos, J. J., Butterfield, P., & Klinnert, M. D. (1985, April). *Cardiac and behavioral differentiation of negative emotional signals: An individual differences perspective.* Presented at the biennial Meeting of the Society for Research in Child Development, Toronto, Canada.

Campos, J. J., Campos, R. G., & Barrett, K. C. (1989). Emergent themes in the study of emotional development and emotion regulation. *Developmental Psychology*, *25*, 394–402.

Campos, J. J., Dahl, A., & He, M. (2010). Beyond breaches and battles: Clarifying important misconceptions about emotion. *Emotion Review*, *2*, 100–104.

Campos, J. J., Frankel, C., & Camras, L. (2004). On the nature of emotion regulation. *Child Development*, *75*, 377–394.

Campos, J. J., Walle, E. A., Dahl, A., & Main, A. (2011). Reconceptualizing emotion regulation. *Emotion Review*, *3*, 26–35.

Camras, L. A. (2011). Differentiation, dynamical integration and functional emotional development. *Emotion Review*, *3*, 138–146.

Camras, L. A., Oster, H., Campos, J. J., & Bakemand, R. (2003). Emotional facial expressions in European-American, Japanese, and Chinese infants. *Annals of the New York Academy of Sciences*, *1000*, 135–151.

Camras, L. A., & Shuster, M. M. (2013). Current emotion research in developmental psychology. *Emotion Review*, *5*, 321–329.

Camras, L. A., & Shutter, J. (2010). Emotional facial expressions in infancy. *Emotion Review, 2*, 120–129.

Camras, L. A., & Witherington, D. C. (2005). Dynamical systems approaches to emotional development. *Developmental Review, 25*, 328–350.

Cantone, E., Piras, A. P., Vellante, M., Preti, A., Daníelsdóttir, S., D'Aloja, E., Lesinskiene, S., Angermeyer, M. C., Carta, M. G., & Bhugra, D. (2015). Interventions on bullying and cyberbullying in schools: A systematic review. *Clinical Practice and Epidemiology in Mental Health, 11* (Suppl 1: M4), 58–76.

Caplan, M., Vespo, J., Pedersen, J., & Hay, D. F. (1991). Conflict and its resolution in small groups of one and two year olds. *Child Development, 62*, 1513–1524.

Carlo, G., Mestre, M. V., McGinley, M. M., Tur-Porcar, A., Samper, P., & Opal, D. (2014). The protective role of prosocial behaviors on antisocial behaviors: The mediating effects of deviant peer affiliation. *Journal of Adolescence, 37*, 359–366.

Caron, A. J., Caron, R. F., & McLean, D. T. (1988). Infant discrimination of naturalistic emotional expressions: The role of face and voice. *Child Development, 59*, 604–616.

Carpendale, J. I. M., Hammond, S. I., & Atwood, S. (2013). A relational developmental systems approach to moral development. *Advances in Child Development and Behavior, 45*, 125–153.

Case, A., Paxson, C., & Ableidinger, J. (2004). Orphans in Africa: Parental death, poverty, and school enrollment. *Demography, 41*, 483–508.

Caspi, A. (1998). Personality development across the life course. In W. Damon & N. Eisenberg (Eds), *Handbook of child psychology, Fifth edition, Volume 2. Social, emotional, and personality development* (pp. 745–800). New York, NY: Wiley.

Caspi, A. (2000). The child is the father of the man: Personality continuities from childhood to adulthood. *Journal of Personality and Social Psychology, 78*, 158–172.

Caspi, A., & Roberts, B. W. (2001). Personality development across the life course: The argument for change and continuity. *Psychological Inquiry, 12*, 49–66.

Caspi, A., Roberts, B. W., & Shiner, R. L. (2005). Personality development: Stability and change. *Annual Review of Psychology, 56*, 453–484.

Caspi, A., Hariri, A. R., Holmes, A., Uher, R., & Moffitt, T. E. (2010). Genetic sensitivity to the environment: The case of the serotonin transporter gene and its implications for studying complex diseases and traits. *Focus, 8*, 398–416.

Caspi, A., Henry, B., McGee, R. O., Moffitt, T. E., & Silva, P. A. (1995). Temperamental origins of child and adolescent behavior problems: From age three to age fifteen. *Child Development, 66*, 55–68.

Caspi, A., McClay, J., Moffitt, T. E., Mill, J., Martin, J., Craig, I. W., Taylor, A., & Poulton, R. (2002). Role of genotype in the cycle of violence in maltreated children. *Science, 297*, 851–854.

Catron, T. F., & Masters, J. C. (1993). Mothers' and children's conceptualizations of corporal punishment. *Child Development, 64*, 1815–1828.

Cheah, C. S. L., & Park, S.-Y. (2006). South Korean mothers' beliefs regarding aggression and social withdrawal in preschoolers. *Early Childhood Research, 21,* 61–75.

Chen, X., & French, D. (2008). Children's social competence in cultural context. *Annual Review of Psychology, 59,* 591–616.

Chen, X., & Schmidt, L. A. (2015). Temperament and personality. In R. M. Lerner, M. E. Lamb & C. G. Coll (Eds), *Handbook of child psychology and developmental science, Seventh edition, Volume 3: Social and emotional development* (pp. 152–200). Hoboken, NJ: Wiley.

Chess, S., & Thomas, A. (1999). *Goodness of fit: Clinical applications from infancy through adult life.* London: Bunner/Mazel.

Chisholm, K. (1998). A three-year follow-up of attachment and indiscriminate friendliness in children adopted from Romanian orphanages. *Child Development, 69,* 1092–1106.

Chronis-Tuscano, A., Rubin, K. H., O'Brien, K. A., Coplan, R. J., Thomas, S. R., Dougherty, L. R., Cheah, C. S., Watts, K., Heverly-Fitt, S., Huggins, S. L., etal. (2015). Preliminary evaluation of a multimodal early intervention program for behaviorally inhibited preschoolers. *Journal of Consulting and Clinical Psychology, 83,* 534–540.

Cicchetti, D. (2013). Annual research review: Resilient functioning in maltreated children–past, present, and future perspectives. *Journal of Child Psychology and Psychiatry, 54* (4), 402–422.

Cicchetti, D. (2016). Socioemotional, personality, and biological development: Illustrations from a multilevel developmental psychopathology perspective on child maltreatment. *Annual Review of Psychology, 67,* 187–211.

Cicchetti, D., & Toth, S. L. (2015). Child maltreatment. In R. M. Lerner, M. E. Lamb & C. G. Coll (Eds), *Hand-book of child psychology and developmental science, Seventh edition, Volume 3: Social and emotional development* (pp. 513–563). Hoboken, NJ: Wiley.

Clarke, A., & Clarke, A. (2000). *Early experience and the life path.* London: Jessica Kingsley.

Cloninger, C. R., Sigvardsson, S., Bohman, M., & Knorring, A. L. von (1982). Predisposition to petty criminality in Swedish adoptees: II. Cross fostering analysis of gene environment interaction. *Archives of General Psychiatry, 39,* 1242–1247.

Colby, A., Kohlberg, L., Gibbs, J., & Lierberman, M. (1983). A longitudinal study of moral development. *Monographs for the Society for Research in Child Development, 48* (1–2).

Cole, P. M. (1986). Children's spontaneous control of facial expression. *Child Development, 57,* 1309–1321.

Cole, P. M., Bruschi, C. J., & Tamang, B. L. (2002). Cultural differences in children's emotional reactions to difficult situations. *Child Development, 73,* 983–996.

Collins, W. A., Maccoby, E. E., Steinberg, L., Hetherington, E. M., & Bornstein, M. H. (2000). Contemporary research on parenting. *American Psychologist, 55,* 218–232.

Collishaw, S. (2015). Annual research review: Secular trends in child and adolescent mental health. *Journal of Child Psychology and Psychiatry, 56,* 370–393.

Coplan, R. J., & Arbeau, K. A. (2008). The stresses of a brave new world: Shyness and adjustment in kindergarten. *Journal of Research in Childhood Education, 22,* 377–389.

Coplan, R. J., Arbeau, K. A., & Armer, M. (2008). Don't fret, be supportive! Maternal characteristics linking child shyness to psychosocial and school adjustment in kindergarten. *Journal of Abnormal Child Psychology, 36,* 359–371.

Corcoran, J., & Hanvey-Phillips, J. (2013). Effective interventions for adolescents with depression. In C. Franklin, M. B. Harris & P. Allen-Meares (Eds), *The school services sourcebook: A guide for school-based professionals* (pp. 149–157). Oxford: Oxford University Press.

Cornell, A. H., & Frick, P. J. (2007). The moderating effects of parenting styles in the association between behavioral inhibition and parent-reported guilt and empathy in preschool children. *Journal of Clinical Child and Adolescent Psychology, 36,* 305–318.

Corrieri. S., Heider, D., Conrad, I., Blume, A., König, H. H., & Riedel-Heller, S. G. (2013). School-based prevention programs for depression and anxiety in adolescence: A systematic review. *Health Promotion International, 29,* 427–441.

Costa, P. T., & McCrae, R. R. (1992). *Revised NEO Personality Inventory (NEO-PI-R) and NEO Five Factor Inventory (NEO-FFI). Professional manual.* Odessa, FL: Psychological Assessment Resources.

Craig, W., Harel-Fisch, Y., Fogel-Grinvald, H., Dostaler, S., Hetland, J., Simons-Morton, B., Molcho, M., de Mato, M. G., Overpeck, M., Due, P., et al. (2009). A cross-national profile of bullying and victimization among adolescents in 40 countries. *International Journal of Public Health, 54,* 216–224.

Cramer, V., Torgersen, S., & Kringlen, E. (2007). Sociodemographic conditions, subjective somatic health, Axis I disorders and personality disorders in the common population: The relationship to quality of life. *Journal of Personality Disorders, 21,* 552–567.

Creed, A. T., Waltman, H. S., Frankel, A. S., & Williston, A. M. (2016). School-based cognitive behavioral therapy: Current status and alternative approaches. *Current Psychiatry Reviews, 12,* 53–64.

Crick, N. R., & Dodge, K. A. (1994). A review and reformulation of social information-processing mechanisms in children's social adjustment. *Psychological Bulletin, 115,* 74–101.

Crockenberg, S. C., & Leerkes, E. (2006). Infant and mother behavior moderate reactivity to novelty to predict anxious behavior at 2.5 years. *Development and Psychopathology, 18,* 1–18.

Crockenberg, S. C., Leerkes, E. M., & Lekka, S. K. (2007). Pathways from marital aggression to infant emotion regulation: The development of withdrawal in infancy. *Infant Behavior and Development, 30,* 97–113.

Cui, L., Morris, A. S., Criss, M. M., Houltberg, B. J., & Silk, J. S. (2014). Parental psychological control and adolescent adjustment: The role of adolescent emotion regulation. *Parenting, 14,* 47–67.

Cummings, E. M. (1987). Coping with background anger in early childhood. *Child Development, 58*, 976–984.

Cummings, E. M., & Davies, P. T. (1994). *Children and marital conflict: The impact of family dispute and resolution.* New York, NY: Guilford Press.

Cummings, E. M., & Davies, P. T. (2002). Effects of marital conflict on children: Recent advances and emerging themes in process-oriented research. *Journal of Child Psychology and Psychiatry, 43*, 31–63.

Cummings, E. M., Ballard, M., & El Sheikh, M. (1991). Responses of children and adolescents to interadult anger as a function of gender, age, and mode of expression. *Merrill-Palmer Quarterly, 37*, 543–560.

Cummings, E. M., Hennessy, K. D., Rabideau, G. J., & Cicchetti, D. (1994). Responses of physically abused boys to interadult anger involving their mothers. *Development and Psychopathology, 6*, 31–41.

Cummings, E. M., El-Sheikh, M., Kouros, C. D., & Buckhalt, J. A. (2009). Children and violence: The role of children's regulation in the marital aggression–child adjustment link. *Clinical Child and Family Psychology Review, 12*, 3–15.

Cummings, E. M., Iannotti, R. J., & Zahn-Waxler, C. (1985). Influence of conflict between adults on the emotions and aggression of young children. *Developmental Psychology, 21*, 495–507.

Cummings, E. M., Merrilees, C. E., Taylor, L. K., & Mondi, C. F. (2017). *Political violence, armed conflict, and youth adjustment.* Cham, Switzerland: Springer.

Cummings, E. M., Vogel, D., Cummings, J. S., & El-Sheikh, M. (1989). Children's responses to different forms of expression of anger between adults. *Child Development, 60*, 1392–1404.

Dagnan, D., & Sandhu, S. (1999). Social comparison, self-esteem and depression in people with intellectual disability. *Journal of Intellectual Disability Research, 43*, 372–379.

Dahl, A. (2014). Definitions and developmental processes in research on infant morality. *Human Development, 57 (4)*, 241–249.

Dahl, A. (2015). The developing social context of infant helping in two US samples. *Child Development, 86*, 1080–1093.

Dahl, A., & Campos, J. J. (2013). Domain differences in early social interactions. *Child Development, 84*, 817–825.

Dahl, A., Campos, J. J., & Witherington, D. (2011). Emotional action and communication in early moral development. *Emotion Review, 3*, 147–157.

Dahl, A., Schuck, R. K., & Campos, J. J. (2013). Do young toddlers act on their social preferences? *Developmental Psychology, 49*, 1964–1970.

Dallaire, D. H., & Weinraub, M. (2005). The stability of parenting behaviors over the first 6 years of life. *Early Childhood Research Quarterly, 20*, 201–219.

Daro, D., & Benedetti, G. (2014). Sustaining progress in preventing child maltreatment: A transformative challenge. In J. E. Korbin & R. D. Krugman (Eds), *Handbook of child maltreatment* (pp. 281–300). Dordrecht, NL: Springer.

Darwin, C. (1872). *The expression of the emotions in man and animals.* London: Oxford University Press (Reprint, 1998).

Davis, M., & Suveg, C. (2014). Focusing on the positive: A review of the role of child positive affect in developmental psychopathology. *Clinical Child and Family Psychology Review, 17*, 97–124.

de Haan, A. D., Prinzie, P., & Dekovic, M. (2009). Mothers' and fathers' personality and parenting: The mediating role of sense of competence. *Developmental Psychology, 45*, 1695–1707.

de Waal, F. B. (2008). Putting the altruism back into altruism: The evolution of empathy. *Annual Review of Psychology, 59*, 279–300.

Degnan, K. A., Hane, A. A., Henderson, H. A., Moas, O. L., Reeb-Sutherland, B. C., & Fox, N. A. (2011). Longitudinal stability of temperamental exuberance and social-emotional outcomes in early childhood. *Developmental Psychology, 47*, 765–780.

DeLoache, J. S., & LoBue, V. (2009). The narrow fellow in the grass: Human infants associate snakes and fear. *Developmental Science, 12*, 201–207.

Denham, S. A. (1986). Social cognition, prosocial behavior, and emotion in preschoolers: Contextual validation. *Child Development, 57*, 194–201.

Denham, S. A. (1989). Maternal affect and toddlers' social emotional competence. *American Journal of Orthopsychiatry, 59*, 368–376.

Denham, S. A. (1993). Maternal emotional responsiveness and toddlers' social emotional competence. *Journal of Child Psychology and Psychiatry, 34*, 715–728.

Denham, S. A. (2007). Dealing with feelings: How children negotiate the worlds of emotions and social relationships. *Cognitions, Brain, Behaviour, 11*, 1–48.

Denham, S. A., & Grout, L. (1993). Socialization of emotion: Pathway to preschoolers' emotional and social competence. *Journal of Nonverbal Behavior, 17*, 205–227.

deVries, M. W., & Sameroff, A. J. (1984). Culture and temperament: Influences on infant temperament in three East African societies. *American Journal of Orthopsychiatry, 54*, 83–96.

Dishion, T. J., & Tipsord, J. M. (2011). Peer contagion in child and adolescent social and emotional development. *Annual Review of Psychology, 62*, 189–214.

Dishion, T. J., McCord, J., & Poulin, F. (1999). When interventions harm: Peer groups and problem behavior. *American Psychologist, 54*, 755–764.

Dix, T., & Meunier, L. N. (2009). Depressive symptoms and parenting competence: An analysis of 13 regulatory processes. *Developmental Review, 29*, 45–68.

Dodge, K. A. (2009). Community intervention and public policy in the prevention of antisocial behavior. *Journal of Child Psychology and Psychiatry, 50*, 194–200.

Dodge, K. A., & Somberg, D. (1987). Hostile attributional biases among aggressive boys are exacerbated under conditions of threats to the self. *Child Development, 58*, 213–224.

Dodge, K. A., Coie, J. D., & Lynam, D. (2006). Aggression and antisocial behavior in youth. In W. Damon, R. M. Lerner & N. Eisenberg (Eds), *Handbook of child psychology, Sixth edition, Volume 3: Social, emotional, and personality development* (pp. 437–472). New York, NY: Wiley.

Dodge, K. A., Malone, P. S., Lansford, J. E., Sorbring, E., Skinner, A. T., Tapanya, S., Tirado, L. M., Zelli, A., Alampay, L. P., Al-Hassan, S. M., etal. (2015). Hostile attributional bias and aggressive behavior in global context. *Proceedings of the National Academy of Sciences of the United States of America, 112*, 9310–9315.

Dolev-Cohen, M., & Barak, A. (2013). Adolescents' use of Instant Messaging as a means of emotional relief. *Computers in Human Behavior, 29*, 58–63.

Doost, H. T. N., Moradi, A. R., Taghavi, M. R., Yule, W., & Dalgleish, T. (1999). The development of a corpus of emotional words produced by children and adolescents. *Personality and Individual Differences, 27*, 433–451.

Dost, A., & Yagmurlu, B. (2008). Are constructiveness and destructiveness essential features of guilt and shame feelings respectively? *Journal for the Theory of Social Behaviour, 38*, 109–129.

Dudeney, J., Sharpe, L., & Hunt, C. (2015). Attentional bias towards threatening stimuli in children with anxiety: A meta-analysis. *Clinical Psychology Review, 40*, 66–75.

Duman, S., & Margolin, G. (2007). Parents' aggressive influences and children's aggressive problem solutions with peers. *Journal of Clinical Child and Adolescent Psychology, 36*, 42–55.

Dumaret, A. C., Coppel-Batsch, M., & Courand, S. (1997). Adult outcome of children reared for long term periods in foster families. *Child Abuse and Neglect, 21*, 911–927.

Dunfield, K. A. (2014). A construct divided: Prosocial behavior as helping, sharing, and comforting subtypes. *Frontiers in Psychology, 5*, 958.

Dunfield, K. A., & Kuhlmeier, V. A. (2010). Intention-mediated selective helping in infancy. *Psychological Science, 21*, 523–527.

Dunfield, K. A., & Kuhlmeier, V. A. (2013). Classifying prosocial behavior: Children's responses to instrumental need, emotional distress, and material desire. *Child Development, 84*, 1766–1776.

Dunn, J. (1988). *The beginnings of social understanding.* Cambridge, MA: Harvard University Press.

Dunn, J. (1995). Children as psychologists: The later correlates of individual differences in understanding of emotions and other minds. *Cognition and Emotion, 9*, 187–201.

Dunn, J. (2014). Moral development in early childhood and social interaction in the family. In M. Killen & J. G. Smetana (Eds), *Handbook of moral development, Second edition* (pp. 135–160). Hove, UK: Psychology Press.

Dunn, J., Bretherton, I., & Munn, P. (1987). Conversations about feeling states between mothers and their young children. *Developmental Psychology, 23*, 132–139.

Dunn, J., Brown, J. R., & Beardsall, J. (1991). Family talk about feeling states and children's later understanding of others' emotions. *Developmental Psychology, 27*, 448–455.

Dunn, J., Brown, J. R., & Maguire, M. (1995). The development of children's moral sensibility: Individual differences and emotion understanding. *Developmental Psychology, 31*, 649–659.

Dweck, C. S. (1999). Caution—praise can be dangerous. *American Educator, 23*, 4–9.

Dyregrov, A., Dyregrov, K., Endsjø, M., & Idsoe, T. (2015). Teachers' perception of bereaved children's academic performance. *Advances in School Mental Health Promotion, 8*, 187–198.

Early, D. M., Rimm-Kaufman, S. E., Cox, M. J., Saluja, G., Pianta, R. C., Bradley, R. H., & Payne, C. C. (2002). Maternal sensitivity and child wariness to the transition to kindergarten. *Parenting: Science and Practice, 2*, 355–377.

Ehntholt, K. A., & Yule, W. (2006). Practitioner Review: Assessment and treatment of refugee children and adolescents who have experienced war-related trauma. *Journal of Child Psychology and Psychiatry, 47*, 1197–1210.

Eibl-Eibesfeldt, I. (1973). The expressive behavior of the deaf-and-blind-born. In M. von Cranach & I. Vine (Eds), *Social communication and movement* (pp. 163–194). London: Academic Press.

Eisenberg, N. (1982). The development and reasoning regarding prosocial behavior. In N. Eisenberg (Ed.), *The development of prosocial behavior* (pp. 219–249). London: Academic Press.

Eisenberg, N. (1991). Meta-analytic contributions to the literature on prosocial behavior. *Personality and Social Psychology Bulletin, 17*, 273–282.

Eisenberg, N. (1992). *The caring child*. London: Harvard University Press.

Eisenberg, N. (2000). Emotion, regulation, and moral development. *Annual Review in Psychology, 51*, 665–697.

Eisenberg, N., Cumberland, A., & Spinrad, T. L. (1998). Parental socialization of emotion. *Psychological Inquiry, 9*, 241–273.

Eisenberg, N., & Fabes, R. A. (1994). Mothers' reaction-sto children's negative emotions: Relations to children's temperament and anger behavior. *Merrill-Palmer Quarterly, 40*, 138–156.

Eisenberg, N., Fabes, R. A., Carlo, G., & Karbon, M. (1992). Emotional responsiveness to other: Behavioral correlates and socialization antecedents. *New Directions for Child Development, 5*, 57–73.

Eisenberg, N., Fabes, R. A., & Spinrad, T. L. (2006). Prosocial development. In W. Damon, R. M. Lerner & N. Eisenberg (Eds), *Handbook of child psychology, Sixth edition, Volume 3. Social, emotional, and personality development* (pp. 646–718). New York: John Wiley.

Eisenberg, N., Murphy, B. C., & Shepard, S. (1997). The development of empathic accuracy. In W. J. Ickes (Ed.), *Empathic accuracy* (pp. 73–116). New York, NY: Guilford Press.

Eisenberg, N., Spinrad, T. L., & Knafo-Noam, A. (2015). Prosocial development. In R. M. Lerner, M. E. Lamb & C. G. Coll (Eds), *Handbook of child psychology and developmental science, Seventh edition, Volume 3: Social and emotional development* (pp. 610–656). Hoboken, NJ: Wiley.

Eisenberg-Berg, N., & Neal, C. (1979). Children's moral reasoning about their own spontaneous prosocial behaviour. *Development Psychology, 15*, 228–229.

Eisenbraun, K. D. (2007). Violence in schools: Prevalence, prediction, and prevention. *Aggression and Violent Behavior, 12*, 459–469.

Eley, T. C., Napolitano, M., Lau, J. Y., & Gregory, A. M. (2010). Does childhood anxiety evoke maternal control? A genetically informed study. *Journal of Child Psychology and Psychiatry, 51*, 772–779.

Elonheimo, H., Gyllenberg, D., Huttunen, J., Ristkari, T., Sillanmäki, L., & Sourander, A. (2014). Criminal offending among males and females between ages 15 and 30 in a population-based nationwide 1981 birth cohort: Results from the FinnCrime Study. *Journal of Adolescence, 37*, 1269–1279.

Emde, R. N. (1992). Social referencing research: Uncertainty, self, and the search for meaning. In S. Feinman (Ed), *Social referencing and the social construction of reality in infancy* (pp. 79–94). London: Plenum.

Emerson, E., & Einfeld, S. (2011). *Challenging behaviour, Third edition.* Cambridge: Cambridge University Press.

Enebrink, P., Danneman, M., Mattsson, V. B., Ulfsdotter, M., Jalling, C., & Lindberg, L. (2015). ABC for parents: Pilot study of a universal 4-session program shows increased parenting skills, self-efficacy and child well-being. *Journal of Child and Family Studies, 24*, 1917–1931.

Erickson, M. F., Egeland, B. R., & Pianta, R. (1989). The effects of maltreatment on the development of young children. In D. Cicchetti & V. Carlson (Eds), *Child maltreatment: Theory and research on the causes and consequences of child abuse and neglect* (pp. 647–684). Cambridge: Cambridge University Press.

Erikson, E. H. (1963). *Childhood and society.* London: Norton.

Erikson, E. H. (1968). *Identity: Youth and crisis and the life cycle.* London: Norton.

Eron, L. D. (1987). The development of aggressive behavior from the perspective of a developing behaviorism. *American Psychologist, 42*, 435–442.

Eysenck, H. J. (1967). *The biological basis of personality.* Springfield, IL: Charles C. Thomas.

Eysenck, H. J. (1992). Four ways five factors are not basic. *Personality and Individual Differences, 13*, 667–673.

Fabes, R., Eisenberg, N., Nyman, M., & Michealieu, Q. (1991). Young children's appraisal of others' spontaneous emotional relations. *Developmental Psychology, 27*, 858–866.

Fagot, B. I., & Hagan, R. (1985). Aggression in toddlers: Responses to the assertive acts of boys and girls. *Sex Roles, 12*, 341–351.

Fanti, K. A., Panayiotou, G., Lazarou, C., Michael, R., & Georgiou, G. (2016). The better of two evils? Evidence that children exhibiting continuous conduct problems high or low on callous–unemotional traits score on opposite directions on physiological and behavioral measures of fear. *Development and Psychopathology, 28*, 185–198.

Farrington, D. P., & Ttofi, M. M. (2009). School-based programs to reduce bullying and victimization. *Campbell Systematic Reviews, 2009*, 6.

Farroni, T., Menon, E., Rigato, S., & Johnson, M. H. (2007). The perception of facial expressions in newborns. *European Journal of Developmental Psychology, 4*, 2–13.

Feigon, S. A., Wladman, I. D., Levy, F., & Hay, A. D. (2001). Genetic and environmental influences on separation anxiety disorder symptoms and their moderation by age and sex. *Behavior Genetics, 31*, 403–411.

Feinman, S., Roberts, D., Hsieh, K.-F., Sawyer, D., & Swanson, D. (1992). A critical review of social referencing in infancy. In S. Feinman (Ed.), *Social referencing and the social construction of reality in infancy* (pp. 15–54). London: Plenum.

Ferguson, T., Stegge, H., & Damhuis, I. (1991). Children's understanding of guilt and shame. *Child Development, 62*, 827–839.

Field, T. (1984). Early interactions between infants and their postpartum depressed mothers. *Infant Behavior and Development, 7*, 517–522.

Field, T. (1994). The effects of mother's physical and emotional unavailability on emotion regulaton. *Monographs of the Society for Research in Child Development, 59 (2–3)*, 208–227.

Field, T., Diego. M., & Hernandez-Reif, M. (2009). Depressed mothers' infants are less responsive to faces and voices. *Infant Behavior and Development, 32*, 239–244.

Field, T., Healy, B., Goldstein, S., Perry, S., Bendell, D., Schanberg, S., Zimmerman, E. A., & Kuhn, C. (1988). Infants of depressed mothers show "depressed" behavior even with nondepressed adults. *Child Development, 59*, 1569–1579.

Field, T., Woodson, R., Greenberg, R., & Cohen, D. (1982). Discrimination and imitation of facial expressions by neonates. *Science, 218*, 179–181.

Fivush, R. (1991). Gender and emotion in mother–child conversations about the past. *Journal of Narrative and Life History, 1*, 325–341.

Fletcher, A., Darling, N., Steinberg. L., & Dornbusch, S. (1995). The company they keep: Relation of adolescents' adjustment and behavior to their friends' perception of authoritative parenting in the social network. *Developmental Psychology, 31*, 300–310.

Foley, D. L., Eaves, L. J., Wormley, B., Silberg, J. L., Maes, H. H., Kuhn. J., & Riley, B. (2004). Childhood adversity, monoamine oxidase a genotype, and risk for conduct disorder. *Archives of General Psychiatry, 61*, 738–744.

Fontaine, R. G., & Dodge, K. A. (2009). Social information processing and aggressive behavior: A transactional perspective. In A. J. Sameroff (Ed.), *The transactional model of development: How children and contexts shape each other* (pp. 117–135). Washington, DC: American Psychological Association.

Forti-Buratti, M. A., Saikia, R., Wilkinson, E. L., & Ramchandani, P. G. (2016). Psychological treatments for depression in pre-adolescent children (12 years and younger): Systematic review and meta-analysis of randomised controlled trials. *European Child and Adolescent Psychiatry, 25*, 1045–1054.

Fox, J. K., Warner, C. M., Lerner, A. B., Ludwig, K., Ryan, J. L., Colognori, D., Lucas, C. P., & Brotman, L. M. (2012). Preventive intervention for anxious preschoolers and their parents: Strengthening early emotional development. *Child Psychiatry and Human Development, 43*, 544–559.

Fox, N. A., & Rutter, M. (2010). Introduction to the special section on the effects of early experience on development. *Child Development, 81,* 23–27.

Fraiberg, S. (1971). Smiling and stranger reaction in blind infants. In J. Hellmuth (Ed.), *The exceptional infant, Volume 2* (pp. 110–127). New York, NY: Brunner/ Mazel.

Fréchette, S. (2016). *Corporal punishment: National trends, longer-term consequences, and parental perceptions of physical discipline.* Doctoral dissertation, University of Ottawa.

Freedman, D. G. (1964). Smiling in blind infants and the issue of innate vs. acquired. *Journal of Child Psychology and Psychiatry, 5,* 171–184.

Freedman, D. G. (1974). *Human infancy: An evolutionary perspective.* Hillsdale, NJ: Erlbaum.

Freud, S. (1895). Project for a scientific psychology. In *The standard edition of the complete works of Sigmund Freud, Volume 1.* London: Hogarth Press.

Freud, S. (1905). *Three essays on the theory of sexuality.* London: Allen and Unwin.

Freud, S. (1916). *A general introduction to psychoanalysis.* New York, NY: Liveright.

Freud, S. (1927). *The ego and the id.* London: Hogarth Press.

Freud, S. (1930). *Civilization and its discontents.* Oxford: Hogarth Press.

Frick, P. J. (2006). Developmental pathways to conduct disorder. *Child and Adolescent Psychiatric Clinics of North America, 1,* 311–331.

Frick, P. J., & Morris, A. S. (2004). Temperament and developmental pathways to conduct problems. *Journal of Clinical Child and Adolescent Psychology, 33,* 54–68.

Frick, P. J., Ray, J. V., Thornton, L. C., & Kahn, R. E. (2014). Annual research review: A developmental psychopathology approach to understanding callous-unemotional traits in children and adolescents with serious conduct problems. *Journal of Child Psychology and Psychiatry, 55,* 532–548.

Fung, H., Lieber, E., & Leung, P. W. L. (2003). Parental beliefs about moral socialization in Taiwan, Hong Kong and United States. In K. S. Yang, K. K. Wang, P. B. Pedersen & I. Daibo (Eds), *Progress psychology: Conceptual and empirical contributions* (pp. 83–109). Westport, CO: Praeger.

Furstenberg, F. F., & Hughes, M. E. (1997). The influence of neighborhoods on children's development: A theoretical perspective and a research agenda. In J. Brooks-Gunn, G. J. Duncan & J. L. Aber (Eds), *Neighborhood poverty, Volume 2* (pp. 23–47). New York, NY: Sage.

Galambos, N. L., Barker, E. T., & Almeida, D. M. (2003). Parents do matter: Trajectories of change in externalizing and internalizing problems in early adolescence. *Child Development, 74,* 578–594.

Gallagher, K. C. (2002). Does child temperament moderate the influence of parenting on adjustment? *Developmental Review, 22,* 623–643.

Gallo, E. A. G., De Mola, C. L., Wehrmeister, F., Gonçalves, H., Kieling, C., & Murray, J. (2017). Childhood maltreatment preceding depressive disorder at age 18 years: A prospective Brazilian birth cohort study. *Journal of Affective Disorders, 217,* 218–224.

Ganiban, J. M., Ulbricht, J., Saudino, K. J., Reiss, D., & Neiderhiser, H. M. (2011). Understanding child-based effects on parenting: Temperament as a moderator of genetic and environmental contributions to parenting. *Developmental Psychology, 47*, 676–692.

Garandeau, C. F., Lee, I. A., & Salmivalli, C. (2014). Differential effects of the KiVa anti-bullying program on popular and unpopular bullies. *Journal of Applied Developmental Psychology, 35*, 44–50.

Garber, J., Frankel, S. A., & Herrington, C. G. (2016). Developmental demands of cognitive behavioral therapy for depression in children and adolescents: Cognitive, social, and emotional processes. *Annual Review of Clinical Psychology, 12*, 181–216.

Gasser, L., & Keller, M. (2009). Are the competent the morally good? Perspective taking and moral motivation of children involved in bullying. *Social Development, 18*, 798–816.

Gavine, A., MacGillivray, S., & Williams, D. J. (2014). Universal community-based social development interventions for preventing community violence by young people 12 to 18 years of age. *The Cochrane Library*, No. 8.

Geangu, E., Benga, O., Stahl, D., & Striano, T. (2010). Contagious crying beyond the first days of life. *Infant Behavior and Development, 33*, 279–288.

Gewirtz, A. H., & Zamir, O. (2014). The impact of parental deployment to war on children: The crucial role of parenting. *Advances in Child Development and Behavior, 46*, 89–112.

Gibbs, J. C., Basinger, K. S., Grime, R. L., & Snary, J. R. (2007b). Moral judgment development across cultures: Revisiting Kohlberg's universality claims. *Developmental Review, 27*, 443–500.

Gillberg, I. C., Helles, A., Billstedt, E., & Gillberg, C. (2016). Boys with Asperger syndrome grow up: Psychiatric and neurodevelopmental disorders 20 years after initial diagnosis. *Journal of Autism and Developmental Disorders, 46*, 74–82.

Gillham, J. E., Reivich, K. J., Freres, D. R., Chaplin, T. M., Shatté, A. J., Samuels, B., Elkon, A. G. L., Litzinger, S., Lascher, M., Gallop, R., & Seligman, M. E. P. (2007). School-based prevention of depressive symptoms: A randomized controlled study of the effectiveness and specificity of the Penn Resiliency Program. *Journal of Consulting and Clinical Psychology, 75*, 9–19.

Gilligan, C. (1982). *In a different voice: Psychological theory and women's development.* Cambridge, MA: Harvard University Press.

Gilmore, K. (2008). Psychoanalytic developmental theory: A contemporary reconsideration. *Journal of the American Psychoanalytic Association, 56*, 885–907.

Gladstone, T. R., & Beardslee, W. R. (2009). The prevention of depression in children and adolescents: A review. *The Canadian Journal of Psychiatry, 54 (4)*, 212–221,

Gnepp, J., & Gould, M. E. (1985). The development of personalized inferences: Understanding other people's emotional reactions in light of their prior experiences. *Child Development, 56*, 1455–1464.

Goldberg, S. (1990). Attachment in infants at risk: Theory, research, and practice. *Infants and Young Children, 2,* 11–20.

Goldsmith, H. H., Lemery, K. S., Buss, K. A., & Campos, J. J. (1999). Genetic analyses of focal aspects of infant temperament. *Developmental Psychology, 35,* 972.

Gosch, E. A., Flannery-Schroeder, E., & Brecher, R. J. (2012). Anxiety disorders: School-based cognitive behavioral interventions. In R. B. Mennuti, R. W. Christner & A. Freeman (Eds), *Cognitive-behavioral interventions in educational settings: A handbook for practice* (pp. 117–160). New York, NY: Routledge.

Greenspan, S. I., & Greenspan, N. T. (1985). *First feelings: Milestones in the emotional development of your infant and child from birth to age 4.* New York, NY: Viking Press.

Gregory, A. M., Caspi, A., Moffitt, T. E., Koenen, K., Eley, T. C., & Poulton, R. (2007). Juvenile mental health histories of adults with anxiety disorders. *American Journal of Psychiatry, 164,* 301–308.

Griggs, R. A. (2015). Psychology's lost boy: Will the real Little Albert please stand up? *Teaching of Psychology, 42,* 14–18.

Gross, A. L., & Bailif, B. (1991). Children's understanding of emotion from facial expressions and situations: A review. *Developmental Review, 11,* 368–398.

Gross, D., & Harris, P. L. (1988). False belifs about emotion: Children's understanding of misleading emotional displays. *International Journal of Behavioral Development, 11,* 475–488.

Gross, J. J., & Barrett, L. F. (2011). Emotion generation and emotion regulation: One or two depends on your point of view. *Emotion Review, 3,* 8–16.

Grusec, J. E. (1982). The socialization of altruism. In N. Eisenberg-Berg (Ed.), *The development of prosocial behavior* (pp. 65–90). London: Academic Press.

Grusec, J. E. (1991). Socializing concern for others in the home. *Developmental Psychology, 27,* 338–342.

Grusec, J. E. (2011). Socialization processes in the family: Social and emotional development. *Annual Review of Psychology, 62,* 243–269.

Guerin, D. W., & Gottfried, A. W. (1994). Temperamental consequences of infant difficultness. *Infant Behavior and Development, 17,* 413–421.

Gunn, J. F., & Goldstein, S. E. (2017). Bullying and suicidal behavior during adolescence: A developmental perspective. *Adolescent Research Review, 2,* 77–97.

Guralnick, M. J. (2011). Why early intervention works: A systems perspective. *Infants and Young Children, 24,* 6–28.

Güroğlu, B., van den Bos, W., & Crone, E. A. (2014). Sharing and giving across adolescence: an experimental study examining the development of prosocial behavior. *Frontiers in Psychology, 5,* 291.

Haidt, J. (2001). The emotional dog and its rational tail: A social intuitionist approach to moral judgment. *Psychological Review, 108,* 814–834.

Haidt, J. (2008). Morality. *Perspectives on Psychological Science, 3,* 65–72.

Haidt, J. (2013). Moral psychology for the twenty-first century. *Journal of Moral Education, 42,* 281–297.

Halberstadt, A. G., & Lozada, F. T. (2011). Emotion development in infancy through the lens of culture. *Emotion Review*, *3*, 158–168.

Halldorsdottir, T., & Ollendick, T. H. (2014). Comorbid ADHD: Implications for the treatment of anxiety disorders in children and adolescents. *Cognitive and Behavioral Practice*, *21*, 310–322.

Hamlin, J. K. (2013). Moral judgment and action in preverbal infants and toddlers: Evidence for an innate moral core. *Current Directions in Psychological Science*, *22*, 186–193.

Hamlin, J. K. (2015). The case for social evaluation in preverbal infants: Gazing toward one's goal drives infants' preferences for Helpers over Hinderers in the hill paradigm. *Frontiers in Psychology*, *5*, 1563.

Hamlin, J. K., & Wynn, K. (2011). Young infants prefer prosocial to antisocial others. *Cognitive Development*, *26*, 30–39.

Hammond, S. I., & Carpendale, J. I. (2015). Helping children help: The relation between maternal scaffolding and children's early help. *Social Development*, *24*, 367–383.

Hanish, L. D., Eisenberg, N., Fabes, R. A., Spinrad, T. L., Ryan, P., & Schmidt, S. (2004). The expression and regulation of negative emotions: Risk factors for young children's peer victimization. *Development and Psychopathology*, *16*, 335–353.

Hankin, B. L. (2012). Future directions in vulnerability to depression among youth: Integrating risk factors and processes across multiple levels of analysis. *Journal of Clinical Child and Adolescent Psychology*, *41*, 695–718.

Hankin, B. L., Gibb, B. E., Abela, J. R., & Flory, K. (2010). Selective attention to affective stimuli and clinical depression among youths: Role of anxiety and specificity of emotion. *Journal of Abnormal Psychology*, *119*, 491–501.

Harlow, H. F. (1963). The maternal affectional system. In B. M. Foss (Ed.), *Determinant of infant behaviour* (pp. 3–29). London: Methuen.

Harris, B. (1979). Whatever happened to Little Albert? *American Psychologist*, *34*, 151–160.

Harter, S. (1987). The determinants and mediation role of global self-worth in children. In N. Eisenberg (Ed.), *Contemporary issues in developmental psychology* (pp. 219–242). New York, NY: Wiley.

Hauser, M. D. (2006). *Moral minds: How nature designed our universal sense of right and wrong*. New York, NY: Ecco Press.

Hay, D. F. (2009). The roots and branches of human altruism. *British Journal of Psychology*, *100*, 473–479.

Heilmann, A., Kelly, Y., & Watt, R. G. (2015). Equally Protected? A review of the evidence on the physical punishment of children. Report commissioned by the NSPCC Scotland, Children 1st, Barnardo's Scotland and the Children and Young People's Commissioner Scotland.

Herpers, P. C., Rommelse, N. N., Bons, D. M., Buitelaar, J. K., & Scheepers, F. E. (2012). Callous–unemotional traits as a cross-disorders construct. *Social Psychiatry and Psychiatric Epidemiology*, *47*, 2045–2064.

Herskind, A., Greisen, G., & Nielsen, J. B. (2015). Early identification and intervention in cerebral palsy. *Developmental Medicine and Child Neurology, 57*, 29–36.

Hertenstein, M. J., & Campos, J. J. (2004). The retention effects of an adult's emotional displays on infant behavior. *Child Development, 75*, 595–613.

Herzhoff, K., Smack, A. J., Reardon, K. W., Martel, M. M., & Tackett, J. L. (2017). Child personality accounts for oppositional defiant disorder comorbidity patterns. *Journal of Abnormal Child Psychology, 45*, 327–335.

Hess, R. D., Kashiwagi, K., Azuma, K., Price, G. G., & Dickson, W. P. (1980). Maternal expectations for mastery of developmental tasks in Japan and the United States. *International Journal of Psychology, 15*, 259–271.

Hetherington, E. M. (2003). Social support and the adjustment of children in divorced and remarried families. *Childhood, 10*, 217–236.

Hetrick, S. E., Cox, G. R., & Merry, S. N. (2015). Where to go from here? An exploratory meta-analysis of the most promising approaches to depression prevention programs for children and adolescents. *International Journal of Environmental Research and Public Health, 12*, 4758–4795.

Hiatt, S. W., Campos, J. J., & Emde, R. N. (1979). Facial patterning and infant emotional expression: Happiness, surprise, and fear. *Child Development, 50*, 1020–1035.

Higgins, E., & O'Sullivan, S. (2015). "What works": Systematic review of the "FRIENDS for Life" programme as a universal school-based intervention programme for the prevention of child and youth anxiety. *Educational Psychology in Practice, 31*, 424–438.

Hill, P. L., & Edmonds, G. W. (2017). Personality in adolescence. In J. Specht (Ed.), *Personality across the life span* (pp. 25–38). London: Elsevier.

Hinde, R. A. (1974). *Biological bases of human social behavior*. New York, NY: McGraw-Hill.

Hinde, R. A. (1989). Temperament as an intervening variable. In G. A. Kohnstamm, J. E. Bates & M. K. Rothbarth (Eds), *Temperament in childhood* (pp. 27–33). Chichester, UK: John Wiley.

Hinde, R. A. (1992). Human social development: An ethological/relationship perspective. In H. McGurk (Ed.), *Childhood social development: Contemporary perspectives* (pp. 13–29). Hove, UK: Lawrence Erlbaum.

Hindle, D., & Smith, M. V. (Eds) (1999). *Personality development: A psychoanalytic perspective*. London: Routledge.

Hirshberg, L. M., & Svejda, M. (1990a). When infants look to their parents: I. Infants' social referencing of mothers compared to fathers. *Child Development, 61*, 1175–1186.

Hirshberg, L. M., & Svejda, M. (1990b). When infants look to their parents: II. Twelve month olds' response to conflicting parental emotional signals. *Child Development, 61*, 1187–1191.

Hoffman, M. L. (1987). The contribution of empathy to justice and moral judgment. In N. Eisenberg & J. Strayer (Eds), *Empathy and its development* (pp. 47–80). Cambridge: Cambridge University Press.

Hoffman, M. L. (2000). *Empathy and moral development*. New York, NY: Cambridge University Press.

Holodynski, M., & Friedlmeier, W. (2006). *Development of emotions and emotion regulation*. New York, NY: Springer.

Horowitz, J. L., & Garber, J. (2006). The prevention of depressive symptoms in children and adolescents: A meta-analytic review. *Journal of Consulting and Clinical Psychology, 74*, 401–415.

House, B. R. (2018). How do social norms influence prosocial development? *Current Opinion in Psychology, 20*, 87–91.

House, B. R., Silk, J. B., Henrich, J., Barrett, H. C., Scelza, B. A., Boyette, A. H., Hewlett, B. S., McElreath, R., & Laurence, S. (2013). Ontogeny of prosocial behavior across diverse societies. *Proceedings of the National Academy of Sciences, 110*, 14586–14591.

Howell, K. H., Shapiro, D. N., Layne, C. M., & Kaplow, J. B. (2015). Individual and psychosocial mechanisms of adaptive functioning in parentally bereaved children. *Death Studies, 39*, 296–306.

Hudson, J. L., Doyle, A. M., & Gar, N. (2009). Child and maternal influence on parenting behavior in clinically anxious children, *Journal of Clinical Child and Adolescent Psychology, 38*, 256–262.

Hudson, J. L., Dodd, H. F., Lyneham, H. J., & Bovopoulous, N. (2011). Temperament and family environment in the development of anxiety disorder: Two-year follow-up. *Journal of the American Academy of Child and Adolescent Psychiatry, 50*, 1255–1264.

Humphreys, A. P., & Smith, P. K. (1987). Rough and tumble, friendship, and dominance in schoolchildren: Evidence for continuity and change with age. *Child Development, 58*, 201–212.

Huurre, T., Junkkari, H., & Aro, H. (2006). Long-term psychosocial effects of parental divorce. *European Archives of Psychiatry and Clinical Neuroscience, 256*, 256–263.

Hyde, L. W., Waller, R., Trentacosta, C. J., Shaw, D. S., Neiderhiser, J. M., Ganiban, J. M., Reiss, D., & Leve, L. D. (2016). Heritable and nonheritable pathways to early callous-unemotional behaviors. *American Journal of Psychiatry, 173*, 903–910.

Ibáñez, M. I., Viruela, A. M., Mezquita, L., Moya, J., Villa, H., Camacho, L., & Ortet, G. (2016). An investigation of five types of personality trait continuity: A two-wave longitudinal study of Spanish adolescents from age 12 to age 15. *Frontiers in Psychology, 7*, 512.

Imamoglu, E. O. (1975). Children's awareness and usage of intention cues. *Child Development, 46*, 39–45.

Izard, C. E. (1991). *The psychology of emotions*. New York, NY: Plenum Press.

Izard, C. E. (2007). Basic emotions, natural kinds, emotion schemas, and a new paradigm. *Perspectives on Psychological Science, 2*, 260–280.

Izard, C. E., Fine, S. E., Mostow, A. J., Trentacosta, C. J., & Campbell, J. (2002). Emotion processes in normal and abnormal development and preventive intervention. *Development and Psychopathology, 14*, 761–787.

Izard, C. E., Hembree, E. A., & Huebner, R. R. (1987). Infants' emotion expressions to acute pain: Developmental change and stability of individual differences. *Developmental Psychology, 23,* 105–113.

Jaffee, S. R., Moffitt, T. E., Caspi, A., & Taylor, A. (2003). Life with (or without) father: The benefits of living with two biological parents depend on the father's antisocial behavior. *Child Development, 74,* 109–126.

Jennings, W. G., & Reingle, J. M. (2012). On the number and shape of developmental/life-course violence, aggression, and delinquency trajectories: A state-of-the-art review. *Journal of Criminal Justice, 40,* 472–489.

Johansson, A., Grant, J. E., Kim, S. W., Odlaug, B. L., & Götestam, K. G. (2009). Risk factors for problematic gambling: A critical literature review. *Journal of Gambling Studies, 25,* 67–92.

Jones, S. S., & Hong, H. W. (2005). How some infant smiles get made. *Infant Behavior and Development, 28,* 194–205.

Jongerden, L., & Bögels, S. M. (2015). Parenting, family functioning and anxiety-disordered children: Compar isons to controls, changes after family versus child CBT. *Journal of Child and Family Studies, 24,* 2046–2059.

Jorgensen, G. (2006). Kohlberg and Gilligan: Duet or duel? *Journal of Moral Education, 35,* 179–196.

Joseph, J. (2013). The use of the classical twin method in the social and behavioral sciences: The fallacy continues. *The Journal of Mind and Behavior, 34,* 1–39.

Joshi, R. M., Padakannaya, P., & Nishanimath, S. (2010), Dyslexia and hyperlexia in bilinguals. *Dyslexia, 16,* 99–118.

Julian, M. M. (2013). Age at adoption from institutional care as a window into the lasting effects of early experiences. *Clinical Child and Family Psychology Review, 16,* 101–145.

Junger-Tas, J. (2012). Delinquent behaviour in 30 countries. In J. Junger-Tas, I. H. Marshall, D. Enzmann, M. Killias, M. Steketee & B. Gruszczynska (Eds), *The many faces of youth crime* (pp. 69–93). New York, NY: Springer.

Kagan, J. (1998). *Three seductive ideas.* Cambridge, MA: Harvard University Press.

Kagan, J., & Fox, N. (2006). Biology, culture, and temperamental biases. In W. Damon, R. M. Lerner & N. Eisenberg (Eds), *Handbook of child psychology, Sixth edition, Volume 3: Social, emotional and personality development* (pp. 167–225). New York, NY: Wiley.

Kagan, J., & Snidman, N. C. (2004). *The long shadow of temperament.* Cambridge, MA: Belknap Press.

Kaitz, M., Meschulach-Sarfaty, O., Auerbach, J., & Eidelman, A. (1988). A reexamination of newborns' ability to imitate facial expressions. *Developmental Psychology, 24,* 3–7.

Kalin, N. H. (1993). The neurobiology of fear. *Scientific American, 268,* 94–101.

Kalmijn, M. (2015). Father-child relations after divorce in four European countries: Patterns and determinants. *Comparative Population Studies, 40,* 251–276.

Kappas, A. (2011). Emotion and regulation are one! *Emotion Review, 3,* 17–25.

Karevold, E., Røysamb, E., Ystrom, E., & Mathiesen, K. S. (2009). Predictors and pathways from infancy to symptoms of anxiety and depression in early adolescence. *Developmental Psychology, 45*, 1051–1060.

Katz, L. F., Hessler, D. M., & Annest, A. (2007). Domestic violence, emotional competence, and child adjustment. *Social Development, 16*, 513–538.

Kawakami, K., Takai-Kawakami, K., Tomonaga, M., Suzuki, J., Kusaka, T., & Okai, T. (2006). Origins of smile and laughter: A preliminary study. *Early Human Development, 82*, 61–66.

Keller, H., & Otto, H. (2009). The cultural socialization of emotion regulation during infancy. *Journal of Cross-Cultural Psychology, 40*, 996–1011.

Kelly-Vance, L., Ryalls, B. O., & Gill-Glover, K. (2002). The use of play assessment to evaluate the cognitive skills of two- and three-year-old children. *School Psychology International, 23*, 169–185.

Kiel, E. J., & Buss, K. A. (2010). Maternal expectations for toddlers' reactions to novelty: Relations of maternal internalizing symptoms and parenting dimensions to expectations and accuracy of expectations. *Parenting, 10*, 202–218.

Kiff, C. J., Lengua, L. J., & Zalewski, M. (2011). Nature and nurturing: Parenting in the context of child temperament. *Clinical Child and Family Psychology Review, 14*, 251–301.

Killen, M., & Dahl, A. (2018). Moral judgment: Reflective, interactive, spontaneous, challenging, and always evolving. In K. Gray & J. Graham (Eds), *Atlas of Moral Psychology (pp. 20–30)*. New York, NY: Guilford Press.

Killen, M., & Smetana, J. G. (Eds). (2014). *Handbook of moral development*, Second edition. Hove, UK: Psychology Press.

Kimonis, E. R., Cross, B., Howard, A., & Donoghue, K. (2013). Maternal care, maltreatment and callous-unemotional traits among urban male juvenile offenders. *Journal of Youth and Adolescence, 42*, 165–177.

Kirschner, S., & Tomasello, M. (2010). Joint music making promotes prosocial behavior in 4-year-old children. *Evolution and Human Behavior, 31*, 354–364.

Klein, D. N., Bufferd, S. J., Dyson, M. W., & Danzig, A. P. (2014). Personality pathology. In M. Lewis & K. D. Rudolph (Eds), *Handbook of developmental psychopathology* (pp. 703–719). Boston, MA: Springer.

Klimstra, T. A., Hale III, W. W., Raaijmakers, Q. A., Branje, S. J., & Meeus, W. H. (2009). Maturation of personality in adolescence. *Journal of Personality and Social Psychology, 96*, 898–912.

Klingzell, I., Fanti, K. A., Colins, O. F., Frogner, L., Andershed, A. K., & Andershed, H. (2016). Early childhood trajectories of conduct problems and callous-unemotional traits: The role of fearlessness and psychopathic personality dimensions. *Child Psychiatry and Human Development, 47*, 236–247.

Kochanska, G. (1997). Multiple pathways to conscience for children with different temperaments: From toddlerhood to age 5. *Developmental Psychology, 33*, 228–240.

Kochanska, G., & Aksan, N. (2004). Development of mutual responsiveness between parents and their young children. *Child Development, 75*, 1657–1676.

Kochanska, G., & Aksan, N. (2006). Children's conscience and self-regulation. *Journal of Personality, 74,* 1587–1618.

Kochanska, G., Brock, R. L., & Boldt, L. J. (2017). A cascade from disregard for rules of conduct at preschool age to parental power assertion at early school age to antisocial behavior in early preadolescence: Interplay with the child's skin conductance level. *Development and Psychopathology, 29,* 875–885.

Kochanska, G., Gross, J. N., Lin, M. H., & Nichols, K. E. (2002). Guilt in young children: Development, determinants, and relations with a broader system of standards. *Child Development, 73,* 461–482.

Kochanska, G., Koenig, J. L., Barry, R. A., Kim, S., & Yoon, J. E. (2010). Children's conscience during toddler and preschool years, moral self, and a competent, adaptive developmental trajectory. *Developmental Psychology, 46,* 1320–1332.

Kohlberg, L. (1963). The development of children's orientations toward a moral order. *Vita Humana, 6,* 11–33.

Kohlberg, L. (1969). Stage and sequence: The cognitive-developmental approach. In D. A. Goslin (Ed.), *Handbook of socialization theory and research* (pp. 347–480). Chicago, IL: Rand McNally.

Kohlberg, L. (1971). Stages of moral development. *Moral Education, 1,* 23–92.

Kohlberg, L. (1976). Moral stages and moralization: The cognitive-developmental approach. In T. Lickona (Ed.), *Moral development and behavior: Theory, research and social issues* (pp. 31–53). New York, NY: Holt, Rinehart and Winston.

Kohlberg, L. (1981). *The philosophy of moral development: Moral stages and the idea of justice.* New York, NY: Harper and Row.

Kohlberg, L., & Hersh, R. H. (1977). Moral development: A review of the theory. *Theory into Practice, 16,* 53–59.

Kohnstamm, G. A., Halverson, C. F., Mervielde, I., & Havill, V. L. (1998). Analyzing parental free descriptions of child personality. In G. A. Kohnstamm, C. F. Halverson, I. Mervielde & V. L. Havill (Eds), *Parental descriptions of child personality: Developmental antecedents of the Big Five?* (pp. 1–19). Mahwah, NJ: Erlbaum.

Kohnstamm, G. A., Mervielde, I., Besevegis, I., & Halverson, C. F. (1995). Tracing the Big Five in parents' free descriptions of their children. *European Journal of Personality, 9,* 283–304.

Kopp, C. B. (1989). Regulation of distress and negative emotions: A developmental view. *Developmental Psychology, 25,* 343–354.

Kornilaki, E. N., & Chlouverakis, G. (2004). The situational antecedents of pride and happiness: Developmental and domain differences. *British Journal of Developmental Psychology, 22,* 605–619.

Kreppner, J. M., O'Connor, T. G., Dunn, J., Andersen-Wood, L., & the English and Romanian Adoptees Study Team (1999). The pretend play and social role play of children exposed to early severe deprivation. *British Journal of Developmental Psychology, 17,* 319–332.

Krettenauer, T., Campbell, S., & Hertz, S. (2013). Moral emotions and the development of the moral self in childhood. *European Journal of Developmental Psychology, 10,* 159–173.

Kring, A. M., & Werner, K. H. (2004). Emotion regulation in psychopathology. In P. Philippot & R. S. Feldman (Eds), *The regulation of emotion* (pp. 359–385). Mahwah, NJ: Erlbaum.

Kruger, A. C. (1992). The effect of peer and adult–child transductive discussions on moral reasoning. *Merrill-Palmer Quarterly, 38*, 191–211.

Kuchuk, A., Vibert, M., & Bornstein, M. H. (1986). The perception of smiling and its experiential correlates in three month old infants. *Child Development, 57*, 1054–1061.

Kuczynski, L., & Knafo, A. (2014). Innovation and continuity in socialization, internalization and acculturation. In M. Killen & J. G. Smetana (Eds), *Handbook of moral development, Second edition* (pp. 93–112). New York, NY: Taylor and Francis.

Kumsta, R., Sonuga-Barke, E., & Rutter, M. (2012). Adolescent callous–unemotional traits and conduct disorder in adoptees exposed to severe early deprivation. *The British Journal of Psychiatry, 200*, 197–201.

Kuusikko, S., Pollock-Wurman, R., Jussila, K., Carter, A. S., Mattila, M. L., Ebeling, H., Pauls, D., & Moilanen, I. (2008). Social anxiety in high-functioning children and adolescents with autism and Asperger syndrome. *Journal of Autism and Developmental Disorders, 38*, 1697–1709.

Kwan, V. S. Y., & Herrmann, S. D. (2015). The interplay between culture and personality. In M. Mikulincer & P. R. Shaver (Eds), *APA handbook of personality and social psychology, Volume 4: Personality processes and individual differences* (pp. 553–574). Washington, DC: American Psychological Association.

LaFreniere, P. J. (2000). *Emotional development.* London: Wadsworth.

Lagattuta, K. H., & Thompson, R. A. (2007). The development of self-conscious emotions: Cognitive processes and social influences. In J. L. Tracy, R. W. Robins & J. P. Tangney (Eds), *The self-conscious emotions: Theory and research* (pp. 91–113). New York, NY: Guilford Press.

Lai, B. S., Kelley, M. L., Harrison, K. M., Thompson, J. E., & Self-Brown, S. (2015). Posttraumatic stress, anxiety, and depression symptoms among children after Hurricane Katrina: A latent profile analysis. *Journal of Child and Family Studies, 24*, 1262–1270.

Laible, D., Eye, J., & Carlo, G. (2008). Dimensions of conscience in mid-adolescence: Links with social behavior, parenting, and temperament. *Journal of Youth and Adolescence, 37*, 875–887.

Lamb, M. E., Chuang, S. S., Wessels, H., Broberg, A. G., & Hwang, C. P. (2002). Emergence and construct validation of the Big Five Factors in early childhood: A longitudinal analysis of their ontogeny in Sweden. *Child Development, 73*, 1517–1524.

Lansford, J. E. (2010). The special problem of cultural differences in effects of corporal punishment. *Law and Contemporary Problems, 73*, 89–106.

Lansford, J. E., Alampay, L. P., Al-Hassan, S., Bacchini, D., Bombi, A. S., Bornstein, M. H., Chang, L., Deater-Deckard, K., Di Giunta, L., Dodge, K. A., et al. (2010). Corporal punishment of children in nine countries as a function of child gender and parent gender. *International Journal of Pediatrics, 2010*, 672780.

Lansford, J. E., Chang, L., Dodge, K. A., Malone, P. S., Oburu, P., Palmérus, K., Bacchini, D., Pastorelli, C., Bombi, A. S., Zelli, A., et al. (2005). Physical discipline and children's adjustment: Cultural normativeness as a moderator. *Child Development, 76,* 1234–1246.

Lansford, J. E., Dodge, K. A., Pettit, G. S., Bates, J. E., Crozier, J., & Kaplow, J. (2002). A 12-year prospective study of the long-term effects of early child physical maltreatment on psychological, behavioral, and academic problems in adolescence. *Archives of Pediatric and Adolescence Medicine, 156,* 824–830.

Larson, R. W., & Ham, M. (1993). Stress and "Storm and Stress" in early adolescence: The relationship of negative events with dysphoric affect. *Developmental Psychology, 29,* 130–140.

Lau, E. X., & Rapee, R. M. (2011). Prevention of anxiety disorders. *Current Psychiatry Reports, 13,* 258–266.

Laugesen, N., Dugas, M. J., & Bukowski, W. M. (2003). Understanding adolescent worry: The application of a cognitive model. *Journal of Abnormal Child Psychology, 31,* 55–64.

Lebowitz, E. R., Scharfstein, L. A., & Jones, J. (2014). Comparing family accommodation in pediatric obsessive-compulsive disorder, anxiety disorders, and nonanxious children. *Depression and Anxiety, 31,* 1018–1025.

Lee, C. L., & Bates, J. E. (1985). Mother–child interaction at age two years and perceived difficult temperament. *Child Development, 56,* 1314–1325.

Lemerise, E. A., & Dodge, K. A. (2008). The development of anger and hostile interactions. In M. Lewis, J. M. Haviland & L. F. Barrett (Eds), *Handbook of emotions, Third edition* (pp. 740–741). New York, NY: Guilford Press.

Lemerise, E. A., & Harper, B. D. (2010). The development of anger from preschool to middle childhood: Expressing, understanding, and regulating anger. In M. Potegal, G. Stemmler & C. Spielberger (Eds) *International handbook of anger constituent and concomitant biological, psychological, and social processes* (pp. 219–229). New York, NY: Springer.

Leno, V. C., Charman, T., Pickles, A., Jones, C. R., Baird, G., Happé, F., & Simonoff, E. (2015). Callous–unemotional traits in adolescents with autism spectrum disorder. *The British Journal of Psychiatry, 207,* 392–399.

Lerner, J. V., & Lerner, R. M. (1983). Temperament and adaptation across life: Theoretical and empirical issues. In P. B. Baltes & O. G. Brim (Eds), *Life-span development and behavior, Volume 5* (pp. 197–231). London: Academic Press.

Levitt, M. J., Weber, R. A., Clark, M. C., & McDonnell, P. (1985). Reciprocity of exchange in toddler sharing behavior. *Developmental Psychology, 21,* 122–123.

Lewis, M. (1993). The emergence of human emotions. In M. Lewis & J. Haviland (Eds), *Handbook of emotions* (pp. 223–235). New York, NY: Guilford Press.

Lewis, M. (2001a). Issues in the study of personality development. *Psychological Inquiry, 12,* 67–83.

Lewis, M. (2001b). Continuity and change: A reply. *Psychological Inquiry, 12,* 110–112.

Lewis, M. (2007). Self-conscious emotional development. In J. L. Tracy, R. W. Robins, & J. P. Tangney (Eds), *The self-conscious emotions: Theory and research* (pp. 134–149). New York, NY: Guilford Press.

Lewis, M., Alessandri, S. M., & Sullivan, M. V. (1990). Violation of expectancy, loss of control and anger expressions in young infants. *Developmental Psychology, 26*, 745–751.

Llabre, M. M., Hadi, F., La Greca, A. M., & Lai, B. S. (2015). Psychological distress in young adults exposed to war-related trauma in childhood. *Journal of Clinical Child and Adolescent Psychology, 44*, 169–180.

LoBue, V. (2009). More than just another face in the crowd: Detection of threatening facial expressions in children and adults. *Developmental Science, 12*, 305–313.

Loeber, R., Jennings, W. G., Ahonen, L., Piquero, A. R., & Farrington, D. P. (2017). *Female delinquency from childhood to young adulthood: Recent results from the Pittsburgh Girls Study*. Cham, Switzerland: Springer.

Loeber, R., Menting, B., Lynam, D. R., Moffitt, T. E., Stouthamer-Loeber, M., Stallings, R., Farrington, D. P., & Pardini, D. (2012). Findings from the Pittsburgh Youth Study: Cognitive impulsivity and intelligence as predictors of the age–crime curve. *Journal of the American Academy of Child and Adolescent Psychiatry, 51*, 1136–1149.

Loeber, R., & Schmaling, K. B. (1985). Empirical evidence for overt and covert patterns of antisocial conduct problems: A meta-analysis. *Journal of Abnormal Child Psychology, 13*, 337–353.

Loeber, R., Wung, P., Keenan, K., Giroux, B., Stouthamer-Loeber, M., van Kammen, W. B., & Maughan, B. (1993). Developmental pathways in disruptive child behavior. *Development and Psychopathology, 5*, 103–133.

Lorenz, K. (1963). *On aggression*. London: Methuen.

Lougheed, J. P., & Hollenstein, T. (2012). A limited repertoire of emotion regulation strategies is associated with internalizing problems in adolescence. *Social Development, 21*, 704–721.

Lourenço, O. M. (2003). Making sense of Turiel's dispute with Kohlberg: The case of the child's moral competence. *New Ideas in Psychology, 21*, 43–68.

Lowther, H., & Newman, E. (2014). Attention bias modification (ABM) as a treatment for child and adolescent anxiety: A systematic review. *Journal of Affective Disorders, 168*, 125–135.

Luborsky, L., & Barrett, M. S. (2006). The history and empirical status of key psychoanalytic concepts. *Annual Review of Clinical Psychology, 2*, 1–19.

Ludemann, P. M. (1991). Generalized discrimination of positive facial expressions by seven- and ten-month-old infants. *Child Development, 62*, 55–67.

Luengo Kanacri, B. P., Pastorelli, C., Eisenberg, N., Zuffianò, A., & Caprara, G. V. (2013). The development of prosociality from adolescence to early adulthood: The role of effortful control. *Journal of Personality, 81*, 302–312.

Luntz, B. K., & Widom, C. S. (1994). Antisocial personality disorder in abused and neglected children grown up. *American Journal of Psychiatry, 151*, 670–674.

Luthar, S. S., Lyman, E. L., & Crossman, E. J. (2014). Resilience and positive psychology. In M. Lewis & K. Rudolph (Eds), *Handbook of developmental psychopathology* (pp. 125–140). New York, NY: Springer.

Lutz, C. (1988). Ethnographic perspectives on the emotion lexicon. In V. Hamilton, G. H. Bower, H. Gordon & N. H. Frijda (Eds), *Cognitive perspectives on emotion and motivation* (pp. 399–419). Norwell, MA: Kluwer.

Lynam, D. R., & Widiger, T. A. (2007). Using a general model of personality to identify the basic elements of psychopathy. *Journal of Personality Disorders, 21*, 160–178.

MacKenzie, M. J., Nicklas, E., Brooks-Gunn, J., & Waldfogel, J. (2015). Spanking and children's externalizing behavior across the first decade of life: Evidence for transactional processes. *Journal of Youth and Adolescence, 44*, 658–669.

Macklem, G. L. (2014). *Preventive mental health at school.* New York, NY: Springer.

MacLeod, C., & Clarke, P. J. (2015). The attentional bias modification approach to anxiety intervention. *Clinical Psychological Science, 3*, 58–78.

Magnus, P., Birke, C., Vejrup, K., Haugan, A., Alsaker, E., Daltveit, A. K., Handal, M., Haugen, M., Høiseth, G., Knudsen, G. P., et al. (2016). Cohort profile update: The Norwegian mother and child cohort study (MoBa). *International Journal of Epidemiology, 45*, 382–388.

Main, M., & George, C. (1985). Responses of abused and disadvantaged toddlers to distress in agemates: A study in the daycare setting. *Developmental Psychology, 21*, 407–412.

Malatesta, C. Z., & Haviland, J. M. (1982). Learning display rules: The socialization of emotion expression in infancy. *Child Development, 53*, 991–1003.

Malti, T., Dys, S., Ongley, S. F., & Colasante, T. (2012). The development of adolescents' emotions in situations involving moral conflict and exclusion. *New Directions for Youth Development, 136*, 12–41.

Malti, T., & Ongley, S. F. (2014). The development of moral emotions and moral reasoning. In M. Killen & J. Smetana (Eds), *Handbook of moral development, Second edition* (pp. 163–183). New York, NY: Psychology Press.

Marsee, M. A., & Frick, P. J. (2010). Callous unemotional traits and aggression in youth. In E. A. William & L. Elizabeth (Eds), *Emotions, aggression and morality in children: Bridging development and psychopathology* (pp. 137–156). Washington: American Psychological Association.

Martin, A., & Olson, K. R. (2015). Beyond good and evil: What motivations underlie children's prosocial behavior? *Perspectives on Psychological Science, 10*, 159–175.

Martinsen, H., Nærland, T., & von Tetzchner, S. (2015). *Språklig høytfungerende barn og voksne med autismespekterforstyrrelse: Prinsipper for opplæring og tilrettelegging, Annen utgave (High functioning children and adults with autism spectrum disorder: Principles for teaching and adaptation, Second edition).* Oslo: Gyldendal Akademisk.

Martinsen, K. D., Kendall, P. C., Stark, K., & Neumer, S. P. (2016). Prevention of anxiety and depression in children: Acceptability and feasibility of the transdiagnostic EMOTION program. *Cognitive and Behavioral Practice, 23*, 1–13.

Masi, G. (1998). Psychiatric illness in mentally retarded adolescents: Clinical features. *Adolescence, 33*, 425–434.

Masten, A. S. (2014). Global perspectives on resilience in children and youth. *Child Development, 85*, 6–20.

Masters, J. C. (1971). Social comparison by young children. *Young Children, 27*, 7–60.

Mathews, A., & MacLeod, C. (2005). Cognitive vulnerability to emotional disorders. *Annual Review of Clinical Psychology, 1*, 167–195.

Mathiesen, K. S., & Tambs, K. (1999). The EAS Temperament Questionnaire – Factor structure, age trends, reliability, and stability in a Norwegian sample. *Journal of Child Psychology and Psychiatry, 40*, 431–439.

Maughan, A., & Cicchetti, D. (2002). Impact of child maltreatment and inter-adult violence on children's emotion regulation abilities and socioemotional adjustment. *Child Development, 73 (5)*, 1525–1542.

Maxwell, C., & Maxwell, S. (2003). Experiencing and witnessing familial aggression and their relationship to physical aggressive behaviors among Filipino adolescents. *Journal of Interpersonal Violence, 18*, 1432–1451.

Mayer, J. D., & Salovey, P. (1997). What is emotional intelligence? In P. Salovey & D. J. Sluyter (Eds), *Emotional development and emotional intelligence* (pp. 3–31). New York, NY: Basic Books.

Mazefsky, C. A., & White, S. W. (2014). Emotion regulation: Concepts and practice in autism spectrum disorder. *Child and Adolescent Psychiatric Clinics of North America, 23*, 15–24.

McCartney, K., Harris, M. J., & Bernieri, F. (1990). Growing up and growing apart: A developmental meta-analysis of twin studies. *Psychological Bulletin, 107*, 226–237.

McClowry, S. G., Rodriguez, E. T., & Koslowitz, R. (2008). Temperament-based intervention: Re-examining goodness of fit. *International Journal of Developmental Science, 2*, 120–135.

McCrae, R. R., & Costa, P. T. (1995). Trait explanations in personality psychology. *European Journal of Personality, 9*, 231–252.

McCrae, R. R., & Costa, P. T. (2008). The Five-Factor Theory of personality. In O. P. John, R. W. Robins & L. A. Pervin (Eds), *Handbook of personality: Theory and research, Third edition* (pp. 159–181). New York, NY: Guilford Press.

McCrory, E. J., & Viding, E. (2015). The theory of latent vulnerability: Reconceptualizing the link between childhood maltreatment and psychiatric disorder. *Development and Psychopathology, 27*, 493–505.

McIntyre, L. L. (2013). Parent training interventions to reduce challenging behavior in children with intellectual and developmental disabilities. *International Review of Research in Developmental Disabilities, 44*, 245–279.

McLaughlin, K. A., & King, K. (2015). Developmental trajectories of anxiety and depression in early adolescence. *Journal of Abnormal Child Psychology, 43*, 311–323.

Meaney, M. J. (2010). Epigenetics and the biological definition of gene × environment interactions. *Child Development, 81*, 41–79.

Meltzoff, A. N. (1993). The centrality of motor coordination and proprioception in social and cognitive development: From shared actions to shared minds. In G. J. P. Savelsbergh (Ed.), *The development of coordination in infancy* (pp. 463–496). Amsterdam, NL: Elsevier.

Meltzoff, A. N., & Moore, M. K. (1999). Persons and representation: Why infant imitation is important for theories of human development. In J. Nadel & G. Butterworth (Eds), *Imitation in infancy* (pp. 9–35). Cambridge: Cambridge University Press.

Merry, S. N., Hetrick, S. E., Cox, G. R., Brudevold-Iversen, T., Bir, J. J., & McDowell, H. (2012). Psychological and educational interventions for preventing depression in children and adolescents. *Evidence-Based Child Health, 7,* 1409–1685.

Mesquita, B., & Karasawa, M. (2004). Self-conscious emotions as dynamic cultural processes. *Psychological Inquiry, 15,* 161–166.

Messer, E. J., Burgess, V., Sinclair, M., Grant, S., Spencer, D., & McGuigan, N. (2017). Young children display an increase in prosocial donating in response to an upwards shift in generosity by a same-aged peer. *Scientific Reports, 7,* 2633.

Miller, R. S. (2007). Is embarrassment a blessing or a curse? In J. L. Tracy, R. W. Robins & J. P. Tangney (Eds), *The self-conscious emotions: Theory and research* (pp. 245–262). New York, NY: Oxford University Press.

Mills, R. S. L. (2003). Possible antecedents and developmental implications of shame in young girls. *Infant and Child Development, 12,* 29–349.

Mills, R. S. L. (2005). Taking stock of the developmental literature on shame. *Developmental Review, 25,* 26–63.

Mills, R. S. L., Arbeau, K. A., Lall, D. I. K., & De Jaeger, A. E. (2010). Parenting and child characteristics in the prediction of shame in early and middle childhood. *Merrill-Palmer Quarterly, 56,* 500–528.

Mischel, W. (1984). Convergences and challenges in the search for consistency. *American Psychologist, 39,* 351–364.

Mischel, W., & Shoda, Y. (2008). Toward a unifying theory of personality: Integrating dispositions and processing dynamics within the cognitive-affective processing system. In L. A. Pervin & O. P. John (Eds), *Handbook of personality: Theory and research*, Third edition (pp. 209–241). New York, NY: Guilford Press.

Mischel, W., & Shoda, Y. (2010). The situated person. In B. Mesquita, L. Feldman Barrett & E. R. Smith (Eds), *The mind in context* (pp. 149–173). New York, NY: Guilford Press.

Mischel, W., Shoda, Y., & Mendoza-Denton, R. (2002). Situation-behavior profiles as a locus of consistency in personality. *Current Directions in Psychological Science, 11,* 50–54.

Miyaki, K., Campos, J., Bradshaw, D., & Kagan, J. (1986). Issues in socioemotional development. In H. Stevenson, H. Azuma & K. Hakuta (Eds), *Child development and education in Japan* (pp. 239–261). New York, NY: Freeman.

Moffitt, T. E. (1993). The neuropsychology of conduct disorder. *Development and Psychopathology, 5,* 135–152.

Moffitt, T. E., Caspi, A., Harkness, A. R., & Silva, P. A. (1993). The natural history of change in intellectual performance: Who changes? How much? Is it meaningful? *Journal of Child Psychology and Psychiatry*, *34*, 455–506.

Moffitt, T. E., Caspi, A., & Rutter, M. (2006). Measured gene–environment interactions in psychopathology: Concepts, research strategies, and implications for research, intervention, and public understanding of genetics. *Perspectives on Psychological Science*, *1*, 5–27.

Montirosso, R., Peverelli, M., Frigerio, E., Crespi, M., & Borgatti, R. (2009). The development of dynamic facial expression recognition at different intensities in 4- to 18-year-olds. *Social Development*, *19*, 71–92.

Moors, A., Ellsworth, P. C., Scherer, K. R., & Frijda, N. H. (2013). Appraisal theories of emotion: State of the art and future development. *Emotion Review*, *5*, 119–124.

Morgado, A. M., & da Luz Vale-Dias, M. (2013). The antisocial phenomenon in adolescence: What is literature telling us? *Aggression and Violent Behavior*, *18*, 436–443.

Morris, A. S., Silk, J. S., Steinberg, L., Myers, S. S., & Robinson, L. R. (2007). The role of the family context in the development of emotion regulation. *Social Development*, *16*, 361–388.

Moskowitz, S. (1985). Longitudinal follow-up of child survivors of the Holocaust. *American Academy of Child Psychiatry*, *24*, 401–407.

Mrug, S., Madan, A., & Windle, M. (2016). Emotional desensitization to violence contributes to adolescents' violent behavior. *Journal of Abnormal Child Psychology*, *44*, 75–86.

Mullin, B. C., & Hinshaw, S. P. (2007). Emotion regulation and externalizing disorders in children and adolescents. In J. J. Gross (Ed.), *Handbook of emotion regulation* (pp. 523–541). New York, NY: Guilford Press.

Mumme, D. L., Fernald, A., & Herrera, C. (1996). Infants' responses to facial and vocal emotional signals in a social referencing paradigm. *Child Development*, *67*, 3219–3237.

Murray, J., & Farrington, D. P. (2010). Risk factors for conduct disorder and delinquency: Key findings from longitudinal studies. *The Canadian Journal of Psychiatry*, *55*, 633–642.

Murray-Close, D., Crick, N. R., & Galotti, K. M. (2006). Children's moral reasoning regarding physical and relational aggression. *Social Development*, *15*, 345–372.

Navarro, R., Yubero, S., & Larrañaga, E. (Eds) (2016). *Cyberbullying across the globe: Gender, family, and mental health*. Cham, Switzerland: Springer.

Neale, M.-C., & Stevenson, J. (1989). Rater bias in the EASI temperament scales: A twin study. *Journal of Personality and Social Psychology*, *56*, 446–455 & 845.

Neil, A. L., & Christensen, H. (2009). Efficacy and effectiveness of school-based prevention and early intervention programs for anxiety. *Clinical Psychology Review*, *29*, 208–215.

Nelson, C. A., & de Haan, M. (1997). A neurobehavioral approach to the recognition of facial expressions in infancy. In J. A. Russell & J. M. Fernandez-Dols

(Eds), *The psychology of facial expression* (pp. 176–204). Cambridge: Cambridge University Press.

Neppl, T. K., Donnellan, M. B., Scaramellac, L. V., Widamand, K. F., Spilmana, S. K., Ontai, L. L., & Conger, R. D. (2010). Differential stability of temperament and personality from toddlerhood to middle childhood. *Journal of Research in Personality, 44,* 386–396.

Newson, J., & Newson, E. (1965). *Patterns of infant care in an urban community.* Harmondsworth, UK: Penguin.

Nigg, J. T. (2000). On inhibition/disinhibition in developmental psychopathology: Views from cognitive and personality psychology and a working inhibition taxonomy. *Psychological Bulletin, 126,* 220–246.

Nigg, J. T. (2006). Temperament and developmental psychopathology. *Journal of Child Psychology and Psychiatry, 47,* 395–422.

Nivard, M. G., Dolan, C. V., Kendler, K. S., Kan, K. J., Willemsen, G., van Beijsterveldt, C. E. M., Lindauer, R. J., van Beek, J. H., Geels, L. M., Bartels, M., etal. (2015). Stability in symptoms of anxiety and depression as a function of genotype and environment: A longitudinal twin study from ages 3 to 63 years. *Psychological Medicine, 45,* 1039–1049.

Novak, G., & Peláez, M. (2004). *Child and adolescent development: A behavioral systems approach.* London: Sage.

Novak, M., & Harlow, H. F. (1975). Social recovery of monkeys isolated for the first year of life: I. Rehabilitation and therapy. *Developmental Psychology, 11,* 453–465.

Nucci, L. P., & Nucci, M. S. (1982a). Children's social interactions in the context of moral and conventional transgressions. *Child Development, 53,* 403–412.

Nucci, L. P., & Nucci, M. S. (1982b). Children's responses to moral and social conventional transgressions in free-play settings. *Child Development, 53,* 1337–1342.

Nucci, L. P., & Turiel, E. (2009). Capturing the complexity of moral development and education. *Mind, Brain, and Education, 3,* 151–159.

O'Brien, K., Daffern, M., Chu, C. M., & Thomas, S. D. (2013). Youth gang affiliation, violence, and criminal activities: A review of motivational, risk, and protective factors. *Aggression and Violent Behavior, 18,* 417–425.

Odgers, C. L., Moffitt, T. E., Broadbent, J. M., Dickson, N. P., Hancox, R., Harrington, H., Poulton, R., Sears, M. R., Thompson, W. M., & Caspi, A. (2008). Female and male antisocial trajectories: From childhood origins to adult outcomes. *Development and Psychopathology, 20,* 673–716.

Ollendick, T. H., & Hirshfeld-Becker, D. R. (2002). The developmental psychopathology of social anxiety disorder. *Biological Psychiatry, 51,* 44–58.

Olweus, D. (1993). *Bullying at school: What we know and what we can do.* Malden, MA: Blackwell.

Olweus, D., & Breivik, K. (2014). The plight of victims of school bullying: The opposite of well-being. In B.-A. Asher, F. Casas, I. Frønes & J. E. Korbin.

(Eds), *Handbook of child well-being* (pp. 2593–2616). Heidelberg, Germany: Springer.

Oster, H., Hegley, D., & Nagel, L. (1992). Adult judgments and fine grained analysis of infant facial expressions: Testing the validity of a priori coding formulas. *Developmental Psychology, 28*, 1115–1131.

Ostrov, J. M., & Crick, N. R. (2007). Forms and functions of aggression during early childhood: A short-term longitudinal study. *School Psychology Review, 36*, 22–43.

Padilla-Walker, L. M., Memmott-Elison, M. K., & Coyne, S. M. (2017). Associations between prosocial and problem behavior from early to late adolescence. *Journal of Youth and Adolescence, 47 (5)*, 961–975.

Pasalich, D. S., Witkiewitz, K., McMahon, R. J., Pinderhughes, E. E., & Conduct Problems Prevention Research Group (2016). Indirect effects of the fast track intervention on conduct disorder symptoms and callous-unemotional traits: Distinct pathways involving discipline and warmth. *Journal of Abnormal Child Psychology, 44*, 587–597.

Patel, P. G., Stark, K. D., Metz, K. L., & Banneyer, K. N. (2014). School-based interventions for depression. In M. D. Weisst, N. A. Lever, C. P. Bradshaw & J. S. Owens (Eds), *Handbook of school mental health* (pp. 369–383). New York, NY: Springer.

Patterson, G. R., DeBaryshe, B. D., & Ramsey, E. (1989). A developmental perspective on antisocial behavior. *American Psychologist, 44*, 329–335.

Paulus, F. W., Backes, A., Sander, C. S., Weber, M., & von Gontard, A. (2015). Anxiety disorders and behavioral inhibition in preschool children: A population-based study. *Child Psychiatry and Human Development, 46*, 150–157.

Paulus, M. (2014). The emergence of prosocial behavior: Why do infants and toddlers help, comfort, and share? *Child Development Perspectives, 8*, 77–81.

Paulus, M., & Moore, C. (2011). Whom to ask for help? Children's developing understanding of other people's action capabilities. *Experimental Brain Research, 211*, 593–600.

Paulus, M., & Moore, C. (2012). Producing and understanding prosocial actions in early childhood. *Advances in Child Development and Behavior, 42*, 271–305.

Paulus, M., & Rosal-Grifoll, B. (2017). Helping and sharing in preschool children with autism. *Experimental Brain Research, 235*, 2081–2088.

Peláez, M., Field, T., Pickens, J. N., & Hart, S. (2008). Disengaged and authoritarian parenting behavior of depressed mothers with their toddlers. *Infant Behavior and Development, 31*, 145–148.

Pellegrini, A. D., & Long, J. D. (2002). A longitudinal study of bullying, dominance, and victimization during the transition from primary school through secondary school. *British Journal of Developmental Psychology, 20*, 259–280.

Pérez-Edgar, K., Reeb-Sutherland, B. C., McDermott, J. M., White, L. K., Henderson, H. A., Degnan, K. A., Hane, A. A., Pine, D. S., & Fox, N. A. (2011).

Attention biases to threat link behavioral inhibition to social withdrawal over time in very young children. *Journal of Abnormal Child Psychology, 39*, 885–895.

Pérez-Edgar, K., Taber-Thomas, B., Auday, E., & Morales, S. (2014). Temperament and attention as core mechanisms in the early emergence of anxiety. In K. H. Lagattutta (Ed.), *Children and emotion* (pp. 42–56). Basel, Switzerland: Karger.

Pervin, L. A., & John, O. P. (1997). *Personality.* New York, NY: John Wiley.

Pervin, L. A., Cervone, D., & John, O. P. (2005). *Personality: Theory and research, Ninth edition.* New York, NY: Wiley.

Pettit, G. S., & Bates, J. E. (1984). Continuity of individual differences in the mother infant relationship from six to thirteen months. *Child Development, 55*, 729–739.

Pettygrove, D. M., Hammond, S. I., Karahuta, E. L., Waugh, W. E., & Brownell, C. A. (2013). From cleaning up to helping out: Parental socialization and children's early prosocial behavior. *Infant Behavior and Development, 36*, 843–846.

Piaget, J. (1932). *The moral judgment of the child.* London: Kegan Paul.

Pianta, R. C., & Nimetz, S. L. (1992). Development of young children in stressful contexts: Theory, assessment, and prevention. In M. Gettinger, S. N. Elliott & T. R. Kratochwill (Eds), *Preschool and early childhood treatment directions* (pp. 151–185). Hillsdale, NJ: Erlbaum.

Piekkola, B. (2011). Traits across cultures: A neo-Allportian perspective. *Journal of Theoretical and Philosophical Psychology, 31*, 2–24.

Pine, D. S., & Fox, N. A. (2015). Childhood antecedents and risk for adult mental disorders. *Annual Review of Psychology, 66*, 459–485.

Pine, D. S., & Klein, R. G. (2015). Anxiety disorders. In A. Thapar, D. S. Pine, F. S. Leckman, S. Scott, M. J. Snowling & E. Taylor (Eds), *Rutter's child and adolescent psychiatry*, Sixth edition (pp. 822–840). Oxford: Wiley.

Piquero, A. R., Carriaga, M. L., Diamond, B., Kazemian, L., & Farrington, D. P. (2012). Stability in aggression revisited. *Aggression and Violent Behavior, 17*, 365–372.

Plomin, R., DeFries, J. C., McClearn, G. E., & Rutter, M. (1997). *Behavioral genetics, Third edition.* New York, NY: W. H. Freeman.

Pluess, M., & Belsky, J. (2010). Differential susceptibility to parenting and quality child care. *Developmental Psychology, 46*, 379–390.

Pomerantz, E. M., & Thompson, R. A. (2008). Parents' role in children's personality development: The psychological resource principle. In O. P. John, R. W. Robins & L. A. Pervin (Eds), *Handbook of personality: Theory and research*, Third edition (pp. 351–374). New York, NY: Guilford Press.

Pons, F., Harris, P. L., & de Rosnay, M. (2004). Emotion comprehension between 3 and 11 years: Developmental periods and hierarchical organization. *European Journal of Developmental Psychology, 1*, 127–152.

Posada, R., & Wainryb, C. (2008). Moral development in a violent society: Colombian children's judgments in the context of survival and revenge. *Child Development, 79*, 882–898.

Poulin, F., & Boivin, M. (2000). Reactive and proactive aggression: Evidence of a two-factor model. *Psychological Assessment, 12,* 115–122.

Poulin, F., Dishion, T. J., & Burraston, B. (2001). Three-year iatrogenic effects associated with aggregating high-risk adolescents in cognitive-behavioral preventive interventions. *Applied Developmental Science, 5,* 214–224.

Provine, R. R. (1997). Yawns, laughs, smiles, tickles, and talking: Naturalistic and laboratory studies of facial action and social communication. In J. A. Russell & J. M. Fernandez-Dols (Eds), *The psychology of facial expression* (pp. 158–175). Cambridge: Cambridge University Press.

Putnam, S. P., Sanson, A. V., & Rothbart, M. K. (2002). Child temperament and parenting. In M. H. Bornstein (Ed.), *Handbook of parenting, Second edition, Volume 1: Children and parenting* (pp. 163–179), Mahwah, NJ: Erlbaum.

Quiggle, N. L., Garber, J., Panak, W. F., & Dodge, K. A. (1992). Social information processing in aggressive and depressed children. *Child Development, 63,* 1305–1320.

Räikkönen, K., Pesonen, A., Heinonen, K., Komsi, N., Järvenpää, A., & Strandberg, T. (2006). Stressed parents: A dyadic perspective on perceived infant temperament. *Infant and Child Development, 15,* 75–87.

Rapee, R. M., Kennedy, S. J., Ingram, M., Edwards, S. L., & Sweeney, L. (2010). Altering the trajectory of anxiety in at-risk young children. *The American Journal of Psychiatry, 167,* 1518–1525.

Rapee, R. M., Schniering, C. A., & Hudson, J. L. (2009). Anxiety disorders during childhood and adolescence: Origins and treatment. *Annual Review of Clinical Psychology, 5,* 311–341.

Raval, V. V., Martini, T. S., & Raval, P. H. (2007). "Would others think it is okay to express my feelings? " Regulation of anger, sadness and physical pain in Gujarati children in India. *Social Development, 16,* 79–105.

Raver, C. C. (2004). Placing emotional self-regulation in sociocultural and socio-economic contexts. *Child Development, 75,* 346–353.

Ray, E., & Heyes, C. (2011). Imitation in infancy: The wealth of the stimulus. *Developmental Science, 14,* 92–105.

Reindl, M., Gniewosz, B., & Reinders, H. (2016). Socialization of emotion regulation strategies through friends. *Journal of Adolescence, 49,* 146–157.

Reinfjell, T., Kårstad, S. B., Berg-Nielsen, T. S., Luby, J. L., & Wichstrøm, L. (2016). Predictors of change in depressive symptoms from preschool to first grade. *Development and Psychopathology, 28,* 1517–1530.

Repacholi, B. M., & Meltzoff, A. N. (2007). Emotional eavesdropping: Infants selectively respond to indirect emotional signals. *Child Development, 78,* 503–521.

Repacholi, B. M., Meltzoff, A. N., Rowe, H., & Toub, T. S. (2014). Infant, control thyself: Infants' integration of multiple social cues to regulate their imitative behavior. *Cognitive Development, 32,* 46–57.

Restifo, K., & Bögels, S. (2009). Family processes in the development of youth depression: Translating the evidence to treatment. *Clinical Psychology Review, 29,* 294–316.

Rice, T. R., & Hoffman, L. (2014). Defense mechanisms and implicit emotion regulation: A comparison of a psychodynamic construct with one from contemporary neuroscience. *Journal of the American Psychoanalytic Association, 62*, 693–708.

Riese, M. L. (1990). Neonatal temperament in monozygotic and dizygotic twin pairs. *Child Development, 61*, 1230–1237.

Robarchek, C. A., & Robarchek, C. J. (1992). Cultures of war and peace: A comparative study of Waorani and Semai. In J. Silverberg & J. P. Gray (Eds), *Aggression and peacefulness in humans and other primates* (pp. 189–213). Oxford: Oxford University Press.

Roberts, B. W., & DelVecchio, J. F. (2000). The rank-order consistency of personality traits from childhood to old age: A quantitative review of longitudinal studies. *Psychological Bulletin, 126*, 3–25.

Roberts, B. W., Walton, K. E., & Viechtbauer, W. (2006). Patterns of mean-level change in personality traits across the life course: A meta-analysis of longitudinal studies. *Psychological Bulletin, 132*, 1–25.

Roberts C. (2015). Depression. In T. Gullotta, R. Plant & M. Evans (Eds), *Handbook of adolescent behavioral problems, Second edition* (pp. 173–191). Boston, MA: Springer.

Roberts, W. L., & Strayer, J. (1987). Parents' responses to the emotional distress of their children: Relations with children's competence. *Developmental Psychology, 23*, 415–422.

Robins, L. N. (1978). Sturdy childhood predictors of adult antisocial behavior: Replications from longitudinal studies. *Psychological Medicine, 8*, 611–622.

Robins, R. W., John, O. P., Stouthamer-Loeber, M., Caspi, A., & Moffitt, T. E. (1996). Resilient, overcontrolled, and undercontrolled boys: Three replicable personality types. *Journal of Personality and Social Psychology, 70*, 157–171.

Rodgers, J. L., Rowe, D. C., & Li, C. (1994). Beyond nature versus nurture: DF analysis of nonshared influences on problem behaviors. *Developmental Psychology, 30*, 374–384.

Rodríguez., M. M. D., Dononvick, M. R., & Crowley, S. L. (2009). Parenting styles in a cultural context: Observations of "protective parenting" in first-generation Latinos. *Family Process, 48*, 195–210.

Rogosch, F. A., & Cicchetti, D. (2004). Child maltreatment and emergent personality organization: Perspectives from the five-factor model. *Journal of Abnormal Child Psychology, 32*, 123–145.

Rosen, L. H., DeOrnellas, K., & Scott, S. R. (Eds) (2017). *Bullying in school: Perspectives from school staff, students, and parents.* New York, NY: Palgrave Macmillan.

Rossman, B. R. (1992). School age children's perceptions of coping with distress: Strategies for emotion regulation and the moderation of adjustment. *Journal of Child Psychology and Psychiatry, 33*, 1373–1397.

Rothbart, M. K., & Bates, J. E. (2006). Temperament. In W. Damon, R. M. Lerner & N. Eisenberg (Eds), *Handbook of child psychology, Sixth edition, Volume*

3: Social, emotional, and personality development (pp. 99–166). New York, NY: John Wiley.

Rottman, J., & Young, L. (2015). Mechanisms of moral development. In J. Decety & T. Wheatley (Eds), *The moral brain: A multidisciplinary perspective* (pp. 123–142). Cambridge, MA: MIT Press.

Rubin, K. H., Bowker, J. C., McDonald, K. L., & Menzer, M. (2013). Peer relationships in childhood. In P. D. Zelazo (Ed.), *The Oxford handbook of developmental psychology, Volume 2* (pp. 242–275). New York, NY: Oxford University Press.

Rubin, K. H., Burgess, K. B., & Hastings, P. D. (2002). Stability and social-behavioral consequences of toddlers' inhibited temperament and parenting. *Child Development, 73*, 483–495.

Rubin, K. H., Cheah, C. S. L., & Menzer, M. (2009). Peer relationships. In M. Bornstein (Ed.), *Handbook of cross-cultural developmental science* (pp. 223–238). New York, NY: Psychology Press.

Rubin, K. H., Nelson, L. J., Hastings, P. D., & Asendorpf, J. (1999). The transaction between parents' perceptions of their children's shyness and their parenting styles. *International Journal of Behavioral Development, 23*, 937–958.

Rutter, M. (1991a). A fresh look at "maternal deprivation". In P. Bateson (Ed.), *The development and integration of behaviour* (pp. 331–374). Cambridge: Cambridge University Press.

Rutter, M. (1991b). Childhood experiences and adult social functioning. In G. R. Bock & J. Whelan (Eds), *The childhood environment and adult disease* (pp. 189–208). Chichester, UK: John Wiley.

Rutter, M. (2004). Pathways of genetic influences on psychopathology. *European Review, 12*, 19–33.

Rutter, M., Colvert, E., Kreppner, J., Beckett, C., Castle, J., Groothues, C., Hawkins, A., O'Connor, T. G., Stevens, S. E., & Sonuga-Barke, E. J. (2007). Early adolescent outcomes for institutionally-deprived and non-deprived adoptees. I: Disinhibited attachment. *Journal of Child Psychology and Psychiatry, 48*, 17–30.

Rutter, M., Giller, H., & Hagell, A. (1998) *Antisocial behavior by young people.* Cambridge: Cambridge University Press.

Rutter, M., Sonuga-Barke, E. J., Beckett, C., Castle, J., Kreppner, J., Kumsta, R., Schlotz, W., Stevens, S., Bell, C. A., & Gunnar, M. R. (2010). Deprivation-specific psychological patterns: Effects of institutional deprivation. *Monographs of the Society for Research in Child Development, 75*, 1.

Rydland, A. B. (2007). *Barneoppdragelse i fjernsynet – en analyse av oppdragelsesstrategier og syn på barns utvikling formidlet i "Nannyhjelpen".* Professional Thesis, University of Oslo, Norway.

Saarni, C. (1984). An observational study of children's attempts to monitor their expressive behaviour. *Child Development, 55*, 1504–1513.

Saarni, C. (1992). Children's emotional expressive behaviors as regulators of others' happy and sad emotional states. *New Directions for Child Development, 55*, 91–106.

Saarni, C., Campos, J. J., Camras, L., & Witherington, D. (2006). Emotional development: Action, communication, and understanding. In W. Damon, R. M. Lerner & N. Eisenberg (Eds), *Handbook of child psychology, Sixth edition, Volume 3: Social, emotional, and personality development* (pp. 226–299). New York, NY: Wiley.

Sachs-Ericsson, N. J., Stanley, I. H., Sheffler, J. L., Selby, E., & Joiner, T. E. (2017). Non-violent and violent forms of childhood abuse in the prediction of suicide attempts: Direct or indirect effects through psychiatric disorders? *Journal of Affective Disorders, 215,* 15–22.

Sadowski, H. S., Ugarte, B., Kolvin, I., Kaplan, C., & Barnes, J. (1999). Early life family disadvantages and major depression in adulthood. *British Journal of Psychiatry, 174,* 112–120.

Salvadori, E., Blazsekova, T., Volein, A., Karap, Z., Tatone, D., Mascaro, O., & Csibra, G. (2015). Probing the strength of infants' preference for helpers over hinderers: Two replication attempts of Hamlin and Wynn (2011). *PloS One, 10,* e0140570.

Sameroff, A. J. (Ed.) (2009). *The transactional model of development: How children and contexts shape each other.* Washington, DC: American Psychological Association.

Sameroff, A. J., & Fiese, B. H. (2000). Models of development and developmental risk. In C. H. Zeanah (Ed.), *Handbook of infant mental health, Second edition* (pp. 3–19). London: Guildford Press.

Sanders, M. R. (1999). Triple P-Positive Parenting Program: Towards an empirically validated multilevel parenting and family support strategy for the prevention of behavior and emotional problems in children. *Clinical Child and Family Psychology Review, 2,* 71–90.

Sanders, M. R., Markie-Dadds, C., Tully, L. A., & Bor, W. (2000). The Triple P-Positive Parenting Program: A comparison of enhanced, standard, and self-directed behavioral family intervention for parents of children with early onset conduct problems. *Journal of Consulting and Clinical Psychology, 68,* 624–640.

Saudino, K. J. (2009). The development of temperament from a behavioral genetics perspective. *Advances in Child Development and Behavior, 37,* 201–231.

Saudino, K. J., & Micalizzi, L. (2015). Emerging trends in behavioral genetic studies of child temperament. *Child Development Perspectives, 9 (3),* 144–148.

Saveanu, R. V., & Nemeroff, C. B. (2012). Etiology of depression: Genetic and environmental factors. *Psychiatric Clinics, 35,* 51–71.

Scarr, S. (1992). Developmental theories for the 1990s: Development and individual differences. *Child Development, 63,* 1–19.

Scarr, S., & McCartney, K. (1983). How people make their own environments: A theory of genotype → environment effects. *Child Development, 54,* 424–435.

Scarr, S., & Salapatek, P. (1970). Patterns of fear development during infancy. *Merrill-Palmer Quarterly, 16,* 53–90.

Schlinger, H. D. (1995). *A behavior analytic view of child development.* New York, NY: Plenum Press.

Schreuder, P., & Alsaker, E. (2014). The Norwegian Mother and Child Cohort Study (MoBa) – Recruitment and logistics. *Norsk Epidemiologi, 24,* 23–27.

Schultz, D. P., & Schultz, S. E. (2016). *Theories of personality.* Boston, MA: Cengage Learning.

Schwartz, G. M., Izard, C. E., & Ansul, S. E. (1985). The 5 month old's ability to discriminate facial expressions of emotion. *Infant Behavior and Development, 8,* 65–77.

Scott, S. (2015). Oppositional and conduct disorders. In A. Thapar, D. S. Fine, J. F. Leckman, S. Scott, M. J. Snowling & E. Taylor (Eds), *Rutter's child and adolescent psychiatry* (pp. 913–930). Chicester, UK: Wiley.

Séguin, J. R., & Tremblay, R. E. (2013). Aggression and antisocial behavior: A developmental perspective. In P. D. Zelazo (Ed.), *The Oxford handbook of developmental psychology, Volume 2: Self and other* (pp. 507–526). Oxford: Oxford University Press.

Seifer R. (2002). What do we learn from parent reports of their children's behavior? Commentary on Vaughn et al.'s critique of early temperament assessments. *Infant Behavior and Development, 25,* 117–120.

Seifer, R., Sameroff, A. J., Barrett, L. C., & Krafchuk, E. (1994). Infant temperament measured by multiple observations and mother report. *Child Development, 65,* 1478–1490.

Selin, H. (2014). *Parenting across cultures.* Dordrecht, The Netherlands: Springer.

Seymour, K. E., Chronis-Tuscano, A., Halldorsdottir, T., Stupica, B., Owens, K., & Sacks, T. (2012). Emotion regulation mediates the relationship between ADHD and depressive symptoms in youth. *Journal of Abnormal Child Psychology, 40,* 595–606.

Shakoor, S., Jaffee, S. R., Bowes, L., Ouellet-Morin, I., Andreou, P., Happé, F., Moffitt, T. E., & Arseneault, L. (2012). A prospective longitudinal study of children's theory of mind and adolescent involvement in bullying. *Journal of Child Psychology and Psychiatry, 53,* 254–261.

Shaw, J. A. (2003). Children exposed to war/terrorism. *Clinical Child and Family Psychology Review, 6,* 237–246.

Shaw, P., Stringaris, A., Nigg, J., & Leibenluft, E. (2014). Emotion dysregulation in attention deficit hyperactivity disorder. *American Journal of Psychiatry, 171,* 276–293.

Shedler, J., & Block, J. (1990). Adolescent drug use and psychological health: A longitudinal inquiry. *American Psychologist, 45,* 612–630.

Shiner, R. L. (2006). Temperament and personality in childhood. In D. K. Mroczek & T. D. Little (Eds), *Handbook of personality development* (pp. 213–230). Mahwah, NJ: Erlbaum.

Shiner, R. L. (2009). The development of personality disorders: Perspectives from normal personality development in childhood and adolescence. *Development and Psychopathology, 21,* 715–734.

Shiner, R. L. (2015). The development of temperament and personality traits in childhood and adolescence. In M. Mikulincer, P. Shaver, M. L. Cooper &

R. Larsen (Eds), *APA handbook of personality and social psychology, Volume 3: Personality processes and individual differences* (pp. 85–105). Washington, DC: American Psychological Association.

Shoda, Y., Mischel, W., & Wright, J. C. (1994). Intraindividual stability in the organization and patterning of behavior: Incorporating psychological situations into the idiographic analysis of personality. *Journal of Personality and Social Psychology, 67,* 674–687.

Silk, J. S., Shaw, D. S., Forbes, E. E., Lane, T. L., & Kovacs, M. (2006). Maternal depression and child internalizing: The moderating role of child emotion regulation. *Journal of Clinical Child and Adolescent Psychology, 35,* 116–126.

Simanowitz, V., & Pearce, P. (2003). *Personality development.* Berkshire, UK: Open University Press.

Skar, A. M. S., von Tetzchner, S., Clucas, C., & Sherr, L. (2015). The long-term effectiveness of the International Child Development Programme (ICDP) implemented as a community-wide parenting programme. *European Journal of Developmental Psychology, 12,* 54–68.

Skinner, B. F. (1971). *Beyond freedom and dignity.* New York, NY: Knopf.

Smetana, J. G. (1993). Understanding of social rules. In M. Bennett (Ed.), *The child as a psychologist* (pp. 111–141). London: Harvester Wheatsheaf.

Smetana, J. G., Jambon, M., & Ball, C. (2014). The social domain approach to children's social and moral judgments. In M. Killen & J. G. Smetana (Eds), *Handbook of moral development, Second edition* (pp. 23–45). Hove, UK: Psychology Press.

Smith, C. L. (2010). Multiple determinants of parenting: Predicting individual differences in maternal parenting behavior with toddlers. *Parenting, 10,* 1–17.

Snarey, J. R. (1985). Cross-cultural universality of social moral development: A critical review of Kohlbergian research. *Psychological Bulletin, 97,* 202–232.

Sorce, J. F., Emde, R. N., Campos, J. J., & Klinnert, M. D. (1985). Maternal emotional signaling: Its effect on the visual cliff behavior of 1-year-olds. *Developmental Psychology, 21,* 195–200.

Sowislo, J. F., & Orth, U. (2013). Does low self-esteem predict depression and anxiety? A meta-analysis of longitudinal studies. *Psychological Bulletin, 139,* 213–240.

Spinrad, T. L., & Stifter, C. A. (2006). Toddlers' empathy-related responding to distress: Predictions from negative emotionality and maternal behavior in infancy. *Infancy, 10,* 97–121.

Sroufe, L. A. (1996). *Emotional development.* Cambridge: Cambridge University Press.

Sroufe, L. A., Carlson, E., & Shulman, S. (1993). Individuals in relationships: Development from infancy through adolescence. In D. C. Funder, R. D. Parke, C. Tomlinson-Keasey & K. Widaman (Eds), *Studying lives through time* (pp. 315–342). Washington, DC: American Psychological Association.

Sroufe, L. A., & Waters, E. (1976). The ontogenesis of smiling and laughter: A perspective on the organization of development in infancy. *Psychological Review, 83,* 173–189.

Steinberg, L., & Silk, J. S. (2002). Parenting adolescents. In M. H. Bornstein (Ed.), *Handbook of parenting, Second edition, Volume 1: Children and parenting* (pp. 103–133). Mahwah, NJ: Erlbaum.

Stenberg, C. R., Campos, J. J., & Emde, R. N. (1983). The facial expression of anger in seven-month-old infants. *Child Development, 54*, 178–184.

Stenberg, G. (2009). Selectivity in infant social referencing. *Infancy, 14*, 457–473.

Stern, D. N. (1998). *The interpersonal world of the infant: A view from psychoanalysis and developmental psychology.* New York, NY: Karnac Books.

Stikkelbroek, Y., Bodden, D. H., Reitz, E., Vollebergh, W. A., & van Baar, A. L. (2016). Mental health of adolescents before and after the death of a parent or sibling. *European Child and Adolescent Psychiatry, 25*, 49–59.

Stipek, D. J., Recchia, S., & McClintic, S. (1992). Self-evaluation in young children. *Monographs of the Society for Research in Child Development, 57*, 1–98.

Størksen, I., Røysamb, E., Moum, T., & Tambs, K. (2005). Adolescents with a childhood experience of parental divorce: A longitudinal study of mental health and adjustment. *Journal of Adolescence, 28*, 725–739.

Strayer, J. (1980). A naturalistic study of empathic behaviours and their relation to affective states and perspective-taking skills in preschool children. *Child Development, 51*, 815–822.

Strohschein, L. (2005). Parental divorce and child mental health trajectories. *Journal of Marriage and Family, 67*, 1286–1300.

Suomi, S. J. (1991). Early stress and adult emotional reactivity in rhesus monkeys. In G. R. Bock & J. Whelan (Eds), *The childhood environment and adult disease* (pp. 171–188). Chichester, UK: John Wiley.

Tackett, J. L., Balsis, S., Oltmanns, T. F., & Krueger, R. F. (2009). A unifying perspective on personality pathology across the life span: Developmental considerations for the fifth edition of the Diagnostic and Statistical Manual of Mental Disorders. *Development and Psychopathology, 21*, 687–713.

Tangney, J. P., Stuewig, J., & Mashek, D. J. (2007). Moral emotions and moral behavior. *Annual Review of Psycholology, 58*, 345–372.

Tarabah, A., Badr, L. K., Usta, J., & Doyle, J. (2016). Exposure to violence and children's desensitization attitudes in Lebanon. *Journal of Interpersonal Violence, 31*, 3017–3038.

Thomas, A., & Chess, S. (1977). *Temperament and development.* New York, NY: Bruner/Mazel.

Thomas, A., & Chess, S. (1986). The New York Longitudinal Study: From infancy to early adult life. In R. Plomin & J. Dunn (Eds), *The study of temperament: Changes, continuities and challenges* (pp. 39–52). London: Erlbaum.

Thompson, R. A. (1991). Emotional regulation and emotional development. *Educational Psychology Review, 3*, 269–307.

Thompson, R. A. (2011). Emotion and emotion regulation: Two sides of the developing coin. *Emotion Review, 3*, 53–61.

Thompson, R. A., Meyer, S., & McGinley, M. (2006). Understanding values in relationships: The development of conscience. In M. Killen & J. G. Smetana (Eds), *Handbook of moral development* (pp. 267–297). Mahwah, NJ: Erlbaum.

Thrasher, C., & LoBue, V. (2016). Do infants find snakes aversive? Infants' physiological responses to "fear-relevant" stimuli. *Journal of Experimental Child Psychology, 142*, 382–390.

Tomkins, S. S., & McCarter, R. (1964). What and where are the primary affects? Some evidence for a theory. *Perceptual and Motor Skills, 18*, 119–158.

Tone, E. B., & Tully, E. C. (2014). Empathy as a "risky strength": A multilevel examination of empathy and risk for internalizing disorders. *Development and Psychopathology, 26 (4pt2)*, 1547–1565.

Torgersen, A. M. (1989). Genetic and environmental influences on temperament development: Longitudinal study of twins from infancy to adolescence. In S. Doxiadis & S. Stewart (Eds), *Early influences shaping the individual* (pp. 269–281). New York, NY: Plenum.

Torgersen, A. M., & Janson, H. (2002). Why do identical twins differ in personality: Shared environment reconsidered. *Twin Research, 5*, 44–52.

Tracy, J. L., & Robins, R. W. (2004). Putting the self into self-conscious emotions: A theoretical model. *Psychological Inquiry, 15*, 103–125.

Tracy, J. L., & Robins, R. W. (2007). Emerging insights into the nature and function of pride. *Current Directions in Psychological Science, 16*, 147–150.

Tracy, J. L., Robins, R. W., & Lagattuta, K. H. (2005). Can children recognize the pride expression? *Emotion, 5*, 251–257.

Trevarthen, C., & Logotheti, K. (1989). Child in society, and society in children: The nature of basic trust. In S. Howell & R. Willis (Eds), *Societies at peace: Anthropological perspectives* (pp. 165–186). London: Routledge.

Troop-Gordon, W. (2017). Peer victimization in adolescence: The nature, progression, and consequences of being bullied within a developmental context. *Journal of Adolescence, 55*, 116–128.

Turiel, E. (2014). Morality, epistemology, development, and social opposition. In M. Killen & J. G. Smetana (Eds), *Handbook of moral development, Second edition* (pp. 3–22). New York, NY: Psychology Press.

Turiel, E. (2015). Moral development. Biology, development, and human systems. In R. M. Lerner, W. F. Overton & P. C. M. Molenaar (Eds), *Handbook of child psychology and developmental science, Seventh edition. Volume 1: Theory and method* (pp. 484–522). New York, NY: Wiley.

Turiel, E., & Killen, M. (2010). Taking emotions seriously: The role of emotions in moral development. In W. Arsenio & E. Lemerise (Eds), *Emotions in aggression and moral development* (pp. 33–52). Washington, DC: American Psychological Association.

Turnbull, C. M. (1972). *The mountain people.* New York, NY: Simon and Schuster.

Twyman, K. A., Saylor, C. F., Saia, D., Macias, M. M., Taylor, L. A., & Spratt, E. (2010). Bullying and ostracism experiences in children with special health care needs. *Journal of Developmental and Behavioral Pediatrics, 31*, 1–8.

Underwood, M. A. (2003). *Social aggression among girls.* New York, NY: Guilford Press.

Vaish, A., Grossmann, T., & Woodward, A. (2008). Not all emotions are created equal: The negativity bias in social-emotional development. *Psychological Bulletin, 134,* 383–403.

Vaish, A., Missana, M., & Tomasello, M. (2011). Three- year-old children intervene in third-party moral transgressions. *British Journal of Developmental Psychology, 29,* 124–130.

Vaish, A., & Tomasello, M. (2014). The early ontogeny of human cooperation and morality. In M. Killen & J. G. Smetana (Eds), *Handbook of moral development* (pp. 279–298). New York, NY: Psychology Press.

Valiente, C., Eisenberg, N., Fabes, R. A., Shepard, S. A., Cumberland, A., & Losoya, S. H. (2004). Prediction of children's empathy-related responding from their effortful control and parents' expressivity. *Developmental Psychology, 40,* 911–926.

van Aken, C., Junger, M., Verhoeven, M., van Aken, M. A. G., & Deković, M. (2007). The interactive effects of temperament and maternal parenting on toddlers' externalizing behaviours. *Infant and Child Development, 16,* 553–572.

van den Akker, A. L., Prinzie, P., & Overbeek, G. (2016). Dimensions of personality pathology in adolescence: Longitudinal associations with Big Five personality dimensions across childhood and adolescence. *Journal of Personality Disorders, 30,* 211–231.

Vasey, M. W., Bosmans, G., & Ollendick, T. H. (2014). The developmental psychopathology of anxiety. In M. Lewis & K. Rudolph (Eds), *Handbook of developmental psychopathology, Third edition* (pp. 543–560). New York, NY: Springer.

Viding, E., Fontaine, N. M., & McCrory, E. J. (2012). Antisocial behaviour in children with and without callous-unemotional traits. *Journal of the Royal Society of Medicine, 105,* 195–200.

Viding, E., & Larsson, H. (2007, November). Aetiology of antisocial behaviour. *International Congress Series, 1304,* 121–132.

Viding, E., & McCrory, E. (2015). Developmental risk for psychopathy. In A. Thapar, D. Pine, J. Leckman, S. Scott, M. Snowling & E. Taylor (Eds), *Rutter's child and adolescent psychiatry,* Sixth edition (pp. 966–980). London: Wiley.

Viken, R. J., Rose, R. J., Kaprio, J., & Koskenvuo, M. (1994). A developmental genetic analysis of adult personality: Extraversion and neuroticism from 18 to 59 years of age. *Journal of Personality and Social Psychology, 66,* 722–730.

von Knorring, A. L., Andersson, O., & Magnusson, D. (1987). Psychiatric care and course of psychiatric disorders from childhood to early adulthood in a representative sample. *Journal of Child Psychology and Psychiatry, 28,* 329–341.

von Tetzchner, S. (2004). Early intervention and prevention of challenging behaviour in children with learning disabilities. *Perspectives in Education, 22,* 85–100.

Wachs, T. D. (1994). Fit, context, and the transition between temperament and personality. In C. F. Halverson, G. A. Kohnstamm & R. P. Martin (Eds), *The developing structure of temperament and personality from infancy to adulthood* (pp. 209–220). Hillsdale, NJ: Lawrence Erlbaum.

Wachs, T. D., & Gruen, G. E. (1982). *Early experience and human development*. New York, NY: Plenum Press.

Wainryb, C., & Pasupathi, M. (2010). Political violence and disruptions in the development of moral agency. *Child Development Perspectives, 4*, 48–54.

Wainryb, C., & Recchia, H. E. (2012). Emotion and the moral lives of adolescents: Vagaries and complexities in the emotional experience of doing harm. *New Directions for Student Leadership, 2012*, 13–26.

Walden, T., & Kim, G. (2005). Infants' social looking toward mothers and strangers. *International Journal of Behavioral Development, 29*, 356–360.

Walden, T. A., & Ogan, T. A. (1988). The development of social referencing. *Child Development, 59*, 1230–1240.

Walker, L. J. (1984). Sex differences in the development of moral reasoning: A critical review. *Child Development, 55*, 677–691.

Walker, L. J., & Hennig, K. H. (1997). Moral development in the broader context of personality. In S. Hala (Ed.), *The development of social cognition* (pp. 297–327). Hove, UK: Psychology Press.

Walker, L. J., de Vries, B., & Trevathan, S. D. (1987). Moral stages and moral orientations in real-life and hypothetical dilemmas. *Child Development, 58*, 842–858.

Walker, L. J., & Taylor, J. H. (1991). Family interactions and the development of moral reasoning. *Child Development, 62*, 264–283.

Walker-Andrews, A. S. (1986). Intermodal perception of expressive behaviors: Relation of eye and voice? *Developmental Psychology, 22*, 373–377.

Walker-Andrews, A. S. (1997). Infants' perception of expressive behaviors: Differentiation of multimodal information. *Psychological Bulletin, 121*, 437–456.

Wall, T. D., Frick, P. J., Fanti, K. A., Kimonis, E. R., & Lordos, A. (2016). Factors differentiating callous-unemotional children with and without conduct problems. *Journal of Child Psychology and Psychiatry, 57*, 976–983.

Walle, E. A., & Campos, J. J. (2012). Interpersonal responding to discrete emotions: A functionalist approach to the development of affect specificity. *Emotion Review, 4*, 413–422.

Waller, R., Gardner, F., Viding, E., Shaw, D. S., Dishion, T. J., Wilson, M. N., & Hyde, L. W. (2014). Bidirectional associations between parental warmth, callous unemotional behavior, and behavior problems in high-risk preschoolers. *Journal of Abnormal Child Psychology, 42*, 1275–1285.

Wallerstein, J. S., & Lewis, J. M. (2004). The unexpected legacy of divorce: Report of a 25-year study. *Psychoanalytic Psychology, 21*, 353–370.

Warneken, F., & Tomasello, M. (2007). Helping and cooperation at 14 months of age. *Infancy, 11*, 271–294.

Warneken, F., & Tomasello, M. (2008). Extrinsic rewards undermine altruistic tendencies in 20-month-olds. *Developmental Psychology, 44*, 1785–1788.

Warneken, F., & Tomasello, M. (2009). The roots of human altruism. *British Journal of Psychology, 100*, 455–471.

Waterhouse, L., Dobash, R. P., & Carnie, J. (1994). *Child sexual abuse*. Edinburgh: The Scottish Office Central Research Unit.

Watson, J. B., & Rayner, R. (1920). Conditioned emotional responses. *Journal of Experimental Psychology, 3*, 1–14.

Webster-Stratton, C. (2006). *The Incredible Years: A trouble-shooting guide for parents of children aged 3–8*. Seattle, WA: Incredible Years Press.

Weems, C. F., & Varela, R. E. (2011). Generalized anxiety disorder. In D. McKay & E. Storch (Eds), *Handbook of child and adolescent anxiety disorders* (pp. 261–274). New York, NY: Springer.

Werner, E. E. (2012). Children and war: Risk, resilience, and recovery. *Development and Psychopathology, 24*, 553–558.

Werner, E. E., & Smith, R. S. (1982). *Vulnerable but invincible*. New York, NY: McGraw-Hill.

Werner-Seidler, A., Perry, Y., Calear, A. L., Newby, J. M., & Christensen, H. (2017). School-based depression and anxiety prevention programs for young people: A systematic review and meta-analysis. *Clinical Psychology Review, 51*, 30–47.

Westen, D., Gabbard, G. O., & Ortigo, K. M. (2008). Psychoanalytic approaches to personality. In O. P. John, R. W. Robins & L. A. Pervin (Eds), *Handbook of personality: Theory and research*, Third edition (pp. 61–113). New York, NY: Guilford Press.

Widen, S. C., Pochedly, J. T., & Russell, J. A. (2015). The development of emotion concepts: A story superiority effect in older children and adolescents. *Journal of Experimental Child Psychology, 131*, 186–192.

Widom, C. S. (2000). Childhood victimization: Early adversity, later psychopathology. *National Institute of Justice Journal, 242*, 3–9.

Williams, L. R., Degnan, K. A., Pérez-Edgar, K., Henderson, H. A., Rubin, K. H., Pine, D. S., Steinberg, L., & Fox, N. A. (2009). Impact of behavioral inhibition and parenting style on internalizing and externalizing problems from early childhood through adolescence. *Journal of Abnormal Child Psychology, 37*, 1063–1075.

Wilson, S., & Durbin, C. E. (2010). Effects of paternal depression on fathers' parenting behaviors: A meta-analytic review. *Clinical Psychology Review, 30*, 167–180.

Wilson, S. L., Raval, V. V., Salvina, J., Raval, P. H., & Panchal, I. N. (2012). Emotional expression and control in school-age children in India and the United States. *Merrill-Palmer Quarterly, 58*, 50–76.

Wolff, P. H. (1963). Observations on early development of smiling. In B. M. Foss (Ed.), *Determinants of infant behaviour, Volume 2* (pp. 113–138). London: Methuen.

Wolff, P. H. (1966). The causes, controls, and organization of behavior in the neonate. *Psychological Issues, 5*, 1–105.

Wynn, K., & Bloom, P. (2014). The moral baby. In M. Killen & J. G. Smetana (Eds), *Handbook of moral development, Second edition* (pp. 435–453). New York, NY: Psychology Press.

Xiong, M., Shi, J., Wu, Z., & Zhang, Z. (2016). Five-year-old preschoolers' sharing is influenced by anticipated reciprocation. *Frontiers in Psychology, 7*, 460.

Yau, J., & Smetana, J. G. (2003). Conceptions of moral, social-conventional, and personal events among Chinese preschoolers in Hong Kong. *Child Development, 74*, 647–658.

Zahn-Waxler, C., & Kochanska, G. (1990). The origins of guilt. In R. A. Thompson (Ed.), *The Nebraska symposium on motivation 1988: Socioemotional development, Volume 36* (pp. 182–258). Lincoln, NE: University of Nebraska Press.

Zahn-Waxler, C., Radke-Yarrow, M., & King, R. A. (1979). Child rearing and children's prosocial initiations toward victims of distress. *Child Development, 50*, 319–330.

Zahn-Waxler, C., Cummings, E. M., Ianotti, R. J., & Radke-Yarrow, M. (1984). Young offspring of depressed parents: A population at risk for affective problems. *New Directions for Child Development, 26*, 81–105.

Zahn-Waxler, C., Radke-Yarrow, M., Wagner, E., & Chapman, M. (1992). Development of concern for others. *Developmental Psychology, 28*, 126–136.

Zeanah, C. H., Egger, H. L., Smyke, A. T., Nelson, C. A., Fox, N. A., Marshall, P. J., & Guthrie, D. (2009). Institutional rearing and psychiatric disorders in Romanian preschool children. *American Journal of Psychiatry, 166*, 777–785.

Zeman, J., Cassano, M., Perry-Parrish, C., & Stegall, S. (2006). Emotion regulation in children and adolescents. *Journal of Developmental and Behavioral Pediatrics, 27*, 155–168.

Zentner, M., & Bates, J. E. (2008). Child temperament: An integrative review of concepts, research programs, and measures. *International Journal of Developmental Science, 2*, 7–37.

Zentner, M., & Shiner, R. (2012). Fifty years of progress in temperament reseach: A synthesis of major themes, findings, and challenges and a look forward. In M. Zentner & R. L. Shiner (Eds), *Handbook of temperament* (pp. 673–700). New York, NY: Guilford Press.

Zheng, Y., Rijsdijk, F., Pingault, J. B., McMahon, R. J., & Unger, J. B. (2016). Developmental changes in genetic and environmental influences on Chinese child and adolescent anxiety and depression. *Psychological Medicine, 46*, 1829–1838.

Zinck, A. (2008). Self-referential emotions. *Consciousness and Cognition, 17*, 496–505.

Index

The **Topics from Child and Adolescent Psychology Series** is drawn from Stephen von Tetzchner's comprehensive textbook for all students of developmental psychology *Child and Adolescent Psychology: Typical and Atypical Development*

Table of Contents

Praise for *Child and Adolescent Psychology: Typical and Atypical Development*

'An extensive overview of the field of developmental psychology. It illustrates how knowledge about typical and atypical development can be integrated and used to highlight fundamental processes of human growth and maturation.'

Dr. John Coleman, *PhD, OBE, UK*

'A broad panoply of understandings of development from a wide diversity of perspectives and disciplines, spanning all the key areas, and forming a comprehensive, detailed and extremely useful text for students and practitioners alike.'

Dr. Graham Music, *Consultant Psychotherapist, Tavistock Clinic London, UK*

'An extraordinary blend of depth of scholarship with a lucid, and engaging, writing style. Its coverage is impressive . . . Both new and advanced students will love the coverage of this text.'

Professor Joseph Campos, *University of California, USA*

'Encyclopedic breadth combined with an unerring eye for the central research across developmental psychology, particularly for the period of its explosive growth since the 1960s. Both a text and a reference work, this will be the go-to resource for any teacher, researcher or student of the discipline for the foreseeable future.'

Professor Andy Lock, *University of Lisbon, Portugal*

It is accompanied by a companion website featuring chapter summaries, glossary, quizzes and instructor resources.